高等职业教育"十二五"实训系列规划教材

国际商务单证实训

主编 牟爱春 李 琳

图书在版编目(CIP)数据

国际商务单证实训 / 牟爱春,李琳主编. —上海：立信会计出版社,2011.11(2025.1重印)
高等职业教育"十二五"实训系列规划教材
ISBN 978-7-5429-3094-1

Ⅰ.①国… Ⅱ.①牟…②李… Ⅲ.①国际贸易—票据—高等职业教育—教材 Ⅳ.①F740.44

中国版本图书馆 CIP 数据核字(2011)第 235815 号

责任编辑　赵志梅
封面设计　周崇文

国际商务单证实训
GUOJI SHANGWU DANZHENG SHIXUN

出版发行	立信会计出版社
地　　址	上海市中山西路 2230 号　邮政编码　200235
电　　话	(021)64411389　传　　真　(021)64411325
网　　址	www.lixinaph.com　电子邮箱　lixinaph2019@126.com
网上书店	http://lixin.jd.com　http://lxkjcbs.tmall.com
经　　销	各地新华书店
印　　刷	苏州市古得堡数码印刷有限公司
开　　本	787 毫米×1092 毫米　1/16
印　　张	15.5
字　　数	338 千字
版　　次	2011 年 11 月第 1 版
印　　次	2025 年 1 月第 4 次
书　　号	ISBN 978-7-5429-3094-1/F
定　　价	45.00 元

如有印订差错,请与本社联系调换

编审委员会

主　任　项家祥
副主任　尹雷方　严玉康
成　员　赵三宝　时启亮　陆爱勤
　　　　　袁雪飞　牟爱春　侯　丹
　　　　　周　曼　高　振　张　强
　　　　　张　瑾　吴谢玲

总序 PREFACE

经济与社会的发展对高等教育的要求越来越高。三十多年来,我国经济的发展使高等教育的毛入学率从5%提高到23%,而对于上海这样经济比较发达的地区,毛入学率更是达到60%。在这种情况下,高等教育逐渐清晰地分为:研究型大学、教学型大学和职业技术大学。在经济发达的美国,真正的研究型大学仅占5%,而职业技术大学则占到60%。

在科学技术日益发展的中国,职业技术教育的重要性日益显现。企业生产的电气化、自动化,生产流水线的普遍化、智能化,对研究、开发人员的科技创新能力要求不断提高,同时,对生产、管理人员的数量和科学素养的要求也越来越高。因此,高等职业技术院校的大发展成为必然。目前,在上海地区,高等职业院校已占高校数量的三分之一,而在校生人数也已占到高校在校生总数的五分之一。

但是,如何办好高等职业技术教育,仍需要我们不断探索和不断进取,切忌把高等职业技术教育简单地改良为普通本科教育的"压缩饼干",简单地把现成的本科教材改编、删减就变成高职教材。教育的目标不同,模式、内容、方法和教材当然不同。高等职业技术教育应极大程度地关注相关职业所需要的基本知识、基本技能,极大程度地了解和剖析专业岗位的操作规范、操作过程。从某种意义上来说,对专业技能和岗位职能训练的要求应远高于对专业理论的要求。而我们目前缺乏的就是这种岗位要求的技能训练教材,是系统而又与生产相吻合的教材,是科学而又容易被操作者掌握的教材。

高等职业教育"十二五"实训系列规划教材就是为此目的而编写的。作者们既是高校具有长期教学经验的教师,又是企业富有管理和生产经验的专家。实训系列规划教材针对不同的行业、不同的岗位要求,搜集了大量信息、题材、案例,让学生身临其境地学习和训练。如果说,实训是高等职业技术院校学生不可缺少的学习环节,那么,这套实训系列规划教材就是高等职业技术院校学生实训前的必修教材。有了它,高职教育可以显现特色;用了它,高职教育可以事半功倍。

愿这套实训系列规划教材为高职教育的改革、发展和创新起到推动作用,愿我们的高职教育为经济和社会的发展作出更大贡献。

  国际商务单证工作贯穿国际商务活动的全过程,是高等院校国际商务、报关与国际货运、物流管理等专业的核心课程。为了使学生了解商务单证领域的前沿信息和最新发展状况,掌握商务单证的审核和缮制方法,我们根据国际商务类专业及其课程设计的特点,组织编写本实训教材,以满足相关专业对国际商务单证实训教学的需要。

  本书以就业为导向,以培养高素质技能型人才为目标,强调基本知识和实用技能相结合,以任务驱动、项目教学、分层指导、综合评价的方式组织和开展教学活动,为商务单证教学提供平台,以适应提升学生的素养、满足劳动就业和继续发展的需要。

  本书是一本注重实务性和操作性的教材,在结构上打破了原学科知识体系,针对实训教学环节进行编写,以国际商务单证员岗位要求为出发点,分解主要的工作环节,通过项目模块教学,强化学生实际动手缮制和审核单证的能力,力求使学生走上工作岗位后能尽快胜任外贸单证缮制工作。本书共分12个项目,充分体现"任务引领,做学一体"的理念。每个项目都由教学活动和体验活动组成,由"实训背景"、"实训指南"、"实训样本"、"实训缮制要求"和"单证模拟实训"五个部分组成。其中,项目一和项目二主要对国际商务单证员工作和单证流转流程作了介绍。项目三到项目十一分别从出口、进口两个大方向入手,对单证流转过程的每个环节的单证操作进行讲解,主要对信用证申请书和信用证、商务单据、保险单证、运输单证、官方单证等相关单据的缮制和审核进行实训。项目十二是国际商务单证的综合模拟操作。本书可以作为高职高专院校国际商务类专业学生的教材或教学参考书,也可作为外贸从业人员的参考用书。

  本书由牟爱春、李琳担任主编,参与本书编写的有牟爱春、李琳、李林海、钱宇,其中,项目一、项目七、项目十一、项目十二由李琳编写,项目二、项目三、项目四、项目九由牟爱春编写,项目五、项目六、项目十由李林海编写,项目八由钱宇编写。本书在编写过程中得到了严玉康教授的大力支持,严教授对教材的体系和编写大纲提出了建设性意见。同时，要感谢上海市国际货运代理协会的大力帮助，在协会秘书长李林海先生的带领下，我们走访了诸多企业，为本书编写提供了大量的实务素材和建议。国际商务、报关与国际货运、物流管理等专业的同学在试用本教材的过程中，也提出了很多宝贵建议。由于经验不足，书中疏忽和不当之处在所难免，恳请使用单位和个人提出宝贵意见和建议。作者 E-mail：1436731761@qq.com。

编 者

2011 年 11 月

目录

项目一　认识国际商务单证员工作 ·· 001
　　工作任务一　掌握国际商务单证的概念 ······································· 001
　　工作任务二　了解单证员岗位工作 ·· 004
　　工作任务三　认识国际商务单证员考试 ······································· 007
　　单证模拟实训一 ··· 009

项目二　进出口合同履行环节及主要单证 ·· 011
　　工作任务一　了解出口合同履行的基本环节及主要单证 ··················· 011
　　工作任务二　了解进口合同履行的基本环节及主要单证 ··················· 030
　　单证模拟实训二 ··· 037

项目三　出口商审核信用证 ·· 038
　　工作任务一　认识销售合同的内容构成 ······································· 038
　　工作任务二　认识信用证的内容构成 ·· 044
　　工作任务三　根据合同审核信用证 ·· 051
　　单证模拟实训三 ··· 057

项目四　出口商务单证 ··· 062
　　工作任务一　缮制商业发票 ··· 062
　　工作任务二　缮制包装单据 ··· 068
　　工作任务三　缮制汇票 ··· 071
　　工作任务四　缮制出口商证明（受益人证明）······························· 074
　　单证模拟实训四 ··· 076

项目五　出口保险单证 ··· 081
　　工作任务一　缮制投保单 ·· 081
　　工作任务二　缮制保险单 ·· 083
　　单证模拟实训五 ··· 089

项目六　出口运输单证——海运单证 ··· 093
　　工作任务一　缮制集装箱货物托运单 ··· 093
　　工作任务二　缮制海运提单 ··· 097

  工作任务三 缮制装运通知 101
  单证模拟实训六 103

项目七 出口运输单证——空运单证和其他 109
  工作任务一 缮制空运托运单 109
  工作任务二 缮制空运单 113
  工作任务三 缮制多式联运单据 118
  工作任务四 了解铁路运单、公路运单、快递单据及邮政收据 120
  单证模拟实训七 125

项目八 出口官方单证——原产地和报检单证 129
  工作任务一 缮制申请书和一般原产地证书 129
  工作任务二 缮制申请书和普惠制原产地证书 135
  工作任务三 缮制出口货物报检单 141
  工作任务四 缮制出口货物通关单 145
  工作任务五 缮制检验证书 146
  单证模拟实训八 149

项目九 出口官方单证——报关及其他单证 158
  工作任务一 缮制出口货物报关单 158
  工作任务二 缮制出口收汇核销单 169
  工作任务三 缮制出口退税单证 171
  单证模拟实训九 176

项目十 进口单证——汇款和开证申请书 181
  工作任务一 缮制购买外汇申请书 181
  工作任务二 缮制汇款申请书 184
  工作任务三 缮制开证申请书 185
  单证模拟实训十 190

项目十一 进口官方单证 196
  工作任务一 缮制进口许可证申请表 196
  工作任务二 缮制进口货物报检单 200
  工作任务三 缮制进口货物报关单 203
  单证模拟实训十一 206

项目十二 进出口单证综合模拟操作 210
  工作任务一 信用证审核综合模拟操作 210
  工作任务二 单据审核综合模拟操作 215
  工作任务三 单据缮制综合模拟操作 223
  单证模拟实训十二 225

参考文献 238

项目一

认识国际商务单证员工作

实训目标

- ◆ 掌握国际商务单证的概念及分类，能区分单证的种类。
- ◆ 了解国际商务单证员岗位工作的基本内容和国际商务单证员岗位的要求，能够掌握国际商务单证工作的要点。
- ◆ 了解国际商务单证员资格考试情况，认识国际商务单证员考试的内容和要求。

实训背景

钱林是某高职院校国际商务专业大学一年级的在校生，立志未来从事外经贸工作。在国际商务单证员、跟单员、外销员、报关员、报检员、货代员等多个外贸职（执、从）业资格证书中，他首选了国际商务单证员。但对于相关情况，他知之甚少。故而，他开始从国际商务单证基础知识、国际商务单证员工作内容和国际商务单证员考试内容开始了解。

工作任务一 掌握国际商务单证的概念

一、国际商务单证介绍

（一）国际商务单证的定义

国际商务单证是指进出口业务中使用的各种单据和证书，如商业发票、提单、保险单和检验检疫证书等，买卖双方凭借这些单证来处理货物的交付、运输、保险、商检和结汇等。国际商务单证有狭义和广义之分：狭义的国际商务单证是指单据和信用证；广义的国际商务单证是指各种文件和凭证。

（二）国际商务单证的作用

国际商务单证在进出口业务中有着重要的作用，主要表现在以下几方面。

1. 单证是货款结算的基本工具

进出口贸易是国与国之间的买卖,是货物与货币的交换。随着国际贸易结算方式的变化,跟单托收和跟单信用证成为国际贸易主要的支付方式。在这种支付条件下,随附的单据成为货款支付的主要凭据。

《跟单信用证统一惯例》(国际商会第 600 号出版物)(Uniform Customs and Practice for Documentary Credits, ICC Publication No. 600)(以下简称《UCP600》)《UCP600》规定,在信用证业务中,各有关方面当事人处理的是单据,而不是单据所涉及的货物、服务或其他行为。《托收统一规则》指出,托收是指银行根据所收到的指示处理金融单据和/或商业单据,以便取得付款和/或承兑。单证是国际贸易结算的基础工具,只有正确、及时地缮制单据,才能保证收汇的安全。

实训案例 1.1

我外贸公司对外出口货物一批,合同规定 2010 年 12 月 6 日交货,信用证规定的最迟装运期为 12 月 6 日。因 12 月 6 日前无船去该国,我方立即与进口商联系延续 20 天。对方表示同意以后,我方在 12 月 21 日装船,12 月 26 日持全套单据向议付行议付。银行审单后,予以拒付。为什么?

2. 单证工作是经营管理的重要环节

单证工作贯穿于整个外贸合同的履行过程中,从合同的签订、信用证的审核、货源的安排到签证认证、投保、运输、交单议付等,单证工作既是为贸易全过程服务,也是为争取安全迅速收汇而进行细致繁琐的工作,这是外贸企业经营管理中的一个重要环节。

实训案例 1.2

某外贸公司与日本客商签订一份销售合同,目的港为大阪。由于单证员疏忽,制单时误填为东京,以致进口货物到达该地。设想一下,这种疏忽会给我方带来什么经济影响?

3. 单证工作是政策性很强的涉外工作

国际贸易是单据贸易,在合同从订立到履行的整个过程中的各种单据,都可以作为在日后发生争议时可以利用的合法手段,外贸企业可以通过出示合格的单据,保护自己的利益不受侵犯。

4. 单证工作是企业业务和素质的体现

单证虽然是商务文件,但却能起到企业对外宣传的作用。优美、整洁、清晰的单证,能展现企业高品位的业务质量,为企业塑造良好的形象,有利于业务的开展。粗劣、杂乱、错讹的单证则必然给企业带来负面效应。

二、国际商务单证的分类

国际贸易业务中涉及的单证很多,根据不同的分类标准,主要有以下几种类别。

（一）根据贸易双方所涉及的单证划分

根据贸易双方所涉及的单证，可分为出口单证和进口单证。

出口单证，即出口国的企业及有关主管部门所涉及的单证。出口单证包括出口配额及出口许可证、商品检验检疫证明、出口报关单、商业发票、包装单据、出口货运单据、保险单、汇票和原产地证明等。

进口单证，即进口国的企业及有关部门涉及的单证。进口单证包括进口许可证、信用证、进口报关单和FOB项下的保险单等。

（二）根据单证的性质划分

根据单证的性质，可分为金融单据和商业单据。

金融单据，即汇票、本票、支票或其他类似用于取得款项的凭证。

商业单据，即发票、运输单据、包装单据等其他任何非金融单据。

（三）根据单证的用途划分

根据单证的用途，可分为资金单据、商业单据、货运单据、保险单据、官方单据和附属单据。

（1）资金单据，即汇票、本票、支票或其他类似支用款项的信用工具。

（2）商业单据，即出口商签发的单据，包括商业发票、形式发票、装箱单和重量单等。

（3）货运单据，即海运提单、不可转让海运单、租船合约提单、多式联运单据、空运单、公路铁路和内河运输单据、专递和邮政收据。

（4）保险单据，即国际货物运输保险单据，由承保人签发，主要有保险单、预保单、保险、证明和投保单等。

（5）官方单据，即由有关的政府职能部门或外国驻中国领事馆签发的单据，如出口许可证、商检证明、原产地证明、海关发票和领事发票等。

（6）附属单据包括受益人证明、寄单证明、装运通知和船公司证明等。

（四）根据业务环节划分

根据进出口贸易环节，可分为托运单证、结汇单证和进口单证等。托运单证主要用来保证货物安全出运，结汇单证用来保证能安全取得货款。

（五）根据单证在结汇时的需要划分

根据单证是否属于结汇时需要的单证，可分为结汇单证和非结汇单证。

结汇单证是指在国际贸易结算中所使用的各种票据、单据和证明的统称，如商业发票、装箱单、运输单据、原产地证明书、汇票和保险单等。

非结汇单证是指在国际贸易中，为了使货物能够顺利出口，在办理相关出口手续时所要使用的各种单据、证书和文件，如出口许可证、配额证明、出口收汇核销单、出口报关单、托运单和货物运输保险投保单等。

（六）根据国际贸易惯例和法律对单证的划分

《UCP600》将单据分为信用证、合同、商业发票、保险单据、运输单据及其他单据。

《URC522》根据性质将单据分为金融单据和商业单据两种。其中，金融单据是指汇票、本票、支票或其他类似的可用于取得款项支付的凭证。商业单据是指发票、运输单据、所有权单据或其他类似的单据,或者不属于金融单据的任何其他单据。

工作任务二　了解单证员岗位工作

一、单证员及其工作内容

单证员是指在对外贸易结算业务中,买卖双方凭借在进出口业务中应用的单据、证书来处理货物的运输、保险、商检和结汇等工作的人员。

单证员的主要工作有审证、制单、审单、交单与归档等一系列业务活动,它贯穿于进出口合同履行的全过程,具有工作量大、涉及面广、时间性强与要求高等特点。单证员工作包括以下内容:

(1) 负责进出口相关单证的制作、管理及信用证审核。

(2) 收集和整理各种单证,完成送货单、订单、提单核对等对单据的各项处理,并进行基础数据录入和归档。

(3) 跟踪每票货物的送货情况,统计核对相关数据。

(4) 及时、准确与货代公司联系装箱,送仓工作。

(5) 在整个过程中,完成与业务员、跟单员以及客户、货代各方面的协调工作。

(6) 协助参与收付汇,外汇核销以及退税的跟踪。

二、单证员工作岗位要求

(一) 单证总要求和依据

单证工作的总要求是"四个一致",即:"单单一致"、"单证一致"、"单货一致"、"单同一致"。"单单一致、单证一致"是信用证业务最基本、最重要的要求,是卖方安全收汇的保障,但在实际业务中卖方还必须做到单据与所交的货物一致以及单据与货物买卖合同相一致。

单证的制作依据以下方面:

(1) 在信用证方式下,单证制作主要以信用证条款为依据。

(2) 在汇付和托收等支付方式下,单证的制作主要以双方签订的合同条款为依据。

(二) 单证制作原则

单证制作原则上应做到"正确、完整、及时、简明、整洁"。

1. 正确

正确是出口单证的前提和核心,单证不正确就不能达到安全收汇的目的。在实际业务中,由于单证不符而遭到国外银行拒付的事情时有发生。

实训案例 1.3

我国 H 公司遭拒付,信用证上受益人名称为,"H Native Produce and Animal By-Products

Import and Export Corporation",而发票上却显示为,"H National Native Produce and Animal By-Products Import and Export Corporation",多加了一个"National",被国际商会认定为与信用证不符。

2. 完整

单证的完整性是构成单证合法性的重要条件之一,单证的完整性一般包括两个方面的内容:

(1) 议付单据应该是一整套单据而不是某一种单据。在信用证业务下,进口商需要哪些单据,每种单据各需多少份,一般都在信用证中表明,出口商只有按规定提交全部合格单据,开证行才保证付款。随着国际贸易的不断发展,进口商为了更好地维护自己的利益,通过信用证要求的单据越来越多,除主要单据外,还要有各种附属证明及办理有关事项的收据。因此,在制单、审单的过程中必须密切注意,及时催办,以防遗漏或误期,以保证全套单据的完整。

实训案例 1.4

以 CIF 术语成交的合同,卖方向买方提交的单据至少应该包括发票、提单和保单三种。遗漏一种,单据就不成套,就可能给出口或进口工作造成影响,银行和进口商也不可能履行议付、承兑或付款的责任。

(2) 每一种单据本身的内容必须完备。任何单证都有其特定的格式、项目、内容、文字和签章等。如果格式使用不当,项目漏填,内容不完整,文字不通,签章不全,就不能构成一份有效的文件,也就不能被银行接受。在实际业务中曾经出现过商业发票因漏打贸易术语、海运提单因漏打运费支付项目而遭拒付的事例。

实训案例 1.5

普惠制产地证表格 A"原产地标准"一栏,虽仅需填一个字母或加上税号或进口成分,但如果漏填或填得不正确,便会使证明书成为一张废纸。

3. 及时

在国际贸易中,出口单证的时间性是很强的。单证工作的及时性要求主要体现在两个方面。

(1) 出单及时。各种单证都要有一个适当的出单日期。同时还应注意各种单证之间日期不能相互矛盾。

(2) 结汇及时。单据制好后,应在信用证的有效期和交单期内送交银行办理议付结汇手续。如信用证没有规定交单议付期,按《UCP600》的规定,受益人应于运输单据出单日期之后的21天内向银行交单,并不得迟于信用证的有效期。

实训案例1.6

议付行将L/C下的全套单据通过DHL寄给开证行,但是开证行说只收到部分单据,而且其中不包括正本海运提单。在这样的情况之下,出口商收不到货款,进口商也提不到货。如何处理,能让出口商收到货款,进口商提到货呢?这个责任应该由谁承担呢?

4. 简明

单据内容应按信用证规定和国际贸易惯例填制,力求简明,力戒繁琐。为简化单证,如《UCP600》规定:"商业发票中货物的描述必须与信用证中的描述相符。在所有其他单据中,货物的描述可使用与信用证对货物的描述无矛盾的统称。"

5. 整洁

单据的布局要美观、大方,其格式的设计和缮制应力求标准化和规范化。如果说正确和完整是单证的内在质量,那么整洁则是单证的外观质量。单证的外观质量在一定程度上反映了一个国家的科技水平和一个企业的业务水平。

(三) 单证更改和管理

1. 单证的更改

各种单证的更改都要有一个限制点,不允许在一份单证上作多次涂改,更改处一定要盖校对章或简签。而有些特殊单证如普惠制产地证表格A和汇票,是不允许有任何更改的,否则就是无效单据。

2. 单证的管理

(1) 商业保密。国际商务单证属于十分重要的商业信息、商业秘密。每个企业、每个员工务必注意保密,提防有损坏公司甚至国家的利益的事情发生。

(2) 存档备查。单证是各个单位和部门最直接的客户档案、商品档案和货源档案,可以随时为企业提供直接的外销业务信息资源,对于总结经验教训,抉择企业未来的业务发展都具有不可缺少的借鉴作用。因此,每一套单据都要收集整理齐全、装订成册,妥善保管。

(四) 单证的发展

1. 制单设计的现代化和国际化

近年来,随着我国进出口贸易迅速发展,出口单证的工作量日益增加,单证工作中明显出现了单证种类多、工作环节多、工作程序复杂、单证流转不快、单证质量不高等一系列问题。纸单证(相对于电子单证)作为进出口贸易的重要凭证已经使用了几百年,然而,纸单证工作效率太低,而且纸单证已经开始给国际贸易的发展带来严重的障碍。一些新的科技工具已逐步应用于贸易领域,如单证制作和管理的电脑化、单证传递的电讯化等,其中最引人注目的是制单中EDI方式的出现及开立信用证中大量使用SWIFT方式。

2. 推广使用国际标准或代码

(1) 运输标志。运输标志由收货人简称、合同号、目的地、件号组成。

(2) 国际和地区代码。国际和地区代码由 2 个英文字母组成,如 CN、GB、US 等。

(3) 货币代码。货币代码由 3 个英文字母组成,前两个符号代表国名,后一个符号代表货币,如人民币 CNY、英镑 GBP、美元 USD、日元 JPY、港币 HKD、欧元 EUR、加拿大元 CAD、澳大利亚元 AUD 等。

(4) 地名代码。地名代码由 5 个英文字母组成,前两个符号代表国名,后三个符号代表地名,如中国上海 CNSHG、英国伦敦 GBLON、美国纽约 USNYC 等。

(5) 日期代码。日期代码用数字表示,如 2010 - 11 - 24。

三、单证员素质要求

由于单证工作在国际贸易业务中的重要作用,所以作为一名合格的单证员,需具备职业素质、职业能力和专业知识等三方面的岗位要求,如下表所示。

外贸单证员素质要求

素质要求	主 要 内 容
职业素质要求	应具备守法意识、责任意识、团队精神、敬业精神、诚信品质等职业素质
职业能力要求	应具备开证审证能力、单证制作能力、单证办理能力、单证审核能力、人际沟通能力等职业能力
专业知识要求	除了要掌握好英语和计算机等基本知识之外,还应熟悉或掌握外贸基础知识、国际结算知识、外贸单证知识、国际贸易惯例、外贸法规政策等专业知识

工作任务三 认识国际商务单证员考试

一、全国国际商务单证员考试背景

随着我国外向型经济的不断发展,外贸业务量迅速增加,各类应用型外贸专业人才供不应求。以外贸单证处理为主要工作内容的国际商务单证员是各企业开展外贸业务的基础性人才之一,然而,如果大量岗上人员未经过较系统的职业培训,企业也很难招聘到符合业务需要的人员,外贸业务风险就会大大增加。

鉴于企业急需大量经过专业教育或培训的国际商务单证人才,商务部中国对外贸易经济合作企业协会于 2004 年在国内推出"全国国际商务单证员"认证项目,它是我国国际商务领域继外销员、国际货代员之后的第三个岗位培训考试和资格认证项目。

二、全国国际商务单证员考试简介

国际商务单证员(International Commercial Vouching Clerk)全国统一考试是由国家商务部中国对外贸易经济合作企业协会组织的全国统一考试,主要是测试应试者从事国际商务单证工作必备的业务知识和能力。

(一) 报考条件

(1) 具有一定的国际商务单证实践经验或已接受过国际商务单证业务培训的从事国际商务单证业务的在职人员。

(2) 具有高中以上学历并有志从事国际商务单证工作的求职人员或在校学生。

(3) 参加上一年中国对外贸易经济合作企业协会组织的国际商务单证员全国统一考试单科未获得通过的人员。

(二) 考试科目和方式

考试科目：国际商务单证基础理论与知识、国际商务单证操作与缮制共两科，每科满分为100分。

考试方式：考试以闭卷笔试答题方式进行。试题由客观性试题和主观性试题组成。

(三) 考试用书

主要依据全国国际商务单证考试办公室编印并由中国商务出版社当年出版的《国际商务单证理论与实务》《全国国际商务单证考试大纲及复习指南》等教材。

三、全国国际商务单证员考试证书

(一) 考试指南

国际商务单证员考试的两个科目中，《国际商务单证基础理论与知识》包括了对国际贸易交易磋商、合同成立、贸易术语、结算支付、货运保险以及国际商务单证的种类、作用、业务计算与相关英语等基础知识的考核；《国际商务单证操作与缮制》则主要考查考生的实际操作能力，包括信用证的审核与修改、单证的审核以及根据信用证或合同规定，准确缮制发票、装箱单、汇票、报检单、报关单、海运提单、保险单、产地证和各种附属单证等，还包括进口单证业务等。

《国际商务单证员》从业资格证书

(二) 合格标准

(1) 全国国际商务单证员培训认证考试的合格分数线为60分(单科)。

(2) 两科均达到60分及以上者方可获得证书。如一门合格，另一门未通过，则合格成绩保留一期，过期作废。

(3) 考试成绩合格的考生，可凭本人身份证向当地考试点领取国际商务单证员资格证书，不再另行向合格考生收取证书工本费。

(三) 合格证书

两项考试全部合格者，即可获得由商务部中国对外贸易经济合作企业协会颁发的《国际商务单证员》从业资格证书。样本如图所示。T]

单证模拟实训一

一、请上网浏览"全国国际商务单证培训认证中心"网站（http://www.icd.net.cn）查询有关全国国际商务单证员考试的相关信息。

二、请根据相关单证基础知识完成下列试题。

（一）单项选择题

1. 单证缮制必须做到正确、完整、及时、简明和整洁，其中（　　）是单证工作的前提。
   A. 正确　　　　　B. 完整　　　　　C. 及时　　　　　D. 简明

2. 各种单据的签发日期应符合逻辑性和国际惯例，通常（　　）日期是确定各单据日期的关键。
   A. 发票　　　　　B. 提单　　　　　C. 许可证　　　　D. 报关单

3. 各种单据的签发日期应符合逻辑性和国际惯例，通常（　　）日期是议付单据出单最早的时间。
   A. 发票　　　　　B. 提单　　　　　C. 保险单　　　　D. 报关单

4. 各种单据的签发日期应符合逻辑性和国际惯例，通常（　　）日期是议付单据出单最晚的时间。
   A. 发票　　　　　B. 报关单　　　　C. 保险单　　　　D. 汇票

5. 根据联合国设计推荐使用的用英文字母表示的货币代码，下列表述中，不正确的是（　　）。
   A. CNY65.00　　　B. GBP65.00　　　C. USD65.00　　　D. RMB65.00

6. 在信用证业务中，有关当事方处理的是（　　）。
   A. 服务　　　　　B. 货物　　　　　C. 单据　　　　　D. 其他行为

7. 狭义的单证是指（　　）。
   A. 单据和文件　　B. 信用证和证书　C. 单据和信用证　D. 信用证和文件

8. 按照贸易双方涉及的单证划分，进口单证包括（　　）。
   A. 商业发票　　　B. 汇票　　　　　C. 信用证　　　　D. 产地证

9. 根据单证的性质，可分为金融单据和商业单据。下列各项中，不是商业单据的是（　　）。
   A. 汇票　　　　　B. 发票　　　　　C. 运输单据　　　D. 包装单据

10. 根据联合国推广使用的国际标准，下列各项中，日期代码表示正确的是（　　）。
    A. 2005/8/4　　　B. 2005-08-04　　C. 04/08/2005　　D. 08/04/2005

（二）多项选择题

1. 所谓单证是指进口业务中使用的各种（　　），如商业发票和提单等，买卖双方凭借这些单据来处理货物的交付、运输、保险、商检和结汇等。
   A. 单据　　　　　B. 证书　　　　　C. 检验检疫证书　D. 保险单

2. 外贸单证工作主要有（　　）等方面的内容，它贯穿于进口合同履行的全过程。
   A. 审证　　　　　B. 制单　　　　　C. 审单　　　　　D. 交单

3. 外贸单证工作具有（　　）等特点，必须仔细、认真、及时地做好这项工作。
   A. 工作量大　　　B. 涉及面广　　　C. 时间性强　　　D. 要求高

4. 单证缮制的具体要求是（　　）。
   A. 正确　　　　　B. 完整　　　　　C. 及时　　　　　D. 简明和简洁

5. 根据推广使用的国际标准，运输标志由（　　）组成。
   A. 收货人简称　　B. 目的地　　　　C. 合同号　　　　D. 件号

6. 货运单据包括（　　）。
   A. 装运通知　　　B. 租船和约提单　C. 报关单　　　　D. 船舱证明

7. 制单中"三相符"的要求包括（　　）。
   A. 单证相符　　　B. 单单相符　　　C. 单货相符　　　D. 货同相符

8. 国际商务单证的工作意义有（　　）。
   A. 单证是国际结算的工具　　　　　B. 它是经营管理的重要环节
   C. 它是企业业务和素质的体现　　　D. 它是政策性很强的涉外工作

9. 下列选项中，属于商业单据的有（　　）。
   A. 发票　　　　　B. 运输单据　　　C. 契据　　　　　D. 保险单

10. 随着海运事业的发展，（　　）发展成为可以转让的结算单据。
    A. 提单　　　　　B. 海运单　　　　C. 大副收据　　　D. 保险单

（三）判断题

1. 单证工作能及时反映货、船、证等业务的管理现状，为了杜绝差错事故的发生，避免带来不必要的经济损失，必须加强工作责任心。　　　　　　　　　　　　　　（　　）

2. 外贸单证员是指外贸业务履行中，根据销售合同、信用证条款进行缮制和出具各种单据、证书的工作人员。　　　　　　　　　　　　　　　　　　　　　　　　（　　）

3. 广义的单证指各种文件和凭证。　　　　　　　　　　　　　　　　　　　（　　）

4. 在国际结算中，货物是贸易双方进行结算的基础和依据。　　　　　　　　（　　）

5. 从商业观点来看，可以说CFR合同的目的不是货物本身，而是与货物有关的单据的买卖。　　　　　　　　　　　　　　　　　　　　　　　　　　　　　　　（　　）

6. 单证"三相符"中最主要的是"单货相符"。　　　　　　　　　　　　　　　（　　）

7. 银行在审单时，如信用证无特殊规定，都是以《UCP600》作为审单的依据。（　　）

8. 单证的完整性是指成套单证的群体的完整性。　　　　　　　　　　　　　（　　）

9. 除交单到期日以外，每个要求运输单据的信用证还应规定一个运输单据出单日期后必须交单付款、承兑的特定期限，银行一般拒收迟于运输单据出单日期21天提交的单据。
　　　　　　　　　　　　　　　　　　　　　　　　　　　　　　　　　　（　　）

10. 根据单证的用途可划分为商业单据和银行单据。　　　　　　　　　　　（　　）

项目二

进出口合同履行环节及主要单证

实训目标

- ◆ 掌握出口合同履行的基本环节,了解出口合同履行的基本环节及相关单证。
- ◆ 掌握进口合同履行的基本环节,了解进口合同履行的基本环节及相关单证。

工作任务一 了解出口合同履行的基本环节及主要单证

实训背景

王杰从某高职院校国际商务专业毕业,进入上海某进出口贸易公司工作,在2011年秋季华交会上遇到了美国Brown Brothers贸易公司的Peter先生,对其公司展览的Wooden Toys很感兴趣,经过磋商,上海进出口公司与Brown Brothers贸易公司会签了出口合同。合同规定,采用CIF术语成交、集装箱班轮运输。王杰负责这笔交易的履行及相关单据的缮制工作。

一、实训指南

出口合同履行的基本环节
(以CIF术语成交、集装箱班轮运输为例)

| 备货 | 安排生产或向供应商采购 |
| 订舱 | 缮制《集装箱货物托运单》(又称十联单),向船公司或其代理订舱 |

如委托货代订舱,需提交《出口货物订舱委托书》,随附《商业发票》、《装箱单》

船公司接受订舱后,在《集装箱货物托运单》的"装货单"联上加盖船公司签单章后,连同《配舱回单》等其他联一并退还

| 报检 | 如货物属于法定检验范围,或进口商要求提交相应检验证书,则需办理出口报检 |

在规定的时间内,向出入境检验检疫机构(Entry-Exit Inspection and Quarantine Bureau)提交《出境货物报检单》,并随附《商业发票》、《装箱单》,办理货物出境报检手续

如委托工厂报检,则需同时提交《报检授权委托书》

货物经检验合格后,出入境检验检疫机构签发《出境货物通关单》和/或《商检证书》

| 投保 | 填制《出口货物投保单》,随附《商业发票》向保险公司投保 |

保险公司接受投保申请后,收取保险费并出具《保险单》

| 认证 | 根据进口商要求,办理出口认证、出证手续 |

例如,进口商要求提交《原产地证明》
填制《一般原产地证明申请书》和《原产地证明》

在规定的时间内,持《一般原产地证明申请书》和《原产地证明》至中国国际贸易促进委员会(CCPIT,简称中国贸促会)申请出证

中国贸促会审核确认无误后,即在《原产地证明》上签字确认并退还

例如,进口商要求提交《普惠制原产地证明》
填制《普惠制原产地证明书申请书》和《普惠制原产地证明》

在规定的时间内,持《普惠制原产地证明书申请书》和《普惠制原产地证明》至出入境检验检疫局 CIQ 申请出证

出入境检验检疫局审核确认无误后,即在《普惠制原产地证明》上签字确认并退还

| 进港 | 出具《集装箱装箱单》(Container Load Plan,简称 CLP),并派集装箱卡车至指定地点装运货物 |

货物运抵海关监管区(港区),场站人员根据 CLP 核对实际装箱情况并签收

报关	在规定的时间内,向海关递交《出口货物报关单》、《集装箱货物托运单》中的"装货单"(Shipping Order s/o 关单,下货纸)、"大副联"、"场站收据"三联、《出口收汇核销单》,并随附《商业发票》、《装箱单》,申报货物出口
	如是法定检验商品,则需同时提交《出境货物通关单》
	如委托货代报关,则需同时提交《报关授权委托书》
	海关查验完毕后,在《集装箱货物托运单》的"装货单"联上加盖海关放行章、连同"大副联"、"场站收据"等联一并退还,在《出口收汇核销单》上加盖海关验讫章后退还
装船	将《集装箱货物托运单》的"装货单"和"大副联"交给船公司,凭此装货
	船方装妥货物,在"大副联"上签字后返还
	凭经船方签署的"大副联"(Mate,Master)向船公司换取正本已装船《提单》
通知	向进口商发出《装船通知》(Shipping Advice) (也有出口商习惯在装船之前发出装船通知)
核销	货款收妥后,收到银行加盖"出口收汇核销专用章"的结汇水单
	结关后,收到海关加盖"验讫章"的《出口货物报关单》"收汇核销联"以及"出口退税专用联"
	在规定的时间内,持银行出具的盖有"出口收汇核销专用章"的结汇水单、盖有验讫章的《出口收汇核销单》及《出口货物报关单》"收汇核销联",向外汇管理部门办理出口收汇核销
	受理核销后,外汇管理部门在《出口收汇核销单》"出口退税专用联"和银行结汇水单上加盖已核销章后退还
退税	向税务机关提供购进货物时的《增值税专用发票》"抵扣联"、盖有验讫章的《出口货物报关单》"出口退税专用联"、盖有已核销的《出口收汇核销单》"出口退税专用联",办理出口退税手续
	税务机关核准后退税

二、单证样本

集装箱货物托运单

Shipper(发货人) DONGHAI TRADING CO.,LTD. ADD: NO 4516, ZHONG SHAN RD., SHANGHAI, CHINA		D/R No.(编号)	
Consignee(收货人) TO SHIPPER'S ORDER			
Notify Party(通知人) NIGROS-GENOSSENSCHAFTS-BUND LIMMATSTRASSE 526 POSTEACH 266 CH8031 ZURICH SWITZERLAND		集装箱货物托运单	
Pre-carriage by(前程运输)	Place of Receipt(收货地点)		
Vessel(船名)Voy. No.(航次)	Port of Loading(装货港) SHANGHAI		
Port of Discharge(卸货港) HAMBURG	Place of Delivery(交货地点)	Final Destination for the Merchant's Reference(目的地)	

Container No. (集装箱号)	Seal No.(封志号) Marks & Nos. (标志与号码) SCHEKERC 06CI-SCH96E HAMBURG C/No.1-300	No. at Containers or Pkgs (箱数或件数) 300 CARTONS	Kind of Packages; Description of Goods (包装种类与货名) STUFFED TOYS	Gross Weight 毛重(千克) 1 527 KGS	Measurement 尺码(立方米) 14.813 CBM
TOTAL NUMBER OF CONTAINERS OR PACKAGES (IN WORDS) 装箱数或件数合计(大写)		SAY THREE HUNDRED AND NINE CARTONS ONLY			
FREIGHT & CHARGES (运费与附加费)	Revenue Tons (运费吨)	Rate (运费率)	Per (每)	Prepaid (运费预付)	Collect (到付)
Ex. Rate. (兑换率)	Prepaid at (预付地点)	Payable at (到付地点)		Place of Issue(签发地点) SHANGHAI	
	Total Prepaid (预付总额)	No. of Original B(s)/L(正本提单份数) THREE			
Service Type on Receiving □-CY □-CFS □-DOOR	Service Type on Delivery □-CY □-CFS □-DOOR	Reefer Temperature Required (冷藏温度) ℉ ℃			
TYPE OF GOODS(种类)	Ordinary □(普通) Liquid □(液体)	Reefer □(冷藏) Live Animal □(活动物)	Dangerous □(危险品) Bulk □(散装)	Auto □(裸装车辆)	危险品	Class: Property: IMDG Code Page UN No.
可否转船: YES		可否分批: YES			
装期: NOV. 31, 2005		效期: DEC. 20, 2005			
金额: USD 65 590.00					
制单日期: OCT. 5, 2005					

出口货物订舱委托书

日期

1) 发货人	4) 信用证号	
	5) 开证银行	
	6) 合同号码	7) 成交金额
	8) 装运口岸	9) 目的港
	10) 转船运输	11) 分批装运
2) 收货人	12) 信用证有效期	13) 装船期限
	14) 运费	15) 成交条件
	16) 联系人	17) 电话/传真
	18) 开户行	19) 账号
3) 通知人	20) 特别要求	

21) 标记唛码　22) 货号规格　23) 包装件数　24) 毛重　25) 净重　26) 数量　27) 单价　28) 总价

29) 总件数　30) 总毛重　31) 总净重　32) 总尺码　33) 总金额

34) 备注

托运单的"装货单"联(船公司配舱后)

Shipper(发货人) DONGHAI TRADING CO.,LTD. ADD: NO.4516, ZHONG SHAN RD., SHANGHAI, CHINA	D/R No.(编号) PONLSHA01836944

装货单

场站收据副本

第五联

Consignee(收货人)
TO SHIPPER'S ORDER

Notify Party(通知人)
NIGROS-GENOSSENSCHAFTS-BUND LIMMATSTRASSE 526 POSTEACH 266 CH8031 ZURICH SWITZERLAND

Pre-carriage by(前程运输)	Place of Receipt(收货地点)

Received by the Carrier the Total number of containers or other packages or units stated below to be transported subject to the terms and conditions of the Carrier's regular form of Bill of Lading (for Combined Transport or port to port shipment) which Date(日期),OCT. 5, 2010

Vessel(船名) Voy. No.(航次) OOCL LONG BEACH V04	Port of Loading(装货港) SHANGHAI

Port of Discharge(卸货港) HAMBURG	Place of Delivery(交货地点)	Final Destination for the Merchant's Reference(目的地)

Container No.(集装箱号)	Seal No.(封志号) Marks & Nos.(标志与号码) SCHEKERC 06CI-SCH96E HAMBURG C/No. 1-300	No. at Containers or Pkgs(箱数或件数) 300 CARTONS	Kind of Packages; Description of Goods(包装种类与货名) STUFFED TOYS	Gross Weight 毛重(千克) 1 527 KGS	Measurement 尺码(立方米) 14.813 CBM

TOTAL NUMBER OF CONTAINERS OR PACKAGES (IN WORDS) 装箱数或件数合计(大写)	SAY THREE HUNDRED AND NINE CARTONS ONLY

Container No.(箱号)	Seal No.(封志号)	Container No.(箱号)	Seal No.(封志号)	Pkgs.(件数)

装船日期:2005年11月15日

	Received(实收)	By Terminal Clerk(场站员签字)

FREIGHT & CHARGS	Prepaid at(预付地点)	Payable at(到付地点)	Place of Issue(签发地点) SHANGHAI
	Total Prepaid(预付总额)	No. of Original B(s)/L(正本提单份数) THREE	Booking(订舱确认) APPROVED BY

签单章 (20)

Service Type on Receiving ☒-Cy ☐-CFS ☐-DOOR	Service Type on Delivery ☒-Cy ☐-CFS ☐-DOOR	Reefer Temperature Required(冷藏温度)		
			°F	℃

TYPE OF GOODS(种类)	☒Ordinary(普通)	☐Reefer(冷藏)	☐Dangerous(危险品)	☐Auto(裸装车辆)	危险品	Class Property IMDG Code Page UN NO.
	☐Liquid(液体)	☐Live Animal(活动物)	☐Bulk(散装)	☐		

项目二　进出口合同履行环节及主要单证

中华人民共和国出入境检验检疫
出境货物报检单

报检单位（加盖公章）：				＊编　号 _____
报检单位登记号：	联系人：	电话：	报检日期：	年　月　日

发货人	（中文）
	（外文）
收货人	（中文）
	（外文）

货物名称(中/外文)	H.S.编码	产地	数/重量	货物总值	包装种类及数量

运输工具名称号码		贸易方式		货物存放地点	
合同号		信用证号		用途	
发货日期		输往国家(地区)		许可证/审批号	
起运地		到达口岸		生产单位注册号	

| 集装箱规格、数量及号码 | |

合同、信用证订立的检验检疫 条款或特殊要求	标　记　及　号　码	随附单据（划"√"或补填）
		□合同　　　　　□包装性能结果单 □信用证　　　　□许可/审批文件 □发票　　　　　□ □换证凭单　　　□ □装箱单　　　　□ □厂检单　　　　□

需要证单名称（划"√"或补填）		＊检验检疫费
□品质证书　　__正__副 □重量证书　　__正__副 □数量证书　　__正__副 □兽医卫生证书__正__副 □健康证书　　__正__副 □卫生证书　　__正__副 □动物卫生证书__正__副	□植物检疫证书　　__正__副 □熏蒸/消毒证书　 __正__副 □出境货物换证凭单__正__副 □ □ □ □	总金额 （人民币元） 计费人 收费人

报检人郑重声明： 　1. 本人被授权报检。 　2. 上列填写内容正确属实，货物无伪造或冒用他人的厂名、标志、认证标志，并承担货物质量责任。 　　　　　　　　　　　　　　　签名：_____	领　取　证　单
	日期 签名

注：有"＊"号栏由出入境检验检疫机关填写　　　　　　◆ 国家出入境检验检疫局制

中华人民共和国出入境检验检疫
出境货物通关单

编号：

1. 发货人		5. 标记及号码
2. 收货人		
3. 合同/信用证号	4. 输往国家或地区	
6. 运输工具名称及号码	7. 发货日期	8. 集装箱规格及数量

9. 货物名称及规格	10. H.S.编码	11. 申报总值	12. 数/重量、包装数量及种类

13. 证明

　　　　上述货物业经检验检疫，请海关予以放行。

　　　　本通关单有效期至　　年　月　日

　　　　　　　　　　　　　　　　　日期：　　年　月　日

签字：

14. 备注
* * *

海运出口货物投保单

1）保险人   2）被保险人

3）标记	4）包装及数量	5）保险货物项目	6）保险货物金额

7）总保险金额：（大写）

8）运输工具：   （船名）   （航次）

9）装运港：   10）目的港：

11）投保险别：   12）货物起运日期：

13）投保日期：   14）投保人签字：

中国贸促会上海市分会
中国国际商会上海商会
一般原产地证明书/加工装配证明书申请书

申请单位注册号为＿＿＿＿＿　　证书号为＿＿＿＿＿　　　全部国产填 P
申请人郑重申明：　　　　　　发票号＿＿＿＿＿　　　　含进口成分填上 W

　　本人被授权代表本企业办理和签署本申请书。
　　本申请书及一般原产地证书/加工装配证明书所列内容正确无误，如发现弄虚作假，冒充证书所列货物，擅改证书，愿按《中华人民共和国出口货物原产地规则》有关规定接受惩处并承担法律责任。现将有关情况申报如下：

商品名称		H.S.编码（八位数）	
商品生产、制造、加工单位、地点			
含进口成分产品主要制造加工工序			
商品 FOB 总值（以美元计）		最终目的国家/地区	
拟出运日期		转口国（地区）	
包装数量或毛重或其他数量			
贸易方式和企业性质			
贸 易 方 式		企 业 性 质	

　　现提交中国出口货物商业发票副本一份，报关单一份或合同/信用证影印件，一般原产地证明书/加工装配证明书一正三副，以及其他附件　份，请予审核签证。

申请单位盖章：　　　　　　　　　　　　　　　　申领人（签名）
　　　　　　　　　　　　　　　　　　　　　　　电话：
　　　　　　　　　　　　　　　　　　　　　　　日期　　年 月 日

如有补发，重发或更改 C.O.证书，请填写背面申请单。

普惠制产地证明书申请书

申请单位(加盖公章): 　　　　　　　　　　　　　　证书号: ……………………

申请人郑重申明: 　　　　　　　　　　　　　　　　注册号: ……………………

本人被正式授权代表本企业办理和签署本申请书的。

本申请书及普惠制产地证明书格式 A 所列内容正确无误,如发现弄虚作假,冒充格式 A 所列货物,擅改证书,自愿接受签发机构的处罚并承担法律责任。现将有关情况申报如下:

生产单位		生产单位联系人电话	
商品名称 (中英文)		H. S. 税目号 (以六位数码计)	
商品 FOB 总值(以美元计)		发票号	
最终销售国	英国	证书种类"√"	加急证书　　　普通证书
货物拟出运日期			

贸易方式和企业性质(请在适用处划"√")

正常贸易 C	来料加工 进 L	补偿贸易 B	中外合资 H	中外合作 Z	外商独资 D	零售 Y	展卖 M

包装数量或毛重或其他数量	

原产地标准:

本项商品系在中国生产,完全符合该给惠国给惠方案规定,其原产地情况符合以下第　　　条:

(1) "P"(完全国产,未使用任何进口原材料);

(2) "W"其 H. S. 税目号为　　　　　(含进口成分);

(3) "F"(对加拿大出口产品,其进口成分不超过产品出厂价值的 40%)。

本批产品系: 1. 直接运输从　上海　到　伦敦　;

　　　　　　2. 转口运输从　　　　　中转国(地区)　　　　到　　　　。

申请人说明	领证人(签名): 电话: 日期:

现提交中国出口商业发票副本一份,普惠制产地证明书格式 A (FORM A)一正二副,以及其他附件一份,请予审核签证。

注: 凡有进口成分的商品,必须要求提交《含进口成分受惠商品成本明细单》。

商 检 局 联 系 记 录

CONTAINER LOAD PLAN
装 箱 单

SINOTRANS
上海中外运船务代理有限公司
CHINA MARINE SHIPPING AGENCY SHANGHAI CO

(5) Shipper's/Packer's Copy
发货人/装箱人联

Class 等级	IMDG Page 危规页码	UN NO. 联合国编号	Flashpoint 闪点	Reefer Temperature Required 冷藏温度		

Ship's Name/Voy No. 船名/航次	Port of Loading 装运	Port of Discharge 卸港	Port of Delivery 交货地	SHIPPER'S/PACKER'S DECLARATIONS: We hereby declare that the container has been thoroughly cleaned without any evidence of previous shipment prior to vanning and cargoes has been properly stuffed and secured.	

Container No. 箱号					

Seal No. 封号	Bill of Loading No. 提单号	Packages & Packing 件数与包装	Gross Weight 毛重	Measurements 尺码	Marks & Numbers 唛头

Cont. Size	Cont. type 箱类			Description of Goods 货名	
20' ( )	DC=普通箱 ( ) OT=开顶箱 ( )				
40' ( )	HC=高箱 ( ) FR=框架箱 ( )	Front 前			
45' ( )	HT=挂衣箱 ( ) PF=平板箱 ( )				
	RE=冷藏箱 ( ) TK=油罐箱 ( )	Door 门			
	RH=冷藏箱 ( ) 高箱 LC=45' ( )				

ISO Code For container Size/Type. 箱型/箱类 ISO 标准代码					

Packer's Name/Address. 装箱人名称/地址			Total Packages 总件数	Total Cargo Wt 总重量	Total Meas. 总尺码

TEL No. 电话号码					

Packing Date. 装箱日期			Received By Drayman 驾驶员签收及车号	Cont. Tare Wt 集装箱皮重	Cgo/Cont. Total Wt 货/箱总重量

Packed By:			Received By Terminals/Date Of Receipt 码头收箱签收和收箱日期	Remarks:备注	

中华人民共和国海关出口货物报关单

预录入编号：　　　　　　　　海关编号：

出口口岸		备案号		出口日期		申报日期	
经营单位		运输方式		运输工具名称		提运单号	
发货单位		贸易方式		征免性质		结汇方式	
许可证号		运抵国（地区）		指运港		境内货源地	
批准文号		成交方式	运费		保费	杂费	
合同协议号		件数	包装种类		毛重（千克）	净重（千克）	
集装箱号		随附单据			生产厂家		
标记唛码及备注							
项号	商品编号	商品名称、规格型号	数量及单位	最终目的国（地区）	单价	总价	币制	征免
税费征收情况								

录入员　　　　录入单位	兹声明以上申报无讹并承担法律责任	海关审单批注及放行日期（签章）	
报关员		审单	审价
单位地址	申报单位（签章）	征税	统计
邮编　　　电话　　　填制日期		查验	放行

出口收汇核销单

出口收汇核销单（出口退税用）

(沪)编号：325623455

出口单位：广州纺织品进出口公司
单位编码：3654984

货物名称	数量	币种总价

报关编号：

外汇局签注栏：

海关盖章

年　月　日（盖章）

出口收汇核销单

(沪)编号：325623455

出口单位：广州纺织品进出口公司
单位编码：3654984

类别	币种金额

银行签注栏：

海关签注栏：

外汇局签注栏：

年　月　日（盖章）

出口收汇核销单（存根）

(沪)编号：325623455

出口单位：广州纺织品进出口公司
单位编码：3654984
出口币种总价：
收汇方式：
约计收款日期：
报关日期：
备注：

此单报关有效截止到　年　月　日

托运单的"装货单"联(海关放行后)

Shipper(发货人) DONGHAI TRADING CO.,LTD. ADD: NO.4516, ZHONG SHAN RD., SHANGHAI, CHINA	D/R No.(编号) PONLSHA01836944	
Consignee (收货人) TO SHIPPER'S ORDER	装货单 场站收据副本	第五联
Notify Party (通知人) NIGROS-GENOSSENSCHAFTS-BUND LIMMATSTRASSE 526 POSTEACH 266 CH8031 ZURICH SWITZERLAND	Received by the Carrier the Total number of containers or other packages or units stated below to be transported subject to the terms and conditions of the Carrier's regular form of Bill of Lading (for Combined Transport or port to port shipment) which Date(日期),OCT. 5, 2010	
Pre-carriage by(前程运输)	Place of Receipt (收货地点)	
Vessel(船名) Voy. No. (航次) OOCL LONG BEACH V04	Port of Loading (装货港) SHANGHAI	
Port of Discharge (卸货港) HAMBURG	Place of Delivery (交货地点)	Final Destination for the Merchant's Reference(目的地)

Container No. (集装箱号)	Seal No.(封志号) Marks & Nos. (标志与号码) SCHEKERC 06CI-SCH96E HAMBURG C/No. 1-300	No. at containers or p'kgs (箱数或件数) 300 CARTONS	Kind of Packages; Description of Goods (包装种类与货名) STUFFED TOYS	Gross Weight 毛重(千克) 1 527 KGS	Measurement 尺码(立方米) 14.813 CBM
TOTAL NUMBER OF CONTAINERS OR PACKAGES (IN WORDS) 装箱数或件数合计(大写)			SAY THREE HUNDRED AND NINE CARTONS ONLY		
Container No.(箱号) Seal No.(封志号)			Container No.(箱号) Seal No.(封志号)		Pkgs.(件数)
装船日期:2005年11月15日			Received(实收)	By Terminal Clerk(场站员签字)	

FREIGHT & CHARGS	Prepaid at (预付地点)	Payable at (到付地点)	Place of Issue(签发地点) SHANGHAI
	Total Prepaid(预付总额)	No. of Original B(s)/L (正本提单份数) THREE	Booking(订舱确认) APPROVED BY

Service Type on Receiving ☒-Cy ☐-CFS ☐-DOOR	Service Type on Delivery ☒-C ☐-CFS ☐-DOOR	Reefer Temperature Required (冷藏温度) °F °C

TYPE OF GOODS (种类)	☒ Ordinary (普通)	☐ Reefer (冷藏)	☐ Dangerous (危险品)	☐ Auto (裸装车辆)	危险品	Class Property IMDG Code Page UN NO.
	☐ Liquid (液体)	☐ Live Animal (活动物)	☐ Bulk (散装)	☐		

澳新银行上海分行出口结汇水单
Payment Advice

出口单位：
SHANGHAI MORNING STAR
TRADING CO., LTD

日期：16JAN2006
我行编号：N0039502/01

出口发票号：051D7905
合约号：
出口核销单号：05879056

	出口币种及金额	：	USD ********50 623.00
减去	国外银行费用	：	USD **********200.00
	信用证通知费	：	USD ************0.00
	信用证修改费	：	USD ************0.00
	议付费	：	USD ***********75.93
	兑换手续费	：	USD ***********75.93
	邮费	：	USD ***********25.00
	电报费	：	USD ***********20.00
	其他费用	：	USD ***********92.58

	净外汇金额	：	USD ********50 133.56
	结汇牌价@	：	
	人民币金额	：	

PLEASE BE NOTED THE PAYMENT TT/CREDITED TO YOUR ACCOUNT NO. 056623500230400125 WITH BOC SHANGHAI BRANCH

摘要：上述款项已于_____年___月___日划入贵公司在_____银行_____分行_____的账户。

备注：其他费用包括

经办：　　　　　　　复核：　　　　　　　核销章：

第一联：出口核销专用联

中华人民共和国海关出口货物报关单

预录入编号：　　　　　　　海关编号：　　　　　　　　　　　收汇核销联

出口口岸		备案号		出口日期	申报日期
经营单位		运输方式	运输工具名称		提运单号
发货单位		贸易方式	征免性质		结汇方式
许可证号	运抵国(地区)		指运港		境内货源地
批准文号	成交方式	运费	保费		杂费
合同协议号	件数	包装种类	毛重(千克)		净重(千克)
集装箱号	随附单据			生产厂家	

标记唛码及备注

项号　商品编号　商品名称、规格型号　数量及单位　最终目的国(地区)单价　总价　币制　征免

税费征收情况

录入员　　　录入单位	兹声明以上申报无讹并承担法律责任	海关审单批注及放行日期(签章)
报关员		审单　　　审价
单位地址	申报单位(签章)	征税　　　统计
邮编　　　电话　　　填制日期		查验　　　放行

中华人民共和国海关出口货物报关单

出口退税专用

预录入编号：　　　　　　　　海关编号：

出口口岸		备案号		出口日期		申报日期	
经营单位		运输方式		运输工具名称		提运单号	
发货单位		贸易方式		征免性质		结汇方式	
许可证号		运抵国(地区)		指运港		境内货源地	
批准文号		成交方式	运费		保费		杂费
合同协议号		件数	包装种类		毛重(千克)		净重(千克)
集装箱号		随附单据			生产厂家		

标记唛码及备注

项号	商品编号	商品名称、规格型号	数量及单位	最终目的国(地区)	单价	总价	币制	征免

税费征收情况

录入员	录入单位	兹声明以上申报无讹并承担法律责任	海关审单批注及放行日期(签章)	
报关员			审单	审价
单位地址		申报单位(签章)	征税	统计
邮编	电话	填制日期	查验	放行

增值税专用发票一式四联,第一联是存根联,第二联是发票联,第三联是抵扣联,第四联是记账联。第一联和第四联由销售方留存,其中第四联是销售方交纳销项增值税的依据,第二联和第三联交给购买方,其中第三联是购买方向税务机关申请抵扣进项增值税的依据。

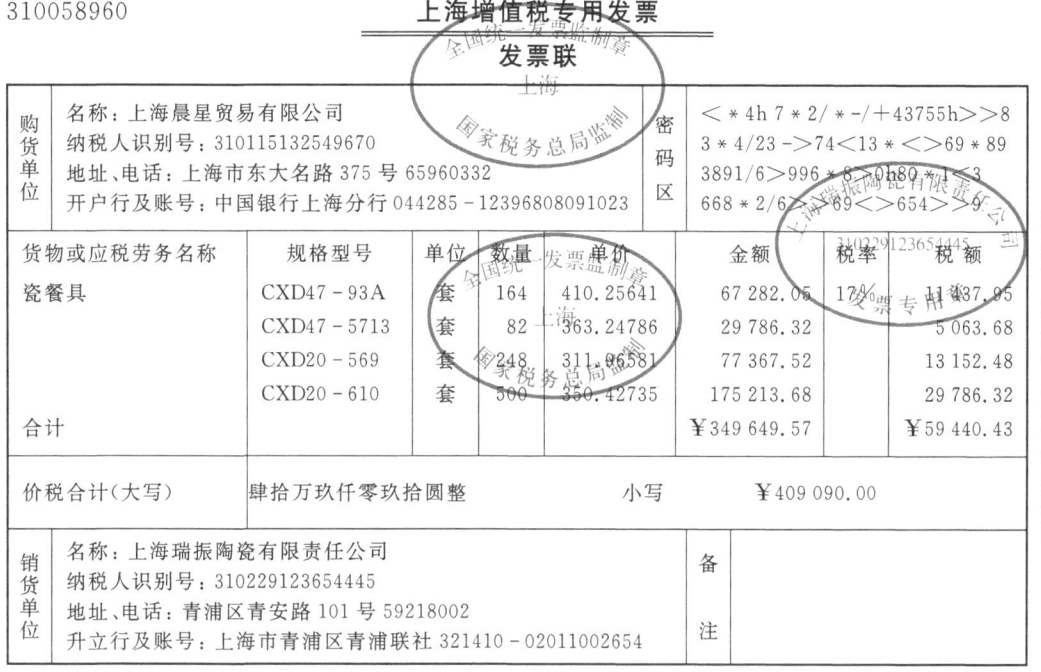

工作任务二　了解进口合同履行的基本环节及主要单证

实训背景

上海进出口贸易公司从日本 Takamra Trading Corporation 进口手动工具一批。为此,上海进出口贸易公司与 Takamra Trading Corporation 进行洽谈,签订了购货合同书,采取 FOB 贸易术语成交,集装箱班轮运输。单证员钱林负责该进口合同履行及相关单证的缮制工作。

一、实训指南

进口合同履行的基本环节

(以 FOB 术语成交、集装箱班轮运输为例)

| 订舱 | 联系出口商、明确备货情况后,及时向船公司办理订舱手续 |

待船公司返还"配舱回单"后,向出口商发出装运指示(Shipping Instruction),明确船名、航次、船期等

或

委托出口商代办订舱手续,及时获取配舱信息

| 投保 | 如与保险公司已事先订立《进口预约保险合同》(Open Cover),则凭出口商发来的装船通知,向保险公司办妥投保手续 |

如无预约保险合同,则在进口货物装船前先与保险公司签订《暂保单》(Cover Note),待出口商发来装船通知后,再向保险公司换取正式《保险单》

| 换单 | 按合同规定安排付款,取得正本《提单》 |

货抵目的港后，凭正本《提单》到船公司或其代理处换取《提货单》(Delivery Order)

| 报检 | 如进口货物属法定检验商品 |

向出入境检验检疫局递交《入境货物报检单》、《提货单》，随附《商业发票》等单证，办理进口货物报检

出入境检验检疫局签发《入境货物通关单》

| 报关 | 在规定的时间内，向海关递交《进口货物报关单》、《提货单》，随附《商业发票》、《装箱单》、《提单》等，办理进口报关手续 |

如进口货物属法定检验商品，则需同时提交《入境货物通关单》

缴纳进口税费

海关验讫，在《提货单》上盖章放行

| 提货 | 凭海关盖章放行的《提货单》提取货物 |

如进口货物属法定检验商品，则提货后至港区指定地点验货

货物出港

二、单证样本

上海市中远集装箱船务代理公司
COSCO SHANGHAI CONTAINER SHIPPING AGENCY CO., LTD

进口集装箱货物提货单

NO. 103845

港区场站　　　　　　　　　　　　　　　　　　　　　　船档号

收货人名称		收货人开户 银行与账户		
船名	航次	起运港	目的港	船舶预计到达时间
提单号	交付条款	卸货地点	进库场日期	第一程运输
标记与集装箱号	货名	集装箱数或件数	重量(KGS)	体积(M³)

船代公司重要提示： 1) 本提货单中有关船、货内容按照提单的相关显示填制； 2) 请当场核查本提货单内容错误之处，否则本公司不承担由此产生的责任和损失；(Error And Omission Excepted) 3) 本提货单仅为向承运人或承运人委托的雇佣人或替承运人保管货物订立合同的人提货的凭证，不得买卖转让；(Non-negotiable) 4) 在本提货单下，承运人代理人及雇佣人的任何行为，均被视为代表承运人的行为，均应享有承运人享有的免责、责任限制和其他任何抗辩理由；(Himalaya Clause) 5) 本提货单所列的船舶预计到达时间，不作为申报进境和计算滞报金、滞箱费、疏港费等起算的依据，货主不及时换和提货造成的损失，责任自负； 6) 本提货单中的中文译文仅供参考。 <div align="center">上海中远集装箱船务代理公司 （盖章有效） 年　月　日</div>	收货人章 1	海关章 2
	检验检疫章 3	4
注意事项： 1) 本提货单需要盖有船代放货章和海关放行章后方始有效。凡属法定检验、检疫的进口商品，必须向检验检疫机构申报。 2) 提货人到码头公司办理提货手续时，应出示单位证明或经办人身份证明，提货人若非本提货单记名收货人时，还应当出示提货单记名收货人开具的证明，以表明其为有权提货人。 3) 货物超过港存期，码头公司可以按《上海港口货物输运管理条例》的有关规定处理。在规定期间无人提取货物，按《海关法》和国家有关规定处理。	5	6

《提货单》共有五联，其分别为：提货单(D/O)、交货记录、费用账单(1)、费用账单(2)、货单留存联。

项目二 进出口合同履行环节及主要单证

中华人民共和国出入境检验检疫
入境货物报检单

报检单位(加盖公章)：   *编号：_____

报检单位登记号：   联系人：   电话：   报检日期： 年 月 日

收货人	(中文)		企业性质(划"√")	□合资 □合作 □外资
	(外文)			
发货人	(中文)			
	(外文)			

货物名称(中/外文)	H.S.编码	原产国	数/重量	货物总值	包装种类及数量

运输工具名称号码		合同号	
贸易方式		贸易国别(地区)		提单/运单号	
到货日期		起运国家(地区)		许可证/审批号	
卸货日期		起运口岸		入境口岸	
索赔有效期至		经停口岸		目的地	
集装箱规格、数量及号码					
合同订立的特殊条款以及其他要求		货物存放地点	
		用 途	
随附单据(划"√"或补填)		标记及号码	*外商投资财产(划"√") □是 □否

随附单据		*检验检疫费
□ 合同 □ 到货通知		
□ 发票 □ 装箱单		
□ 提/运单 □ 质保书		总金额
□ 兽医卫生证书 □ 理货清单		(人民币元)
□ 植物检疫证书 □ 磅码单		
□ 动物检验证书 □ 验收报告		计费人
□ 卫生证书		
□ 原产地证		收费人
□ 许可/审批文件		

报检人郑重声明：	领取证单	
1. 本人被授权报检。	日期	
2. 上列填写内容正确属实。 签名：_____	签名	

注：有"*"号栏由出入境检验检疫机关填写   ◆ 国家出入境检验检疫局制

中华人民共和国出入境检验检疫
入境货物通关单

编号：

1. 收货人	5. 标记及号码
2. 发货人	
3. 合同/提(运)单号	4. 输出国家或地区	
6. 运输工具名称及号码	7. 目的地	8. 集装箱规格及数量
9. 货物名称及规格	10. H.S.编码	11. 申报总值	12. 数/重量、包装数量及种类

13. 内容

　　　　　上述货物业经检验检疫，请海关予以放行。

　　　　　本通关单有效期至　　年　月　日

　　　　　　　　　　　　　　　　　　　日期：　　年　月　日

签字：

14. 备注

中华人民共和国海关进口货物报关单

预录入编号：　　　　　　　　海关编号：

出口口岸		备案号		出口日期		申报日期	
经营单位		运输方式		运输工具名称		提运单号	
收货单位		贸易方式		征免性质		征税比例	
许可证号		运抵国（地区）		指运港		境内货源地	
批准文号		成交方式	运费		保费		杂费
合同协议号		件数	包装种类		毛重（千克）		净重（千克）
集装箱号		随附单据			用途		
标记唛码及备注							
项号　商品编号　商品名称、规格型号　数量及单位　最终目的国（地区）单价　总价　币制　征免							
税费征收情况							
录入员　　　录入单位			兹声明以上申报无讹并承担法律责任		海关审单批注及放行日期（签章）		
报关员					审单　　　　审价		
单位地址			申报单位（签章）		征税　　　　统计		
邮编　　　　电话　　　　填制日期					查验　　　　放行		

上海 海关 进口关税		**专用缴款书**					
收入系统： 海关系统 填发日期： 2005年9月22日 号码 No.(0309)038520451-A01 48							

收款单位	收入机关	中央金库			缴款单位	名称	上海市东汇贸易有限公司
	科目	进口关税	预算级次	中央		账号	
	收款国库	043023-工行市分营业部				开户银行	

税号	货物名称	数量	单位	完税价格(¥)	税率(%)	税款金额(¥)
1.84829900	袖套	1 350.26	千克	220.630	6.0	13 237.80

金额人民币（大写）壹万叁仟贰佰叁拾柒元捌角整			合计(¥)	13 237.80
申请单位编号	3848295598	报关单编号	0838948244	填制单位 收款国库(银行)
合同(批文)号		运输工具(号)	EVER BRIGHT 02	交通银行上海分行 黄浦支行 2011.05.30 业务章
缴款期限	2005年10月8日前	提/装货单号	SH385930580180	
备注	一般征税 照章征税 20050918 进 USD 8.0123000 国际代码：384729593724632 成交：CIF (1) 48935			制单人2967 复核人

从填发缴款书之日起限15日缴纳（期末如遇法定节假日顺延），逾期按日征收税款总额万分之五的滞纳金

上海 海关 进口关税		**专用缴款书**					
收入系统： 海关系统 填发日期： 2005年9月22日 号码 No.(0309)038520451-L02 59							

收款单位	收入机关	中央金库			缴款单位	名称	上海市东汇贸易有限公司
	科目	进口关税	预算级次	中央		账号	
	收款国库	043023-工行市分营业部				开户银行	

税号	货物名称	数量	单位	完税价格(¥)	税率(%)	税款金额(¥)
1.84829900	袖套	1 350.26	千克	233.868	17.0	39 757.56

金额人民币（大写）叁万玖仟柒佰伍拾柒元伍角陆分			合计(¥)	39 757.56
申请单位编号	3848295598	报关单编号	0838948244	填制单位 收款国库(银行)
合同(批文)号		运输工具(号)	EVER BRIGHT 02	交通银行上海分行 黄浦支行 2011.05.30 业务章
缴款期限	2005年10月8日前	提/装货单号	SH385930580180	
备注	一般征税 照章征税 20050918 进 USD 8.0123000 国际代码：384729593724632 成交：CIF (1) 48935			制单人2967 复核人

从填发缴款书之日起限15日缴纳（期末如遇法定节假日顺延），逾期按日征收税款总额万分之五的滞纳金

单证模拟实训二

1. 请写出在 CIF 合同履行中,出口商涉及的部分单据的出单机构。

合同履行阶段	单 据 的 名 称	出 单 机 构
1. 办理运输	海运货物委托书	
	海运出口托运单	
	海运提单	
2. 办理保险	投保单	
	保险单	
3. 办理商检	出境货物报检单	
	商检证书/通关单	
4. 办理报关	出口报关单	
	商业发票	
	装箱单	

2. 选择合适的当事人完成即期议付信用证完整的货物交付及货款收付流程。

     出口商 进口商 出口地银行 进口地银行

(1) ( )与( )签订销售合同,规定以即期议付信用证的方式结算货款。
(2) ( )向( )申请开立即期议付信用证。
(3) ( )向( )开立信用证并委托其通知。
(4) ( )向( )提交信用证。
(5) 在审证无误后,( )向( )发运货物并准备单据。
(6) ( )向( )提交信用证规定的单据,要求议付。
(7) 在审单无误后,( )向( )垫付货款。
(8) ( )向( )交付单据,提出索偿。
(9) 在审单无误后,( )向( )偿付货款。
(10) ( )向( )提示单据,要求付款。

项目三

出口商审核信用证

实训目标

- ◆ 掌握典型销售合同的内容构成，能熟练翻译合同条款。
- ◆ 掌握跟单信用证条款的内容，能看懂 SWIFT 格式的信用证。
- ◆ 掌握出口商根据合同和《UCP600》审核信用证的要点与技巧。

工作任务一　认识销售合同的内容构成

实训背景

王杰从某高职院校国际商务专业毕业后，进入上海进出口贸易公司工作。该公司与美国 Brown Brothers 贸易公司签订了 Wooden Toys 商品的出口合同，CIF 贸易术语成交，集装箱海运，信用证付款方式，在合同签订后不久，Brown Brothers 贸易公司通过美国的 First National Bank of San Diego 银行开来了信用证。单证员王杰的任务是对照销售合同和《UCP600》的规定，修改信用证。

一、实训指南

典型的销售合同一般由以下内容构成。

（一）约首

SALES CONFIRMATION　　　　　——① 合同名称
SHKEL - FL05515　　　　　　　　——② 合同号码
AUG. 17. 2024　　　　　　　　　——③ 合同日期
The Seller：Shanghai Lanked International Trading Co. , Ltd.
Address： Rm. 604B Phoenix Building, No. 18 Huangyang Rd.
　　　　　Pudong, Shanghai 201206, P. R. China　　　　④ 合同当事人信息
The Buyer： IMMENSE INC
Address： Suite 209, Keele St. , Toronto, Canada

(二) 正文

1. 品质条款(Quality)

8065		Coffee POT 900 ML	
116602	① 货号(Art. No.)	Tea Kettle 600 ML	② 商品名称、规格
119303		S/S Cup 300 ML	

2. 数量条款(Quantity)

一般应写明商品各货号的数量和使用的计量单位。

8065	240		PCS	
116602	480	① 数量	PCS	② 计量单位
119303	400		PCS	

3. 价格条款(Price)

    Unit Price   Amount

             CIF TORONTO——② 价格术语

8065	USD 23.95		USD 5 748.00	
116602	USD 28.00	① 单价	USD13 440.00	
119303	USD 6.50		USD 2 600.00	

             USD 21 788.00——③ 合同金额(小写)

Total Amount in Words：——④ 合同金额(大写)

Say Us Dollars Twenty One Thousand Seven Hundred and Eighty Eight Only.

4. 包装条款(Packing)

Art. No. 8065 to be packed in <u>cartons</u> of 12 pcs each only. ——① 装箱方式

                   ——② 包装种类

Art. No. 116602 to be packed in cartons of 24 pcs each only.

Art. No. 119303 to be packed in cartons of 40 pcs each only.

Total 50 cartons   ——③ 包装件总数

5. 装运条款(Shipment)

FROM：Shanghai, China   ——① 起运地/港

TO：Toronto, Canada   ——② 目的地/港

To be effected before Nov. 20th, 2024 ——③ 装运期

With partial shipments not allowed and transshipment allowed.

               ——④ 对分批和转运的规定

6. 支付条款(Payment)

The Buyer should open through a bank acceptable to the Seller.

             ——① 开证银行

an Irrevocable L/C payable at 30 days after B/L date ——② 信用证种类及付款期限

for 100% of total contract value　　　　　　——③ 信用证金额

to reach the seller before Sep. 15th, 2025　　——④ 到证时间

valid for negotiation in china　　　　　　　——⑤ 到期地点

until the 15th day after the date of shipment　——⑥ 到期日

7. 保险条款(Insurance)

The seller should cover insurance　　　　　——① 投保人

For 110% of the total invoice value　　　　　——② 保险金额

against Institute cargo clauses(B)　　　　　——③ 投保险别

as per. I.C.C dated 1/1/2009.　　　　　　——④ 保险条款及生效时间

8. 检验和索赔(Inspection & Claims)

In case of any discrepancy in Quality, claims should be filed by the buyer within 30 days after the arrival of the goods at port of destination;

While for quantity discrepancy claims should be filed by the buyer within 15 days after the arrival of the goods at port of destination.

检验条款通常包含有关检验权的规定、检验或复验的时间和地点、检验机构、检验证书等内容。

索赔条款通常包含索赔依据、索赔期限等。

9. 不可抗力(Force Majeure)

The seller shall not hold liable for non-delivery or delay in delivery of the entire lot or a portion of the goods hereunder by reason of natural disasters, war or other causes of Force Majeure. However, the Seller shall notify the buyer as soon as possible and furnish the buyer within 15 days by registered airmail with a certificate issued by the china council for the promotion of International Trade attesting such event(s).

通常包含不可抗力事件的范围、对不可抗力事件的处理原则和方法、不可抗力事件发生后通知对方的期限和方式、出具证明文件的机构等内容。

10. 争议解决(Dispute Settlement)

All disputes arising out of the performance of, or relating to this contract, shall be settled through negotiation. In case no settlement can be reached through negotiation. The case shall then be submitted to the China International Economic and Trade Arbitration Commission for arbitration in accordance with its arbitral rules. The arbitration shall take place in Shanghai. The arbitral award is final and binding upon both parties.

通常包含争议解决方式、提请仲裁的仲裁地点、仲裁机构、仲裁规则、裁决效力等内容。

(三) 约尾

1. The Contract is made out in two original copies, one copy to be held by each party.

　　　　　　　　　　　　　　　　　　　　——合同份数及归属

2.

Confirmed by:

THE SELLER	THE BUYER
Shanghai Lanked International Trading Co., Ltd.	IMMENSE INC.

(Signature) (Signature)

——合同双方签字确认

二、实训样本

SALES CONFIRMATION

S/C NO.: SHKEL-FL05515
Date: Aug. 17, 2020

The Seller: Shanghai Lanked International Trading Co., Ltd.
Address: RM. 640B Phoenix Building, No. 18 Huangyang Rd.
Pudong, Shanghai 201206, P. R. China
Tel: 0086-21-58348433
Fax: 0086-21-58380910

The Buyer: IMMENSE INC.
Address: Suite 209, keele St., Toronto, Canada
zip: M6M 3Z2
Tel: +1 416 901 9776
Fax: +1 416 901 9778

ART. NO	NAME OF COMMODITY & SPECIFICATIONS	QUANTITY	UNIT PRICE	AMOUNT
8065	COFFEE POT 900 ML	240 PCS	CIF TORONTO USD 23.95	USD 5 748.00
116602	TEA KETTLE 600 ML	480 PCS	USD 28.00	USD 13 440.00
119393	S/S CUP 300 ML	400 PCS	USD 6.50	USD 2 600.00
				USD 21 788.00

Total Amount in words: **SAY US DOLLARS TWENTY ONE THOUSAND SEVEN HUNDRED AND EIGHTY EIGHT ONLY**

TERMS OF PACKING: ART. NO. 8065 TO BE PACKED IN CARTONS OF 12 PCS EACH ONLY
ART. NO. 116602 TO BE PACKED IN CARTONS OF 24 PCS EACH ONLY
ART. NO. 119303 TO BE PACKED IN CARTONS OF 40 PCS EACH ONLY
TOTAL 50 CARTONS
TERMS OF SHIPMENT: FROM: SHANGHAI, CHINA
TO: TORONTO, CANADA
TO BE EFFECTED BEFORE NOV. 20, 2020
WITH PARTIAL SHIPMENTS NOT ALLOWED AND TRANSSHIPMENT ALLOWED
TERMS OF PAYMENT: THE BUYER SHOULD OPEN THROUGH A BANK ACCEPTABLE TO THE SELLER
AN IRREVOCABLE L/C PAYABLE AT 30 DAYS AFTER B/L DATE
FOR 100% OF TOTAL CONTRACT VALUE
TO REACH THE SELLER BEFORE SEP. 15, 2020
AND VALID FOR NEGOTIATION IN CHINA
UNTIL THE 15TH DAY AFTER THE DATE OF SHIPMENT
TERMS OF INSURANCE: THE SELLER SHOULD COVER INSURANCE
FOR 110% OF THE TOTAL INVOICE VALUE
AGAINST INSTITUTE CARGO CLAUSES(B)
AS PER I.C.C DATED 1/1/2009

The contract is made out in two original copies, one copy to be held by each party
Confirmed by.

THE SELLER _____ THE BUYER _____
Shanghai Lanked International Trading Co., Ltd.
(signature) (signature)

三、拟写合同条款的常用术语

1. 品质条款常用术语

样品：	Sample
原样：	Original Sample
标准样品：	Type sample
留样：	Keep Sample
回样：	Return Sample
凭卖方样品买卖：	Sale by Seller's Sample
凭买方样品买卖：	Sale by Buyer's Sample
品质公差：	Quality Tolerance

2. 常用计量单位

千克	Kilogram, kg	公吨	Metric Ton, m/t	磅	Pound
公升	Liter, l	加仑	Gallon, gal.	只	Piece, Pc
双	Pair	台、套	Set	打	Dozen, doz.
桶	Barrel, drum	袋	Bag	码	Yard, yd
平方米	Square Meter, m^2	平方英尺	Square Foot, ft^2	立方米	Cubic Meter, m^3

3. 常用包装种类

纸箱	Carton	木箱	Wooden case
麻袋	Gunny bag	塑料袋	Plastic Bag
包	Bundle/bale	铁桶	Iron drum
木桶	Wooden Cask	瓶	Bottle
板条箱	Crate	罐	Can
托盘	Pallet	集装箱	Container

4. 常用警示性运输标志

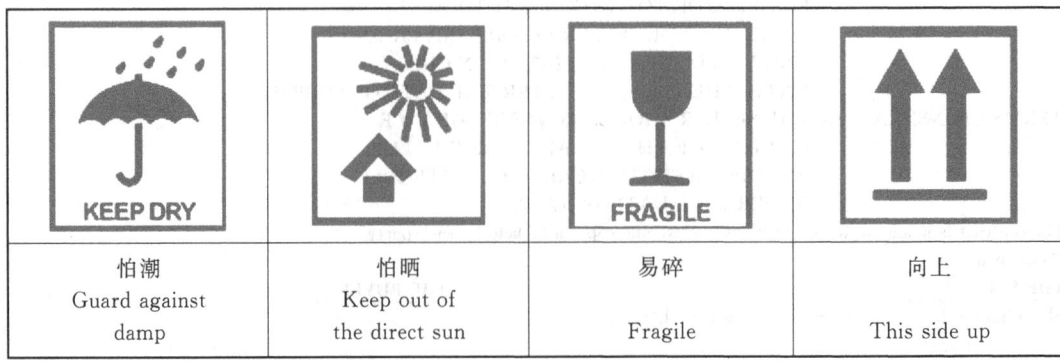

怕潮	怕晒	易碎	向上
Guard against damp	Keep out of the direct sun	Fragile	This side up

5. 保险条款常用术语

	中国保险条款	协会货物条款
英文全称	China Insurance Clauses	Institute Cargo Clauses
英文缩写	C.I.C	I.C.C
颁布机构	中国人民保险公司	英国伦敦保险业协会
生效时间	1981年1月1日	1982年1月1日
基本险别	平安险 Free from Particular Average FPA	协会货物(A)险 Institute Cargo Clauses(A) ICC(A)
	水渍险 With Particular Average WPA	协会货物(B)险 Institute Cargo Clauses(B) ICC(B)
	一切险 All Risks	协会货物(C)险 Institute Cargo Clauses(C) ICC(C)
附加险	战争险 War Risks	协会战争险 Institute War Clauses-cargo
	罢工险 Strike Risks	协会罢工险 Institute strike Clauses-cargo

6. 国际贸易支付方式简介

1) 前T/T与后T/T

交货前电汇付款在贸易界俗称"前T/T",交货后电汇付款俗称"后T/T",而交货时电汇付款,即进口商在收到提单传真件后电汇货款,一般也被称为"前T/T"。

2) 信汇

信汇(Mail Transfer,M/T)结算方式与电汇结算方式的业务流程基本一致,主要区别在于汇出行以邮寄信汇委托书(M/T Advice)的方式向汇入行发出付款指示。与电汇相比,信汇周期较长,收费较低。

3) 票汇

票汇结算的一般程序为:进口商向进口地银行申请开立银行汇票/银行本票,或自行签发支票,然后将票据自行邮寄或亲自带给出口商。在进口业务中,票汇常用于小额货款结算或支付订金、费用等。

4) 即期付款交单与远期付款交单的比较

远期付款交单和即期付款交单的交单条件是相同的,即进口商必须付款,才能取得代表货物所有权的单据。但是两者的付款时间不同。在即期付款变单(D/P at Sight)条件下,代收银行向进口商提示单据后,进口商将见票(和单据)立即付款赎单;而在远期付款交单

(D/P at ×××Day's Sight)条件下,代收银行向进口商提示后,进口商将见票(和单据)先承兑,于汇票到期日再付款赎单。

5) 远期付款交单与远期承兑交单的比较

远期付款交单和远期承兑交单的付款时间是相同的,即在汇票到期日,进口商才向代收银行支付款项。但是两者的交单条件不同。在远期付款变单(D/P at ×××Day's Sight)条件下,当进口商在汇票到期日完成付款后,代收银行才将代表货物所有权的单据交给进口商;而在远期承兑交单(D/A at ×××Day's Sight)条件下,当进口商在远期汇票上作承兑后,代收银行就将代表货物所有权的单据交给进口商。

6) 议付与付款的区别

出口商所在地的银行收到出口商交来的单据,经与信用证核对相符后,即将汇票金额在扣除议付日到估计收款日的利息和手续费后,付给进口方。出口地银行的这一审单、买单、垫款过程称为"议付",办理议付的银行则叫做议付行。议付行议付单据后,即可根据信用证的规定向开证行或其指定的银行索偿。由于议付行的议付属垫款性质,所以当开证行拒付时,议付行可以向出口商行使追索权。而开证行或付款行的付款是终局性的,一旦支付,不得追索。

7) 即期议付信用证与远期议付信用证的比较

受益人(出口商)取得议付的时间相同,只要出口商将全套单据提交给议付行,议付行审单无误后,立即向受益人议付。但是,议付行可从开证行获得偿付的时间是不同的。在即期议付信用证条件下,开证行见票、审单无误后立即向议付行进行偿付;而在远期议付信用证条件下,开证行见票、审单无误后则先向议付行承兑,在汇票到期日才进行偿付。开证申请人(进口商)取得信用证项下单据的条件也是不同的。在即期议付信用证条件下,申请人必须向开证行付款后才能取得单据;而在远期议付信用证条件下,通常申请人在承兑后即可取得单据。

工作任务二 认识信用证的内容构成

一、实训指南

(一) 跟单信用证的定义

《UCP600》第二条对跟单信用证(Letter of Credit,简称 L/C)所下的定义是:信用证指一项不可撤销的安排,无论其名称或描述如何,该项安排构成开证行对相符交单予以承付的确定承诺。

信用证是开证行根据开证申请人的要求和指示或其为其自身业务需要,向受益人开立的在一定条件下保证付款的凭证,其条件是受益人提交符合信用证条款规定的单据。付款人既可以是开证行自己,也可以是开证行指定的其他银行;收款人既可以是受益人本人,也可以是指定人,例如议付行或其往来银行。

(二) 跟单信用证的当事人

在信用证业务中,最基本的当事人是开证申请人、开证行、保兑行(如果存在的话)和受益人。信用证的开立、修改一般都需要经过这四者的同意方可执行。此外,根据业务需要,还会出现通知行、议付行、付款行、偿付行等当事人。

1. 开证申请人(Applicant)

开证申请人是指要求开立信用证的一方。在国际贸易结算中,通常是进口商,也就是买卖合同的买方。从法律责任而言,开证申请人必须依据买卖合同的规定向其往来银行申请开立信用证。

2. 受益人(Beneficiary)

受益人是指信用证指定的唯一享有凭信用证交付单据、支取款项权利的人,一般为出口商,也就是买卖合同的卖方。受益人通常也是信用证的收件人(Addressee)、货运单据的发货人(Shipper)、汇票的出票人(Drawer)与发票和装箱单的制作人。只要履行了按信用证条款发货制单的义务,就有向信用证指定的付款银行提交单据收取价款的权利。可转让信用证的受益人通常为中间商,其转让信用证时就成为可转让信用证的转让人或称第一受益人,供货方为受让人或第二受益人。

3. 开证行(Opening Bank;Issuing Bank)

开证行是指应申请人要求开立信用证、承担保证付款责任的银行。一般是进口地银行。

4. 通知行(Advising Bank;Notifying Bank)

通知行是指应开证行的要求通知信用证的银行。通知行一般是开证行在出口商所在地的代理行。通知行除应合理审慎地鉴别所通知的信用证及其修改书的表面真实性并及时、准确地将信用证及其修改书通知受益人以外,无须承担其他义务。

5. 议付行(Negotiating Bank)

议付行又称押汇银行,是指受开证行的委托,应受益人要求对所提交的单据进行审核并付款的银行。议付行一般是通知行或出口商所在地的其他银行。除非信用证限定某一指定银行为议付行,否则受益人可选择在当地的任何一家往来银行议付。议付行议付后对受益人有追索权。

6. 付款行(Paying Bank)

付款行通常是开证行自身或开证行指定的担任信用证项下付款或充当汇票付款人的银行,是承担信用证最终付款责任的银行。由于付款行通常是信用证业务中汇票的受票人,故亦称受票银行(Drawee Bank)。

7. 保兑行(Confirming Bank)

保兑行是指根据开证行的授权或要求对信用证加具保兑,即在开证行承诺之外作出承付或议付相符交单的确定承诺的银行。保兑行具有与开证行相同的责任和地位。保兑行自对信用证加具保兑之时起,即不可撤销地对受益人承担承付或议付的责任。

8. 偿付行(Reimbursement Bank)

偿付行是指受开证行的委托或授权,对有关指定银行(索偿行)清偿垫款的银行。偿付行是开证行的偿付代理人,有开证行的存款账户。

(三) MT700 格式跟单信用证主要内容

Tag(代号)	Field Name(栏目名称)	说　明
*27	Sequence of Total(报文页次)	
*40A	Form of Documentary Credit(跟单信用证类别)	根据《UCP600》,Irrevocable 不可撤销
*20	Documentary Credit Number(信用证编号)	
*31C	Date of Issue(开证日期)	
*31D	Date and Place of Expiry(信用证的到期日及到期地点)	最迟交单日期和交单地点
*50	Applicant(开证申请人)	进口商
52A	Issuing Bank(开证行)	进口商所在地银行
57A	Advising Through Bank(通知行)	出口商所在地银行
*59	Beneficiary(受益人)	出口商
*32B	Currency Code, Amount(信用证的币种与金额)	
39A	Percentage Credit Amount(信用证金额允许浮动的范围)	数值表示百分比的数值,如:5/5,表示上下浮动最大为5%,39B 与 39A 不能同时出现
39B	Maximum Credit Amount Tolerance(最高信用证金额)	
39C	Additional Amounts Covered(可附加金额)	
*41A	Available With … By …(指定的有关银行及信用证的付款方式)	(1) 银行:With Any Bank 自由议付信用证 (2) 兑付的方式有:By Payment(即期付款);By Acceptance(远期承兑);By Negotiation(议付);By Def Payment(延期付款)
*42C	Drafts at…(汇票付款日期)	
42A	Drawee - BIC(汇票付款人——银行代码,用于限制议付信用证)	
42D	Drawee(汇票付款人,用于自由议付信用证)	
42M	Mixed Payment Details(混合付款指示)	
42P	Deferred Payment Details(延迟付款指示)	

(续表)

Tag(代号)	Field Name(栏目名称)	说　　明
*43P	Partial Shipments(分批装运)	Allowed,Permit,表示允许 Prohibited 表示不允许
*43T	Transshipment(转船)	
*44A	Loading on Board/Dispatch/Taking in Charge(装船/发运/接受监管地点)	
*44B	For Transportation to …(货物运往最终目的地)	
*44C	Latest Date of Shipment(最迟装运日)	
44D	Shipment Period(装运期)	
44E	Port of Discharge/Airport of Destination(卸货港/目的地机场)	
*45A	Description of Goods and/or Services(货物描述)	货物的情况、价格条款如 FOB、CIF 等
*46A	Documents Required(单据要求)	表明该信用证下受益人应向银行提交哪些单据及对单据制作的具体要求
*47A	Additional Conditions(附加条款)	
*71B	Details of Charges(费用负担)	
*48	Period for Presentation(交单期限)	表明开立运输单据后多少天内交单。若未使用该项目,根据《UCP600》在开立运输单据后 21 天内交单
*49	Confirmation Instructions(保兑指示)	Without：不保兑信用证
53A	Reimbursing Bank(偿付行)	
78	Instructions to Paying/Accepting/Negotiating Bank(银行间指示)	
72	Sender to Receiver Information(附言)	

"*"表示必填项目。

二、实训样本

（一）信用证的注意点

请根据以下信用证,作出正确的选择。

ISSUE OF A DOCUMENTARY CREDIT

　　　　　　　　　　　　　　　　　　＊ BANQUE LEUMI FRANCE S. A.
　　　　　　　　　　　　　　　　　　＊ PARIS

SEQUENCE OF TOTAL	＊27：	1/1
FORM OF DOC. CREDIT	＊40A：	IRREVOCABLE
DOC. CREDIT NUMBER	＊20：	55583
DATE OF ISSUE	＊31C：	200826
EXPIRY	＊31D：	DATE 051004 PLACE IN CHINA
APPLICANT	＊50：	BOUTONNERIE SAINT DENTS
		193 RUE SAINT DENIS
		75002 PARIS
BENEFICIARY	＊59：	CHEN HUA IMPORT/EXPORT CO.
		NO. 869 GUANGZHONG ROAD, SHANGHAI, CHINA
AMOUNT	＊32B：	CURRENCY USD AMOUNT 52050.00
PERCENTAGE CREDIT		
AVAILABLE WITH/BY	＊41D：	AT SIGHT BY PAYMENT
PARTIAL SHIPMENTS	43P：	PROHIBITED
TRANSSHIPMENT	43T：	PROHIBITED
LOADING IN CHARGE	44A：	SHANGHAI
FOR TRANSPORT TO …	44B：	MARSEILLES
LATEST DATE OF SHIP	44C：	200919 BY SINOTRANS
DESCRIPT. OF GOODS	45A：	NYLON HOOK AND LOOP FASTENERS
		PRICE TERM： CIF MARSEILLES
DOCUMENTS REQUIRED	46A：	

　　＋ORIGINALLY MANUALLY SIGNED COMMERCIAL INVOICE IN 6 FOLD STATING GOODS, DESTINATION, QUANTITIES AND UNIT PRICE STRICTLY CONFORM TO PROFORMA INVOICE DATED 20.08.18
　　　＋PACKING LIST IN 4 FOLD
　　　＋WEIGHT MEMO IN 4 FOLD
　　　＋FULL SET CLEAN ON BOARD OCEAN BILL OF LADING MADE OUT THE ORDER AND NOTIFY BOUTONNERIE SAINT DENIS 193 RUE SAINT DENIS 75002 PARIS MARKED FREIGHT PREPAID SHOWING "SHIPPED ON BOARD" DULY DATED AND SIGNED BY THE CARRIER AND QUOTE BANQUE LEUMI FRANCE SA DOCUMENTARY CREDIT NO. 55583
　　＋ORIGINAL PLUS COPY OR PHOTOCOPY CERTIFICATE OF ORIGIN FORM A GSP
　　＋2 ORIGINAL INSURANCE POLICY COVERING ALL RISKS FOR 110 PCT INVOICED GOODS VALUE. CLAIMS PAYABLE IN FRANCE BY USD
　　＋BENEFICIARY'S STATEMENT IN 2 FOLD STATING NO MARK OF COUNTRY/ORIGIN INDICATED ON SHIPPED GOODS OR ON CARTONS

ADDITIONAL COND.　　　　47A：
1. IN CASE OF PRESENTATION OF DISCREPANT DOCUMENTS EUR 55(OR COUNTER VALUE) HANDLING CHARGES FOR EACH SET OF DISCREPANT DOCUMENTS AND EUR 22 (OR COUNTER VALUE) FOR EACH TELEX OR SWIFT WILL BE ON BENEFICIARY'S ACCOUNT AND DEDUCTED FROM THE PROCEEDS.

2. ANY OF OUR PAYMENT EFFECTED AGAINST DISCREPANT DOCUMENTS NOT CONSTITUTE AN AMENDMENT OF THIS L/C, NOR OUR AUTHORIZATION TO NEGOTIATE/PAY WITH DISCREPANT DOCUMENTS APPLY TO FUTURE DRAWINGS 3.5 PCT MORE OR LESS IN SHIPPING QUANTITY IS ACCEPTABLE.

DETAILS OF CHARGES　　　　71B：ABROAD/BENEF. AS WELL AS OUR AMENDMENT CHARGES
PRESENTATION PERIOD　　　48：WITHIN 15 DAYS AFTER ON BOARD B/L DATE

该信用证应注意以下问题：

(1) 这张信用证是由"BANQUE LEUMI FRANCE S. A."开立的。

(2) 这张信用证的类型为即期付款信用证。

(3) CHEN HUA IMPORT/EXPORT CO. 是信用证的受益人。

(4) 该信用证规定货物运达的目的港为"马赛"。

(5) 这张信用证项下对汇票的要求为无需提交汇票。

(6) 根据这张信用证，出口运费应在离起运港前由出口商支付。

(7) 根据信用证规定，可以承运货物的船公司为SINOTRANS。

(8) 在这张信用证上规定受益人提交的原产地证明为普惠制产地证明。

(9) 按照这张信用证的规定，由受益人承担单据不符点的费用。

(10) 这张信用证规定受益人提交的提单上的收货人是由发货人指定。

(11) 这张信用证规定提单上必须注明信用证号码。

(12) 信用证要求发票上的货物描述应与形式发票一致。

(13) 开证银行用SWIFT的方式将信用证传递到通知行。

(14) 这张信用证规定的到期地点为受益人所在国家。

(15) 根据这张信用证可以判断出数量允许有溢短装。

(16) 这张信用证规定受益人向银行提交单据的期限为提单签发后15天。

(17) 信用证中规定如有货损，可以在法国用美元赔付。

(18) 这张信用证规定提交保单份数为一式两份。

(19) 这张信用证对货物运输的规定为不允许分运和转运。

(20) 这张信用证中的保险单注明投保中国人民保险公司的一切险。

（二）根据信用证内容填制信用证分析单

IRREVOCABLE DOCUMENTARY CREDIT

SEQUENCE OF TOTAL　　　　　＊27　：1/1
FORM OF DOC, CREDIT　　　　＊40A：IRREVOCABLE
DOC. CREDIT NUMBER　　　　＊20　：XT370
DATE OF ISSUE　　　　　　　　31C　：200210
DATE AND PLACE OF EXPIRY　＊31D：DATE 200420 IN UK
APPLICANT　　　　　　　　　　＊50　：MANDARS IMPORTS CO., LTD.
　　　　　　　　　　　　　　　　　　　38 QUEENSWAY, 2008 UK
ISSUING BANK　　　　　　　　　52A　：BANK OF LONDON
　　　　　　　　　　　　　　　　　　　205 QUEENWAY, LONDON UK

BENEFICIARY	*59	: SHANGHAI IMP. & EXP. CO.
		21 WEST ZHONGSHAN ROAD SHANGHAI CHINA
AMOUNT	*32B	: CURRENCY EUR AMOUNT 126000.00
AVAILABLE WITH/BY	*41D	: ANY BANK IN CHINA BY NEGOTIATION
DRAFTS AT …	42C	: DRAFTS AT 60 DAYS AFTER SIGHT FOR FULL INVOICE COST
DRAWEE	42A	: BANK OF LONDON
PARTIAL SHIPMENTS	43P	: ALLOWED
TRANSSHIPMENT	43T	: NOT ALLOWED
PORT OF LOADING/	44 E	: SHANGHAI PORT
FOR TRANSPORTATION TO …	44B	: LONDON PORT
LATEST DATE OF SHIPMENT	44C	: 200331
DESCRIPT OF GOODS	45A	: LADIES DENIM SKIRT FABRIC; 99% COTTON 1% ELASTIC
DOCUMENTS REQUIRED	46A	: Trade Terms: CIF LONDON

+ SIGNED COMMERCIAL INVOICE, 2 ORIGINAL AND 4 COPIES.
+ FULL SET OF B/L CLEAN ON BOARD, MADE OUT TO ORDER OF SHIPPER AND BLANK ENDORSED AND MARKED "FREIGHT COLLECT" AND NOTIFY APPLICANT.
+ PACKING LIST, 2 ORIGINAL AND 4 COPIES.
+ CERTIFICATE OF ORIGIN GSP CHINA FORM A AND EEC, ISSUED BY THE CHAMBER OF COMMERCE OR OTHER AUTHORITY DULY ENTITLED FOR THIS PURPOSE.
+ FULL SET OF NEGOTIABLE INSURANCE POLICY OR CERTIFICATE BLANK ENDORSED FOR 110 PERCENT OF THE INVOICE VALUE COVERING W.P.A.

CHARGES	71B	: ALL BANKING CHARGES OUTSIDE UK ARE FOR ACCOUNT OF BENEFICIARY.
PERIOD FOR PRESENTATION	48	: DOCUMENTS MUST BE PRESENTED WITHIN 15 DAYS AFTER THE DATE OF SHIPMENT BUT WITHIN THE VALIDITY OF THE CREDIT.
CONFIRMATION INSTRUCTIONS	49	: WITHOUT.

信用分析单

1. 信用证文本格式　　　　　□信开　□电开　□SWIFT
2. 信用证编码　　　　　　　_____
3. 通知银行编号　　　　　　_____□未注明
4. 开证日　　　　　　　　　_____
5. 到期日　　　　　　　　　_____
6. 到期地点　　　　　　　　_____□未注明
7. 付款方式　　　　　　　　□付款　□承兑　□议付
8. 货币　　　　　　　　　　_____
9. 金额(具体数额)　　　　　_____
10. 最高限额(规定具体数额)　_____□未注明
11. 金额允许增减幅度　　　　_____□未注明
12. 交单期(中文)　　　　　　_____

13. 开证申请人(名称) _____
14. 受益人(名称) _____
15. 开证银行(名称) _____
16. 通知银行(名称) _____ □未注明
17. 议付银行(名称) _____ □未注明
18. 付款偿付银行(名称) _____ □未注明
19. 货物名称 _____
20. 合同/订单/形式发票号码 _____ □未注明
21. 合同/订单/形式发票日期 _____ □未注明
22. 价格/交货/贸易术语 _____ □未注明
23. 最迟装运日 _____
24. 装运港 _____
25. 目的港 _____
26. 分批装运 □允许 □不允许
27. 转运 □允许 □不允许
28. 运输标志 _____ □未注明
29. 运输方式 □海运 □空运 □陆运
30. 向银行提交单据列表(用阿拉伯数字表示)

名称	汇票	发票	装箱单	重量单	尺码单	承运人证明	船公司证明	航程证明	受益人证明	寄单证明	装船通知
份数											
名称	海运提单	空运提单	产地证	贸促会产地证	普惠制产地证	商检证	官方商检证	商会商检证	保险单	投保通知	寄单快件收据
份数											

工作任务三　根据合同审核信用证

一、实训指南

对出口商而言,信用证的操作主要涉及以下两个业务环节:

第一,对信用证进行审核,以决定是否需要提出修改;

第二,根据信用证(及信用证修改书)缮制单据,向银行提交请求付款。

信用证的审核要点如下。

1. 检查信用证的付款保证是否有效

如出现下述任何一种情况,则说明该付款保证不是有效的或存在缺陷。

(1)信用证未生效或者对生效有限制条件的信用证,如"待获得进口许可证后生效"。This credit will become operative provided that the necessary authorization is obtained by the applicant from the Exchange Authorities.(软条款。如果申请人无法获得使用外汇的授

权,信用证就无法生效,因此,信用证没有生效前,绝不能因为装运期紧迫,仓促发货)

(2) 应该保兑的信用证未按要求由有关银行进行保兑。

2. 检查信用证的付款时间(DRAFTS AT … 42C)是否与合同(TERMS OF PAYMENT)的规定相一致

(1) 如果信用证中规定有关款项必须在向银行交单后若干天内或见票后若干天内付款,那么需要核对此类付款时间是否符合合同的规定。

(2) 信用证规定在国外到期(PLACE OF EXPIRY ＊31D)。这意味着有关单据必须寄送国外。由于受益人无法掌握单据到达国外银行所需的时间,容易造成延误或丢失,有相当的风险,因此通常受益人应要求在国内交单、到期。

(3) 信用证中的最迟装运日(LATEST DATE OF SHIPMENT)和到期日(DATE AND PLACE OF EXPIRY ＊31D)是同一天。这就是通常所说的"双到期"。在此情况下,受益人不可能在信用证规定的最迟装运日进行装运,而必须将装运期提前一定的时间(一般在到期日前的10~15天),以便腾出合理充分的时间来制单结汇。因此,受益人应比照合同的装运条款,并结合实际情况考虑是否可以接受,否则,应要求修改到期日。

3. 检查信用证受益人和开证申请人的名称和地址是否完整正确

受益人应特别注意信用证中的受益人名称和地址是否与其印就的文件上的名称和地址相一致,以及买方的公司名称和地址写法是否完全正确。如果不正确,则会给今后的收汇带来不便。

4. 检查装运的有关规定是否符合要求

(1) 能否在信用证规定的装期内备妥有关货物并按期出运。如果到证时间与装运期太近,无法如期装运,就应及时与开证申请人联系修改。逾期装运的运输单据将构成单证不符,银行有权不付款。

(2) 如果信用证中规定了分批出运的时间和数量,应注意能否悉数办到,否则,如果任何一批未能按期出运,以后各期即告失效。

5. 检查能否在信用证规定的交单期内提交单据

交单期(Period for Presentation)通常按下列原则处理:

(1) 信用证有规定的,应按信用证规定的交单期向银行交单。

(2) 信用证没有规定的,根据《UCP600》,向银行交单的日期不得迟于运输单据出具日后21天。

应充分考虑办理下列事宜对交单期的影响:

(1) 生产及包装所需的时间。

(2) 内陆运输或集港运输所需的时间。

(3) 进行必要的检验(如法定商检或客检)所需的时间。

(4) 申领检验证明书,如SGS验货报告、OMIC LETTER或其他验货报告(如客检证)等所需的时间。

(5) 申领出口许可证/原产地证明所需的时间(如果需要)。

(6) 报关查验所需的时间。

(7) 船期安排所需的时间。

(8) 到商会和/或领事馆办理认证或出具有关证明所需的时间(如果需要)。

(9) 制造、整理、审核信用证规定的文件所需的时间。

(10) 单据送交银行所需的时间,包括单据送交银行后经审核发现有误退回更正的时间。

6. 检查信用证的金额、币别是否符合合同规定

(1) 信用证的金额是否与事先协商的相一致。

(2) 信用证中的单价与总值是否准确,大小写是否一致。

(3) 如果合同规定数量上允许有一定的伸缩幅度,那么信用证应允许支付金额有相应的增减幅度。如信用证在金额前使用了"About"(大约)一词,则意味着允许金额有10%的增减。

(4) 检查币别是否正确。如合同中规定使用英镑结算,但信用证中使用的是美元,就应要求修改。

7. 检查信用证中的数量是否与合同规定相一致

(1) 除非信用证规定数量不得有增减,那么在支付金额不超过信用证金额的情况下,货物数量可以允许有5%的增减(仅适用大宗散装货物)。

(2) 对于以包装单位或以个体为计算单位的货物不适用。例如,信用证中的货物描述为"5 000 PCS 100% COTTON SHIRTS"(5 000件全棉衬衫),由于数量单位是"PC"(件),则在实际交货时只能是5 000件,而不允许有5%的增减。

8. 检查价格条款是否符合合同规定

不同的价格条款将会涉及具体的费用(如运费、保险费)由谁承担。例如,合同中规定FOB SHANGHAI@USD 50.00/PC,根据此价格条款有关的运费和保险费应由买方(即开证申请人)承担,但如果信用证中的价格条款显示为CIF NEW YORK @USD 50.00/PC,则应要求修改,否则受益人就将承担有关的运费和保险费。

9. 检查货物是否允许分批出运

如果信用证中没有明确规定,应理解为货物是允许分批装运的。如果信用证中还规定了每一批货物出运的确切时间,则必须按此办理;如无法做到,则应立即要求修改。

10. 检查货物是否允许转运

除非信用证另有规定,货物是允许转运的。

11. 检查有关费用条款

(1) 信用证中规定的有关费用(如运费或检验费等)应事先协商一致,否则,对于额外的费用,受益人原则上不应承担。

(2) 银行费用如事先未商定,应以双方共同承担为宜,一般受益人将承担开证国以外发生的银行费用。

12. 检查信用证规定的文件能否及时提供

(1) 一些需要认证的单据,特别是使馆认证等,能否及时办理和提供。

(2) 由其他机构或部门出具的有关文件,如出口许可证、运费收据、检验证明等,能否及时提供。

(3) 信用证中指定船龄、船籍、船公司或不准在某港口转船等条款能否办到。

13. 检查信用证中有无影响收款的软条款

(1) 1/3 正本提单直接寄送客户的条款。如果接受此条款,若信用证项下付款不成功,受益人将面临货、款两空的风险。

(2) 将客户检验证书作为提交单据的条款。如果接受此条款,将影响受益人正常处理信用证业务的主动权,若客户不出具或拖延出具该证书,受益人将无法安全收汇。

14. 检查信用证中有无矛盾之处

例如,航空运输,但要求提供海运提单;价格条款是 FOB,但要求提供保险单;价格条款是 CFR,但要求提单上显示"运费到付"。

二、信用证常见软条款举例

所谓"软条款",是指能够使得不可撤销的信用证无法生效的条款,当然也包括能够使得信用证下的某些承诺可能无法"兑现"的条款。如果信用证含有这类条款,则受益人必须要求修改信用证。

(1) This credit will become operative provided that the necessary authorization is obtained by the applicant from the Exchange Authorities.

软条款。如果申请人无法获得使用外汇的授权,信用证就无法生效,因此,信用证没有生效前,绝不能因为装运期紧迫,仓促发货。

(2) Documents must be presented to us at the date of shipment.

运输单据一般很难在装运日签发并向银行提示。除非信用证要求的单据确实都可以在装运前制备,否则该条款无法操作。

(3) One set of N/N shipping documents has been sent to the opening bank and the bank's telex confirming the receipt is required.

开证行如不发出或不及时发出电传确认书,受益人无法交单。

(4) Sample Receipt issued by the applicant certifying that the shipment samples have been received.

同样,申请人如果不出具或不及时出具船货样品收据,受益人将无法交单。

(5) We confirm this L/C subject to the opening bank's sufficient deposit in our bank.

这可能是"假保兑"。如果开证行在保兑行没有足够的存款,保兑无法生效。受益人很难知道开证行在保兑行的存款状况,何况账户上的存款额时时可能会变化。

(6) 90% of the total L/C amount is payable at sight and 10% will be payable when the applicant issue a no objection certificate.

如果申请人不签发无异议证明,受益人将无法获取剩下的 10% 的货款。

(7) Beneficiary's Certificate stating that one(1/3) original bill of lading has been air

mailed to the applicant one day after shipment.

正本提单如果已经空白背书,申请人获得后即可提货。如果受益人交单发生问题,将钱货两空。因此,有必要核查提单抬头的做法。另外,装运后1日内交单也非常仓促:承运人可能无法及时签出提单,即使仓促签出,如以后向银行交单前发现单据有误,受益人也无法要求承运人更改提单。因为具有同等效力的三份正本如要更改,必须同时更改。

(8) At the time of negotiation, 5% commission to be deducted from the invoice value and shall be remitted by the negotiating bank in the form of a bank draft in favor of ABC Co..

国际贸易中,一般应该争取采用"收妥付佣"的原则。议付行的议付并不等于开证行付款,除非议付行是保兑行。在没有收取"对价"的情况下,议付行一般也不会开立自己的银行汇票。

(9) L/C amount represents 50% of the value of shipment, while the remaining 50% on D/P 60 days after sight 5% commission of invoice value to be deducted form the amount negotiated under this L/C.

D/P下仅涉及商业信用,如果佣金在托收下扣除,有利于约束代理人督促买方支付50%托收下的货款。

(10) … bill of lading made out to order and blankly endorsed showing ABC Co., Hong Kong, as shipper.

这里的香港ABC公司指的是信用证申请人。正如前面分析所提及,空白背书需要由发货人做出。这样的规定操作起来很困难,并且如果发货人做成申请人,受益人将失去提单下的发货人应有的权利。

(11) Except the commercial invoice and draft, documents presented can not show the invoice number.

有些官方或半官方单据要求必须显示有关发票的编号及出票日期,比如,出入境检验检疫局签发的产地证。因此,如果涉及这类单据,本条款无法操作。有些商业单据,比如保险单,尽管也有"发票编号"栏目,但保险公司允许按受益人要求留空。因此可见,审证人熟悉单据的栏目内容以及填写要求非常重要。

(12) Insurance Policy … showing Denny & Jones Co. as the survey agent.

信用证指定了保险检验理赔代理。如果保险公司和该公司没有代理业务关系,绝不会在保险单指定它为理赔代理。

(13) Inspection Certificate issued and signed by two experts nominated by the applicant, the specimen signatures of the individual who were authorized to sign the certificate were being kept by us.

申请人指定的专家如不出具并签署检验证明,则受益人无法交单。即使出具并签署了检验证书,由于受益人手中并没有指定专家签名的样本,无法判断提交的检验证明会不会被开证行以签名不符而拒付。

(14) 32B Currency Code,Amount：USD 4 000.00

……

45A Description of Goods：200 Metric Tons of Sun Flower Seeds with 10 percent more or less at USD 20/MT,FOB Shanghai.

注意,尽管数量有10%的,但信用证金额却没有容差。所以装运时,只能装180公吨至200公吨,不可多装。

(15) 44A　Loading on Board/Dispatch/Taking in Charge at/from：China Port

　　　44B For Transportation to：Chicago

　　　45A Description of Goods：2 000 pcs of Ladies' Coats at USD35.00/pc CIF Chicago as per S/C No. 04－DHN3456

　　　46A Documents Required：+…

　　　　　　　　　　　　　　　+ Full set of clean shipped bill of lading made out to order and endorsed in blank marked freight prepaid notifying us and applicant.

芝加哥并非海港城市,使用CIF术语已经不妥,要求提交海运提单,更无法操作。必须要求修改信用证。

单证模拟实训三

一、根据合同审核信用证，指出信用证存在的问题并说明应如何修改（共 10 处）

SALES CONTRACT

NO.：SAC059
DATE：2008-2-20

THE SELLER：SHANGHAI TEXTILES IMP & EXP CORPORATION
Address：455 NINGXIA ROAD SHANGHAI CHINA

THE BUYER：WBD & CO., LTD
Address：NAKANOMACHI 1-10-15, MIYAKOJIMA-KU OSAKA, JAPAN

This contract is made by and agreed between the BUYER and SELLER, in accordance with the terms and conditions stipulated below：

ITEM NO.	Commodity & Specification	Unit	Quantity	Unit Price	Amount
	APRON			CFR OSAKA	
1	ART NO. 49395(014426)	PC	2 776	USD1.00	USD 2 776.00
2	ART NO. 49394(014427)	PC	3 312	USD1.00	USD 3 312.00
3	ART NO. 49393(014428)	PC	3 699	USD1.00	USD 3 699.00
4	ART NO. 55305(014429)	PC	1 600	USD1.25	USD 2 000.00
					USD 11 787.00

Total：SAY US DOLLARS ELEVEN THOUSAND SEVEN HUNDRED EIGHTY SEVEN ONLY

With 10% More or less of shipment allowed at the sellers' option

TO BE PACKED IN STRONG EXPORT CARTONS

Packing ART NO. 49395(014426) AND ART NO. 55305(014429) IN CARTONS OF 8 PCS EACH
ART NO. 49394(014427) AND ART NO. 49393(014428) IN CARTONS OF 9 PCS EACH

Port of loading & destination FROM SHANGHAI TO OSAKA

Time of Shipment SHIPMENT TO BE EFFECTED BEFORE APR. 30, 2008
WITH PARTIAL SHIPMENT AND TRANSHIPMENT PROHIBITED

Terms of Payment THE BUYER SHALL OPEN THROUGH A BANK ACCEPTABLE TO THE SELLER AN IRREVOCABLE SIGHT LETTER OF CREDIT WHICH REMAIN VALID FOR NEGOTIATION IN CHINA UNTIL THE 15TH DAY AFTER THE DATE OF SHIPMENT

Insurance TO BE COVERED BY THE BUYER

Remarks

Confirmed by

The Seller
SHANGHAI TEXTILES IMP. & EXP. CORPORATION
___蔡昌永___
（signature）

The Buyer
WBD & CO., LTD
___Takeru Takaishi___
（signature）

ISSUE OF A DOCUMENTARY CREDIT

APPLICATION HEADER		0 700 1547 050225 SAIBJPJTCXXX 3846 992024 050225 1447
		* ASAHI BANK LTD
		* TOKYO
SEQUENCE OF TOTAL	* 27	: 1/1
FORM OF DOC CREDIT	* 40	: REVOCABLE
DOC DREDIT NUMBER	* 20	: LC-410-392216
DATE OF ISSUE	* 31C	: 080225
EXPIRY	* 31D	: DATE 080515
		PLACE IN THE COUNTRY OF THE APPLICANT
APPLICANT	* 50	: WBD & CO., LTD
		NAKANOMACHI 1-10-15, MIYAKOJIMA-KU
		OSAKA JAPAN
BENENFICIARY	* 59	: SHANGHAI TEXTILES IMP. & EXP. CORPORATION
		455 NINGXIA ROAD
		SHANGHAI CHINA
AMOUNT	* 32B	: CURRENCY USD AMOUNT 11787,00
MAX CREDIT AMOUNT	* 39B	: UP TO
AVAILABLE WITH/BY	* 41D	: ANY BANK
		BY NEGOTIATION
DRAFTS AT …	* 42C	: DRAFTS AT SIGHT FOR FULL INVOICE VALUE
DRAWEE	* 42A	: ASAHI BANK LTD
		TOKYO
PARTIAL SHIPMENT	* 43P	: ALLOWED
TRANSSHIPMENT	* 43T	: NOT ALLOWED
LOADING IN CHARGE	* 44A	: SHIPMENT FROM CHINESE PORT(S)
FOR TRANSPORT TO	* 44B	: TO OSAKA JAPAN
LATEST DATE OF SHIP	* 44C	: 080430
DESCRIP OF GOODS	* 45A	

(1) 2766 PIECES OF APRON ART NO. 49395(014426) AT USD 2 766.00
(2) 8611 PIECES OF APRON

ART NO.	QUANTITY	UNIT PRICE
49394(014427)	3312 PIECES	USD1.00
49393(014428)	3699 PIECES	USD1.00
55305(014429)	1600 PIECES	USD1.25

PRICE TERM: CIF

DOCUMENTS REQUIRED　　*46A
+3/3 SET OF ORIGINAL CLEAN ON BOARD OCEAN BILLS OF LADING MADE OUT TO ORDER OF SHIPPER AND BLANK ENDORSED MARKED "FREIGHT TO COLLECT" AND NOTIFY APPLICANT

+ORIGINAL SIGNED COMMERCIAL INVOICE IN 5 FOLD INDICATING CONTRACT NO.

+INSURANCE POLICY OR CERTIFICATE, ENDORSED IN BLANK, FOR 110PCT OF THE INVOICE VALUE INCLUDING: THE INSTITUTE CARGO CLAUSE(A), THE INSTITUTE WAR CLAUSE AND THE INSTITUTE STRIKES, ROIT AND CIVIL MOTIONS CLAUSES, INSURANCE CLAIMS TO BE PAYABLE IN JAPAN

+CERTIFICATE OF ORIGIN IN 1 ORIGINAL AND 1 COPY

+PACKING LIST IN 3 FOLD

+WEIGHT LIST IN 3 FOLD

ADDITIONAL COND.　　*47
　　　　1. T.T. REIMBURSEMENT IS PROHIBITED
　　　　2. 5PCT MORE OR LESS IN QUANTITY ACCEPTABLE
　　　　3. THE GOODS TO BE PACKED IN STRONG EXPORT CARTONS

DETAILS OF CHARGES　　*71B : ALL BANKING CHARGES OUTSIDE JAPAN INCLUDING REIMBURSEMENT COMMISSIONS ARE FOR ACCOUNT OF BENEFICIARY.

PRESENTATION PERIOD　　*48 : DOCUMENTS TO BE PRESENTED WITHIN 5 DAYS AFTER THE DATE OF SHIPMENT, BUT WITHIN THE VALIDITY OF THE CREDIT.

CONFIRMATION　　*49 : WITHOUT

INSTRUCTIONS　　*78 :
　　　　THIS CREDIT IS NON-OPERATIVE UNLESS THE OPENING BANK GIVE FURTHER ADVICE.
　　　　THE NEGOTIATION BANK MUST FORWARD THE DRAFTS AND ALL DOCUMENTS BY REGISTERED AIRMAIL DIRECT TO US (INT'L OPERATIONS CENTER MAIL ADDRESS: C.P.O. BOX NO. 800 TOKYO 100-91 JAPAN) IN TWO CONSECUTIVE LOTS, UPON RECEIPT OF THE DRAFTS AND DOCUMENTS IN ORDER, WE WILL REIMBURSE THE NEGOTIATING BANK IN ACCORDANCE WITH THEIR INSTRUCTION.

二、根据合同审核信用证，指出信用证存在的问题并说明应如何修改（共 18 处）

SALES CONTRACT

THE SELLER: NO. YH08039
SHANDONG YIHAI IMP. & EXP. CO., LTD. DATE: DEC. 1, 2008
NO. 51 JINSHUI ROAD, QINGDAO, CHINA SIGNED AT: QINGDAO, CHINA

THE BUYER:
LINSA PUBLICIDAD, S. A.
VALENCIA, 195 BAJOS. 08011. BARCELONA, SPAIN

This Sales Contract is made by and between the Sellers and the Buyers, whereby the sellers agree to sell and the buyers agree to buy the under-mentioned goods according to the terms and conditions stipulated below:

Commodity & Specification	Quantity	Price Terms	
		Unit price	Amount
CARDHOLDER DYED COW LEATHER BLACK BROWN	5 000 PCS 8 000 PCS	FOB QINGDAO USD1.45/PC USD1.50/PC	USD7 250.00 USD12 000.00 USD19 250.00
Total amount: U. S. DOLLARS NINETEEN THOUSAND TWO HUNDRED AND FIFTY ONLY			

Packing: 1PC/POLYBAG, 500 PCS/CTN   Shipping Mark: L. P.
Time of Shipment: DURING JAN. 2009 BY SEA   BARCELONA
                                 NOS. 1-26
Loading Port and Destination: FROM QINGDAO TO BARCELONA
Partial Shipment and Transshipment: ALLOWED
Insurance: TO BE EFFECTED BY THE BUYER.
Terms of Payment: THE BUYER SHALL OPEN THROUGH A BANK ACCEPTABLE TO THE SELLER AN IRREVOCABLE SIGHT LETTER OF CREDIT TO REACH THE SELLER 30 DAYS BEFORE THE MONTH OF SHIPMENT AND TO REMAIN VALID FOR NEGOTIATION IN CHINA UNTIL THE 15TH DAY AFTER THE FORESAID TIME OF SHIPMENT.

ISSUE OF DOCUMENTARY CREDIT

27: SEQUENCE OF TOTAL: 1/1
40A: FORM OF DOC. CREDIT: IRREVOCABLE
20: DOC. CREDIT NUMBER: 103CD137273
31C: DATE OF ISSUE: 081215
40E: APPLICABLE RULES: UCP LATEST VERSION
31D: DATE AND PLACE OF EXPIRY: DATE 090202 PLACE IN SPAIN
51D: APPLICANT BANK: BANCO SANTANDER, S. A.
            28660 BOADILLA DEL BARCELONA, SPAIN
50: APPLICANT: LINSAPUBLICIDAD, S. A.
            VALENCIA, 195 BAJOS. 08011. BARCELONA, SPAIN
59: BENEFICIARY: SHANDONG YIHAN IMP. & EXP. CO., LTD
            NO. 51 JINSHU1 ROAD, QINGDAO, CHINA
32B: AMOUNT: CURRENCYEURAMOUNT 19250.00

41A: AVAILABLE WITH…BY   ANY BANK IN CHINA BY NEGOTIATION
42C: DRAFTS AT… 30 DAYS AFTER SIGHT
42A: DRAWEE: LINSA PUBLICIDAD, S. A.
43P: PARTIAL SHIPMTS: NOT ALLOWED
43T: TRANSSHIPMENT: NOT ALLOWED
44E: PORT OF LOADING: ANY CHINESE PORT
44F: PORT OF DISCHARGE: VALENCIA, SPAIN
44C: LATEST DATE OF SHIPMENT: 090115
45A: DESCRIPTION OF GOODS
    GOODS AS PER S/C NO. YH08036 DATED ON DEC. 1, 2008
    CARDHOLDER DYED COW LEATHER
    BLACK COLOUR/8 000 PCS AT USD 1.45/PC FOB QINGDAO
    BROWN COLOUR/5 000 PCS AT USD 1.50/PC FOB QINGDAO
    PACKING: 200PCS/CTN
46A: DOCUMENTS REQUIRED
    + SIGNED COMMERCIAL INVOICE IN 3 COPIES
    + CERTIFICATE OF ORIGIN GSP FORM A ISSUED BY OFFICIAL AUTHORITIES
    + PACKING LIST IN 3 COPIES
    + FULL SET CLEAN ON BOARD BILLS OF LADING MADE OUT TO ORDER MARKED FREIGHT PREPAID AND NOTIFY APPLICANT
    + INSURANCE POLICY/CERTIFICATE IN DUPLICATE ENDORSED IN BLANK FOR 110% INVOICE VALUE COVERING ALL RISKS AND WAR RISK AS PER CIC.
47A: ADDITIONAL CONDITIONS
    BILL OF LADING ONLY ACCEPTABLE IF ISSUED BY ONE OF THE FOLLOWING SHIPPING COMPANIES: KUEHNE-NAGEL (BLUE ANCHOR LINE) VILTRANS (CHINA) INT'L FORWARDING LTD. OR VILTRANS SHIPPING (HK) CO., LTD.
71B: CHARGES: ALL CHARGES ARE TO BE BORN BY BENEFICIARY
48: PERIOD FOR PRESENTATION: WITHIN 5 DAYS AFTER THE DATE OF SHIPMENT, BUT WITHIN THE VALIDITY OF THIS CREDIT
49: CONFIRMATION INSTRUCTION: WITHOUT

经审核信用证存在如下问题：

项目四

出口商务单证

实训目标

◆ 了解商业发票、海关发票、形式发票、领事发票和厂商发票的概念和作用,掌握商业发票的内容以及缮制要求,并学会独立缮制商业发票。
◆ 了解包装单据填制要求,学会填制各种包装单据。
◆ 了解信用证项下汇票和托收项下汇票缮制要求,学会缮制汇票。
◆ 了解出口商证明(受益人证明)缮制要求,学会缮制各种出口商证明(受益人证明)。

工作任务一 缮制商业发票

实训背景

王杰从某高职院校国际商务专业毕业后,进入上海进出口贸易公司工作。该公司与美国 Brown Brothers 贸易公司签订了 Wooden Toys 商品的出口合同,CIF 贸易术语成交,集装箱海运,信用证付款方式,在货物装船后,王杰需要缮制全套单据向银行交单议付。

一、实训指南

商业发票(Commercial Invoice)简称发票,是出口商向进口商开出的载明销售货物详情的单据。

其主要作用有:

(1)收付货款和记账的凭证。
(2)办理订舱、报关、报检等手续时对货物的说明。
(3)卖方缮制其他单据的依据。

二、实训样本

ISSUER DALIAN TAISHAN SUITCASE & BAG CO., LTD 66 ZHONGSHAN ROAD DALIAN 116001, CHINA	商业发票		
TO ORTAI CO., LTD. 30 EAST 40TH STREET, NEW YORK 10016 TEL: 001-212-992-9788 FAX: 001-212-992-9789	COMMERCIAL INVOICE		
	NO. TSI0801005	DATE Aug. 5, 2020	
TRANSPORT DETAILS FROM DALIAN CHINA TO NEW YORK U.S.A BY SEA	S/C NO. TSSC0801005	L/C NO. N5632405TH11808	
	TERMS OF PAYMENT L/C		
Marks and Numbers	Number and kind of package Description of goods	Quantity	Unit Price	Amount
ORTAI TSI0801005 NEW YORK C/NO. 1-1231	CIF NEWYORK			
	Trolley Cases TS503214 TS503215 TS503216	1 104 PCS 1 149 PCS 1 440 PCS	USD 6.50/PC USD 6.00/PC USD 5.80/PC	USD 7 176.00 USD 6 894.00 USD 8 352.00
	TOTAL:	3 693 PCS		USD 22 422.00
TOTAL: SAY U.S. DOLLARS TWENTY TWO THOUSAND FOUR HUNDRED AND TWENTY TWO ONLY WE HEREBY CERTIFY THAT THE CONTENTS IN THIS INVOICE ARE TRUE AND CORRECT. DALIAN TAISHAN SUITCASE & BAG CO., LTD.				

三、实训缮制要求

商业发票一般无统一格式,由出口商自行设计,但内容必须要符合信用证或合同的要求。其基本内容及制单要点如下。

1. 出票人的名称与地址

根据《UCP600》,发票的出票人必须为信用证的受益人(Beneficiary),其名称和地址相对固定,故出口商通常将此项内容事先印制在发票的上方或右下方。

2. 发票的名称

单据上一般标明"发票"(Invoice)或"商业发票"(Commercial Invoice)字样,用粗题字印刷在单据的明显位置。

3. 出票的日期和地点

发票一般早于装运日。由于申请产地证等,必须提交发票,所以,发票日期早于这些单据。发票日期不得晚于交单日。发票日期最好不要晚于提单的出具日期而且要在信用证规定的议付期之前。此外,卖方经常签订合同后即开立发票,出具日期也就早于信用证开立日期,根据《UCP600》的规定,这是允许的。

4. 发票编号、合同编号和信用证编号

发票编号一般由出口公司自行编制,在发票号码的顺序数字中能看出这一票业务是哪个部门及谁做的,具体的年份,以便于日后查找。为了便于核对,一般还注明有关的合同和信用证编号。

S/C No.：Sales contract,销售合同号。

P/O No.：Purchase Order,采购订单号。

如果 L/C 中要求："ALL DOCUMENTS MUST SHOW THE CREDIT NO."所有单据都要注明信用证号,必须要注明信用证号。

当采用托收和其他支付方式时,此项也可不填。

5. 起运地及目的地

如货物需要转运,则注明转运地。有的还注明运输方式"from…(装货港)to…(目的港)by vessel(海运)"。

如果货物需经转运,应把转运港的名称打上。如：Shipment from Shanghai to Hamburg with transshipment(W/T) at Hong Kong by vessel.(装运自上海到汉堡,在香港转运)或者 from Shanghai Via Hong Kong to Hamburg。

6. 抬头人

即收货人,此栏前通常印有"To"或"Sold to"等字样。根据《UCP600》,发票抬头必须为开证申请人(Applicant),即买方的名称和地址。如：

L/C："… INVOICE IN THE NAME OF ABC CO."或者"… INVOICE ADDRESS TO ABC CO.",此栏应为 ABC CO.

当采用托收或其他方式支付货款时,填写合同买方的名称和地址。填写时需注意的是,公司名称和地址要分两行打,而且必须打上名称和地址的全称。名称一般一行打完,不能换行,地址则可合理分行。

7. 唛头(Shipping Marks)和编号

该栏一般注明包装的运输标记和集装箱号(Container No.)及封号(Seal No.)。ISO 建议,唛头由收货人名称缩写、合同号、目的港、件数号等四行部分,如货物还要转运到内陆目的地,可打上"IN TRANSIT TO×××"等字样,一般由卖方自行设计。若信用证或合同中有规定,必须按规定填写,并与提单、托运单等单据严格一致。如果无唛头,或者裸装货、散装货等,则应填写"NO MARKS"(缩写 N/M)。

8. 品名和货物描述

该栏一般印有"Description of Goods"的字样,在其下一般注明具体装运的货物的名称、品质、规格及包装状况等内容。内容必须与信用证规定的货物描述完全一致,必要时要照信用证原样打印,不得随意减少内容,否则有可能被银行视为不符点。

Commodity,Merchandise 等也可以表示货物。ART No. 翻译为货号。As per contract no…,As per P/O No…翻译为:根据……号合同或采购订单。

9. 数量、单价和总价

单价(Unit Price)包括计价货币、具体价格数、计价单位、贸易术语四部分。根据《UCP600》,商业发票货币必须与信用证货币相同。

总价(Amount)不能超过信用证规定的最高金额。但是信用证总值前有"约"、"大概"、"大约"或类似词语的,允许有10%的增减幅度。一般由大小写组成。

如果合同单价含有佣金(Commission)或折扣(Discount),发票上一般也会注明。

如信用证规定发票金额要扣除相应佣金的,例如,信用证条款规定"5% COMMISSION TO BE DEDUCTED FROM INVOICE VALUE"或有其他类似的条款规定的话,商业发票总金额应按规定表示扣除佣金,同时在扣除后计算净额。

QTY.	Unit Price	Amount
100pcs	CIF C5 NEW YORK USD 100/pc Less 5% Commission: CIF NET VALUE:	USD 10 000.00 USD 500.00 USD 9 500.00

另外,有时根据买方的要求,对按照 CIF、CIP 或者 CFR、CPT 成交的,发票上还分别列明运费(Freight)、保费(Premium)和 FOB 或者 FCA 价值。

信用证下的发票金额不应超过信用证金额。

10. E.&O.E(有错当查)字句

有些发票下端印有 E.&O.E 字句,此系签发人事先声明,一旦发票有误,可以更正。若发票加注了证实所列内容真实无误的证明文句,则应将 E.&O.E 字样删除。

11. 声明文句

声明文句是根据不同国家(地区)及不同信用证的要求缮写的,要求确切、通顺、简洁。如:

WE HEREBY CERTIFY THAT THE ABOVE MENTIONED GOODS ARE OF CHINESE ORIGIN.(兹证明上述产品在中国制造。)

WE CERTIFY THAT THE GOODS NAMED ABOVE HAVE BEEN SUPPLIED IN CONFORMITY WITH ORDER NO.12345.

(兹证明本发票所列货物与合同号 12345 相符。)

12. 支付方式

支付方式(Terms of Payment)。填写交易合同所采用的支付方式,如信用证、汇付、托收等。

13. 出票人签章

签字盖章处一般位于发票的右下方。根据《UCP600》第 18 条的规定,商业发票无须签署,但如果信用证要求提交签署的发票"SIGNED COMMERCIAL INVOICE"或手签的发票"MANUALLY SIGNED",则发票必须签署,且后者还必须由发票授权签字人手签。我国出口企业一般手签或手签并盖章,并注明公司名称。

四、其他类型发票

(一) 加拿大海关发票

 Revenue Canada   **CANADA CUSTOMS INVOICE**

1. Vendor(Name and Address)	2. Date of Direct Shipment to Canada		
	3. Other References(Include Purchaser's Order No.)		
4. Consignee(Name and Address)	5. Purchaser's Name and Address(If other than Consignee)		
	6. Country of Transshipment		
	7. Country of Origin of Goods	IF SHIPMENT INCLUDES GOODS OF DIFFERENT ORIGINSENTER ORIGINS AGAINST ITEMS IN 12	
8. Transportation: Gave Mode and Place of Direct Shipment to Canada	9. Conditions of Sale and Terms of Payment		
	10. Currency of Settlement		
11. No. of Pkgs	12. Specification of Commodities (Kind of Packages, Marks and Numbers, General Description and Characteristics, i. e. Grade, Quality)	13. Quantity (State Unit)	Selling Price
			14. Unit Price / 15. Total
16. If any fields 1 to 17 are included on an attached commercial invoice, check this box ☐ Commercial Invoice No. _____	17. Total weight		18. Invoice Total
	Net	Gross	
19. Exporter's Name and Address(If other than Vendor)	20. Originator(Name and Address)		
21. Departmental Ruling(if applicable)	22. If fields 23 to 25 are not applicable, check this box ☐		
23. If included in field 17 indicate amount: (i) Transportation charges, expenses and insurance from the place of direct shipment to Canada $ _____ (ii) Costs for construction, erection and assembly incurred after importation into Canada $ _____ (iii) Export packing $ _____	24. If not included in field 17 indicate amount: (i) Transportation charges, expenses and insurance to the place of direct shipment to Canada $ _____ (ii) Amount for commissions other than buying commissions $ _____ (iii) Export packing $ _____		25. Check(if applicable): (i) Royalty payments or subsequent proceeds are paid or payable by the purchaser ☐ (ii) The purchaser has supplied goods or services for use in the production of these goods ☐

(二) 形式发票

Issuer: (1) SHANGHAI LUCKY SAFETY SCREENS CO., LTD. UNIT C 2/F JINGMAO TOWER SHANGHAI, CHINA.		**PROFORMA INVOICE**	
To: (2) RAM PLASTICS 201, HAUZ RANI, MALVIYA NAGAR, NEW DELHI 110017, INDIA		No. (3) LU80518	Date: (4) May 18, 2010
Transport details: (5) From Shanghai China to Nhava Sheva India by sea		S/C No. (6) LU0805	
^		Terms of payment: (7) Advanced T/T	
Marks & Nos.	Description of goods and Quantity	Unit Price	Amount
(8) R. P. LU80518 Nhava Sheva Nos 1-up	(9) 200 mm×2 mm×50 m transparent normal 120 rolls 200 mm×2 mm×50 m transparent normal ribbed 10 rolls 200 mm×3 mm×50 m transparent normal 20 rolls 300 mm×3 mm×50 m transparent normal 30 rolls 300 mm×3 mm×50 m transparent normal ribbed 20 rolls 200 rolls	(10) CIF Nhava Sheva USD 86.00/roll USD 98.00/roll USD 92.00/roll USD 108.00/roll USD 116.00/roll	(11) USD 10 320.00 USD 980.00 USD 1 840.00 USD 3 240.00 USD 2 320.00 USD 18 700.00

(12) DETAILS OF OUR BANK:
　　　BANK OF CHINA, SHANGHAI BRANCH,
　　　NO. 4 Zhongshan road, Shanghai, P. R. CHINA
　　　SWIFT CODE: BKCHCNBJ530
　　　BENEFICIARY: SHANGHAI LUCKY SAFETY SCREENS CO., LTD.
　　　ACCOUNT NO: 1281 2242012 7091 015
　　　ADDRESS: UNIT C 2/F JINGMAO TOWER SHANGHAI, CHINA
　　　　　　　　SHANGHAI LUCKY SAFETY SCREENS CO., LTD.
　　　　　　　　　　　　　　　　　　　　　　　　　　　×××

五、补充资料

1. 月份及缩写

月份	英文	缩写	月份	英文	缩写
一月	January	Jan.	二月	February	Feb.
三月	March	Mar.	四月	April	Apr.
五月	May	May	六月	June	Jun.
七月	July	Jul.	八月	August	Aug.
九月	September	Sep.	十月	October	Oct.
十一月	November	Nov.	十二月	December	Dec.

2. 商业发票常用英语

美元	U. S. Dollars	百	Hundred
千	Thousand	百万	Million

3. 常见付款方式(TERMS OF PAYMENT)

L/C	信用证	T/T	电汇(汇付)
D/P	付款交单(托收)	M/T	信汇(汇付)
D/A	承兑交单(托收)	D/D	票汇(汇付)

工作任务二 缮制包装单据

一、实训指南

除散装货物外,包装商品一般都需要提供包装单据。

包装单据是指一切记载或描述货物包装情况的单据,是商业发票的附属单据,也是货运单据中一种重要单据,其主要作用是弥补商业发票的不足。包装单据的种类很多,主要有以下几种:

(1) 装箱单(Packing List)。装箱单是信用证经常要求的单据之一,是表明出口货物的包装形式、包装内容、数量、重量、体积或件数的单据。其主要作用有:

① 补充商业发票内容不足。

② 通过填制包装件数(箱号)、装箱方式以及重量、运输标志等信息,便于买方了解货物的详情和提货。

③ 供海关查验核对。

(2) 重量单/磅码单(Weight Memo/List/Note)。一般以重量计价的商品,收货人对商品的重量比较重视,或当商品的重量对其质量能有一定的反映时,一般会要求重量单。

(3) 尺码单(Measurement List)。尺码单偏重于说明所装运货物的体积,即每件商品的包装尺码以及总尺码。

(4) 详细装箱单(Detailed Packing List)。

(5) 包装声明(Packing Declaration)。有些国家对进口货物的包装有一些特殊规定,如新西兰、澳大利亚等国规定,凡进口货物使用木材为包装材料,木材必须无虫、无菌、经过熏蒸处理才准许入境。对美国、加拿大出口,木质包装货物均需进行杀虫处理,按《国际植物保护公约》,对木质包装进行热处理时,一般要求温度达到56度,并持续30分钟以上,还建议对有些木质包装采取烘干或化学处理,熏蒸时要采用甲基溴化处理。凡是向以上这些国家出口时,就需要采用包装声明。

(6) 规格单(Specification List)。规格单从内容上来讲,与 Packing List 基本一致,只是从名称的要求上要与规定相符,并重点说明包装的规格,如:每箱装 24 打,每两打装一小盒,每打用塑料袋包装等细节。

(7) 花色搭配单(Assortment List)。花色搭配单是说明商品花色搭配情况的单据。之所以有这样一些形式起因于进口商对所购商品的某一或某几方面比较关注,希望出口方重点提供该方面的单据;这类单据由受益人用英文制作,格式自定义,内容繁简应以满足合同或信用证规定、符合银行惯例和适应客户需要为准。

二、实训样本

DETAILED PACKING LIST

TO: GREEN TRADE CO. INVOICE NO. ET335
22 MARK STREET, OSLO, NORWAY   DATE: APR. 10, 2020
S/C NO. 05SUG0012
L/C NO. 123456

SHIPPING MARKS:
GREEN
05SUG0012
OSLO
CTN. 1-1125

C/NOS.	NOS & KINDS OF PKGS	QUANTITY	G. W. (KGS)	N. W. (KGS)	MEAS. (M³)
ART NO. 1018 C/NOS. 1~500	500 CARTONS	5 000 SETS	6 000 KGS	5 000 KGS	100 M³
ART NO. 1019 C/NOS. 501~1125	625 CARTONS	5 000 SETS	6 250 KGS	5 000 KGS	62.5 M³
TOTAL	1 125 CARTONS	10 000 SETS	12 250 KGS	10 000 KGS	162.5 M³

SAY ONE THOUSAND ONE HUNDRED AND TWENTY FIVE CARTIONS ONLY

ZHONGCHENG INTERNATIONAL TRADE CO., LTD.

三、实训缮制要求

装箱单与商业发票一样,由出口商根据信用证的要求和货物特点自行设计,无统一固定的格式。

1. 单据的名称

单据的名称按信用证要求的类型和名称提供,通常印刷在单证上方。如要求 Neutral Packing list(中性装箱单),单证名称仍为"Packing List",但装箱单上无出单人名称及签章,即为中性包装单。

2. 出单人名称与地址

出单人名称与地址一般同发票的出票人名称及地址,通常在装箱单上方印就。

3. 抬头人

装箱单的抬头指明向谁开立的,一般与商业发票相同,即买方的名称及地址。有的装箱单列明"As per Inv."(根据发票)或"To whom it may concern"(致有关人)。

4. 装箱单据的号码、日期

装箱单据的号码、日期(No.,Date)。一般填写发票号码、日期。

5. 箱号

箱号(C/NOS)即包装件号,应根据实际按序编写。有的信用证规定箱单中应注明"1~UP",这里的 UP 应理解为总箱数待定。内容相同的包装可以使它们的序号相连并填写在相同的一行,如:10~20,表示第10箱至第20箱内容相同,记载在同一行中。

6. 唛头

唛头(Shipping Mark)与发票和信用证上的规定一致,也可以只注明"as per invoice No.×××"(根据第"×××"号发票)。

7. 商品数量

商品数量(No and Kinds of Packages)。注明每种货物的包装件数,同时注明合计数。该数量为运输包装单位的数量,而不是计价单位的数量。如:信用证规定、每件装一个塑料袋、每打装一盒、每20打装一个纸箱,则须注明:"Packing each piece in a poly bag, one dozen in a cardboard box and then 20 dozens in a carton."

8. 商品名称

装箱单中所标明的货物应为发票中所描述的货物,一般只填统称。通常也对包装情况作简要说明。有时对包装材料作特殊说明,如"拆散后装入木箱"(Packed in wooden case, C.K.)。

9. 商品的毛重、净重和体积

毛重(Gross Weight,GW)应注明每个包装件的毛重和此包装件内不同规格、品种、花色货物各自的总毛重(subtotal),最后在合计栏处标注所有货物的总毛重;净重(Net Weight,NW)应注明每个包装件的净重和此包装件内不同规格、品种、花色货物各自的总净重,最后在合计栏处标注所有货物总净重;体积(Measurement,Meas)则要求注明每个包装件的尺寸和总体积。

10. 签署

装箱单上一般不用签署,除非信用证条款中有特别指示。

四、参考资料

1. 常见货物外包装的中英文表示方法

纸 箱	CARTON	木 箱	WOODEN CASE
板条箱	CRATE	袋	BAG
麻袋	GUNNY BAG	布袋	CLOTH BAG

(续表)

纸　箱	CARTON	木　箱	WOODEN CASE
塑料袋	PLASTIC BAG	集装箱	CONTAINER
瓶	BOTTLE	托盘	PALLET
卷	ROLL	包,捆	BUNDLE,BALE
篓,篮	BASKET	包裹,件	PACKAGE

2. 单据份数的英文表示方法

In Duplicate	2 - Fold	一式二份
In Triplicate	3 - Fold	一式三份
In Quadruplicate	4 - Fold	一式四份

工作任务三　缮制汇票

一、实训指南

根据我国《票据法》的规定,汇票(Bill of Exchange)是出票人签发的,委托付款人在见票时或者在指定日期无条件支付确定金额给收款人或持票人的票据。

在国际结算中,如果涉及票汇方式付款,使用的是银行汇票;如果涉及托收或信用证方式付款,一般使用以卖方或受益人为出票人,以买方或银行为受票人的商业汇票。

二、实训样本

信用证下的汇票:

```
Drawn under  XYZ INTERNATIONAL BANK, LTD., HONGKONG    L/C No.  TST9-01563
Dated  14 FEB, 2020  Payable with interest @ ........%
No.  DC-H4566    Exchange for  US$8,700.00    Shanghai,  30 APRIL  20 20
At  60DAYS  sight of this FIRST of Exchange (Second of Exchange
being unpaid) Pay to the order of           BANK OF CHINA, SHANGHAI
the sum of       US DOLLARS EIGHT THOUSAND AND SEVEN HUNDRED ONLY

                                         上海东旭有限公司
To:   XYZ INTERNATIONAL BANK, LTD.       SHANGHAI DONGXU CORP
      HONGKONG
                                              布帆
```

托收下的汇票：

```
DRAWN UNDER S/C NO.123 FOR COLLECTION
No.   KC2053   Exchange for  USD 1,600.00    Shanghai, 12TH JULY 20 20
D/P At        45 DAYS        sight of this FIRST of Exchange (Second of Exchange
being unpaid) Pay to the order of   BANK OF CHINA, SINGAPORE         the sum of
SAY  UNITED STATES DOLLARS ONE THOUSAND SIX HUNDRED ONLY

To:                       SHANGHAI AAA IMPORT & EXPORT CORP
     GLOBAL TEXTILES CO.,
     78 FLIGHT STREET,
     SINGAPORE                   Xu Di
```

三、实训缮制要求

（一）信用证下的汇票

付款信用证一般不需要汇票。即期议付信用证可能要求即期汇票，远期议付信用证或承兑信用证中汇票必不可少。

1. 出票条款

出票条款（Drawn Under）又称出票根据，信用证汇票必须有出票条款，说明与某银行某日期开出的某号信用证的关系。如：

Draw under XYZ Bank，Singapore（填开证行名称）L/C No.12345（填信用证号）dated May 5,2011（填开证日期）。

2. 汇票编号

很多外贸公司采用和发票编号相同的汇票编号（No.），以便日后核查。

3. 汇票金额

（1）一般汇票金额（小写 for；大写 the sum of）应该按信用证规定填写。汇票金额不得大于信用证金额。如果信用证规定"…for full invoice value"，则汇票应该和发票金额一致。

（2）汇票如果同时有大小写金额，则大写必须准确反映小写表示的金额，同时显示信用证规定的币种。

（3）一般大写金额应该用"SAY…ONLY"框起。如：

19 600.75 美元，写为：USD 19 600.75，SAY U. S. DOLLARS NINETEEN THOUSAND SIX HUNDRED AND CENTS SEVENTY FIVE ONLY. 或…AND POINT SEVENTY FIVE ONLY.

4. 出票地点及出票日期

出票地点一般应在出口商所在地，和出票日期相连。出票日习惯填交单日。因此，出票日必须在信用证规定的有效期(EXPIRY)即交单期(PRESENTATION PERIOD)内,并且一般应在装运日(提单日)后。

日期需用英文表述,不能全部使用阿拉伯数字。

5. 付款期限

付款期限(At…Sight)按照信用证要求缮制。

① 即期付款,在汇票上的付款期限处,加打三个或六个"﹡"。如:AT﹡﹡﹡SIGHT。

② 远期付款,在汇票上的付款期限处,加打远期天数和起算期。通常有以下三种填写方法:

- 见票后定期付款:AT 30 DAYS AFTER SIGHT;
- 出票日后定期付款:AT 30 DAYS AFTER DATE;
- 提单日后定期付款:AT 30 DAYS AFTER B/L DATE。

③ 定期付款:则应填上将来具体的付款到期日,如 At 31 Dec. 2021 fixed,并将汇票上的"Sight"划去。

6. 收(受)款人

收(受)款人(Pay to)也称汇票抬头人。汇票上通常做成记名抬头(或称指示性抬头)。

信用证下汇票的收款人,外贸企业一般是写成议付行(中国银行出口商所在地分行)名称。如:Pay to the order of Bank of China Shanghai Branch。

7. 付款人

付款人(To)又称受票人,一般都位于汇票的左下角。汇票必须以信用证规定的人为付款人(信用证中汇票条款中,介词 on 后的即为指定的付款人)。根据《UCP600》信用证不应要求提交以开证申请人为付款人的汇票。如果信用证没指定受票人,应以开证行为受票人。

8. 出票人

一般位于汇票右下角。汇票必须由信用证的受益人出票。信用证中一般明确规定"available by beneficiary's draft…"或"available by your draft…"(信用证中第二人称一般指的是受益人)。出票人出票后须加盖出票人公司及授权人的签章。

(二) 托收下的汇票

托收下的汇票应按照合同条款的要求缮制。汇票的金额不能超过合同规定的金额。

托收汇票的出票条款可以表明相应的合同号,也可以说明有关商品,如果需要,还可以标明用以托收。如"Drawn under S/C No. 135 dated Apr. 28, 2021, Covering 3 000 pcs of Ladies Skirts for Collection"。如果托收下使用的汇票没有印制出票条款栏目,出票条款可以在汇票上方空白处注明。

托收下汇票的受票人应该是买卖合同的买方;出票人应该是卖方。托收汇票的票期栏前必须按合同约定,注明代收行交单条件,如"D/P"或"D/A"。

托收汇票的其他栏目的缮制方法,可参考信用证下汇票的相应说明。

另外,信用证中常见汇票的规定如下:

…available by ① …'s draft at ② …sight on ③ …[(payable) to ④ …]for ⑤ …,(⑥ …)

① 出票人。

② 付款期。

③ 付款人(受票人)。

④ 收款人。

⑤ 汇票金额。

⑥ 利息说明。

工作任务四　缮制出口商证明(受益人证明)

一、实训指南

出口商证明也称受益人证明,是出口商根据信用证的要求出具的证明已经履行某种义务或办理某项工作的单据。常见的受益人证明,一般是关于商品品种、包装、已发装船通知、已寄单、已寄样品等情况的证明。

二、实训样本

例如,信用证的单据要求(46A)中规定:

"…BENEFICIARY'S CERTIFICATE CERTIFYING THAT ONE SET OF NON-NEGOTIABLE SHIPPING DOCUMENTS HAS BEEN SENT TO APPLICANT WHTHIN 3 DAYS AFTER SHIPMENT."

受益人证明缮制要求如下:

DALIAN TAISHAN SUITCASE & BAG CO., LTD.
66 ZHONGSHAN ROAD DALIAN 116001, CHINA
TEL: 0086 - 0411 - 84524789

BENEFICIARY'S CERTIFICATE

DATE: AUG. 24, 2010

TO WHOM IT MAY CONCERN,

RE: INVOICE NO. TSI0801005　　　　　　　　L/C NO.: N5632405TH11808

WE HEHEBY CERTIFY THAT ONE SET OF NON-NEGOTIABLE SHIPPING DOCUMENTS HAS BEEN SENT TO APPLICANT WHTHIN 3 DAYS AFTER SHIPMENT.

DALIAN TAISHAN SUITCASE & BAG CO., LTD.

×××

三、实训缮制要求

受益人证明缮制要求如下:

填制栏目	填制内容和要求
单据名称(Title)	根据信用证的要求标注,如:BENEFICIARY'S CERTIFICATE
日期(Date)	根据证明的内容而定,但必须符合信用证要求
抬头人(TO)	除非信用证另有规定,通常填写为"TO WHOM IT MAY CONCERN"
事由(RE)	一般填写信用证名称或货物名称
证明文句	按照信用证要求的内容写
受益人签章	通常在证明的右下方注明受益人的公司名称,并加盖公章

单证模拟实训四

试根据以下出口货物明细及信用证,缮制汇票、商业发票、装箱单和受益人证明

出口货物明细

货 号	数量	计量单位	CIFC2 单价 (US$)	包装种类	装箱方式 (打/箱)	包装重量(KGS)		包装尺码(CM)		
						毛重	净重	长	宽	高
YW4002	128	打	48.50	纸箱	2	20	18	68	46	62
YW4004	340	打	25.00	纸箱	4	23	21	68	48	45
YW4006	822	打	32.00	纸箱	6	22	20	75	38	32
YW4008	288	打	35.00	纸箱	4	22	20	64	52	52

合同日期　　　　　　　　合同号码　　　　　　　　发票日期　　　　　　　　发票号码
3 - Jan - 20　　　　　　　SC080103　　　　　　　　22 - Feb - 20　　　　　　BB - SC080103

装船日期　　　　　　　　承运船名　　　　　　　　航次　　　　　　　　　　提单号码
10 - Mar - 20　　　　　　P. LUDER　　　　　　　　V. 38　　　　　　　　　　Q65498769353

产地证申请日期　　　　　产地证号　　　　　　　　税则号　　　　　　　　　保单号码
4 - Mar - 20　　　　　　　834573892　　　　　　　 9505 9000　　　　　　　　69857540020

运输标记
B. B. TRADING
TIANSHI 649572
LONG BEACH
C/NO. 1 - UP

ADVICE OF A THIRD BANK'S DOCUMENTARY CREDIT

APPLICATION HEADER　　0 710 1229 200117 USBKUS26EHID 7295 3053756 060118 0500 N

　　　　　　　　　　　　＊U. S. BANK

　　　　　　　　　　　　＊PORTLAND,OR

　　　　　　　　　　　　＊(PORTLAND INTERNATIONAL DEPARTMENT)

SEQUENCE OF TOTAL　　＊27　　：1/1
FORM OF DOC CREDIT　　＊40　　：IRREVOCABLE

                            WITHOUT OUR CONFIRMATION

DOC DREDIT NUMBER   *20   : 83955729
DATE OF ISSUE   *31C : 200117
EXPIRY   *31D : DATE 200328
                              PLACE AT BENFICARY'S COUNTRY
ISSUING BANK   *52D : FIRST NATIONAL BANK OF SAN DIEGO
                              410 WEST A STREET
                              SAN DIEGO CA 92101

APPLICANT   *50   : BROWN BROTHERS TRADING CO.
                              1056 LOMA AVE.
                              CORONADO, CA 91228

BENEFICIARY   *59   : SHANGHAI TIANSHI TOYS CO., LTD
                              NO. 88 HUANGPI N. ROAD   SHANGHAI CHINA

AMOUNT   *32B : CURRENCY USD AMOUNT 50070.16
MAX CREDIT AMOUNT   *39B : NO EXCEEDING

AVAILABLE WITH/BY   *41D : ANY BANK
                              BY NEGOTIATION
DRAFTS AT …   *42C : SIGHT
DRAWEE   *42A : FIRST NATIONAL BANK OF SAN DIEGO
                              410 WEST A STREET
                              SAN DIEGO CA 92101

PARTIAL SHIPMENT   *43P : ALLOWED
TRANSSHIPMENT   *43T : ALLOWED
LOADING IN CHARGE   *44A : SHANGHAI, CHINA PORT
FOR TRANSPORT TO   *44B : LONG BEACH CALIFORNIA USA
LATEST DATE OF SHIP   *44C : 200313

DESCRIP OF GOODS   *45A
                              1578 DOZENS WOODEN TOYS
                              AS PER P/O NO. 649672
                              SHIPPING TERMS: CIF LONG BEACH CALIFORNIA USA

DOCUMENTS REQUIRED   *46A:
| ONE ORIGINAL COMMERCIAL INVOICE MANUALLY SIGNED CERTIFYING THAT MERCHANDISE IS AS PER P/O NO. 649672 AND MUST SHOW THAT LOGOS HAVE BEEN IMPRINTED ON EACH ITEM AS INDICATED BY B. B., AND COPIES IN DUPLICATE

 +ONE ORIGINAL PACKING LIST AND COPIES IN DUPLICATE

 + ONE ORIGINAL COUNTRY OF ORIGIN CERTIFICATE ISSUED BY CHAMBER OF

COMMERCE AND COPIES IN DUPLICATE

+FULL SET OF CLEAN "ON BOARD" BILLS OF LADING MARKED FREIGHT PREPAID CONSIGNED TO THE ORDER OF THE APPLICANT AND NOTIFY APPLICANT AND COPIES IN DUPLICATE

+ORIGINAL INSURANCE POLICY OR CERTIFICATE FOR 120PCT OF THE INVOICE VALUE COVERING: ALL RISKS AND WAR RISKS AND COPIES IN DUPLICATE

+BENEFICIARY'S CERTIFICATE CERTIFYING THAT ONE SET OF COPIES OFSHIPPING DOCUMENTS HAS BEEN SENT TO APPLICANT WHTHIN 5 DAYS AFTER SHIPMENT

ADDITIONAL COND.   *47   : ALL DOCUMENTS MUST INDICATE LETTER OF CREDIT NOS. 83955729 AND ULCLMW002836

DETAILS OF CHARGES   *71B   : BENEFICIARY RESPONSIBLE FOR ALL BANKING CHARGES OUTSIDE OF OUR COUNTERS

PRESENTATION PERIOD   *48   : DOCUMENTS TO BE PRESENTED WITHIN 5 DAYS AFTER THE DATE OF SHIPMENT, BUT NOT LATER THAN THE EXPIRY DATE

CONFIRMATION   *49   : WITHOUT

INSTRUCTIONS   *78   :
THE AMOUNT OF THE DRAFTS MUST BE ENDORSED ON THE REVERSE OF THIS CREDIT. COURIER ALL DOCUMENTS IN ONE MAILING UNDER OUR COVER LETTER FOR PAYMENT TO FIRST NATIONAL BANK OF SAN DIEGO,
111 SW FIFTH AVE., SUITE 500, PORTLAND, OR 97204
PHONE (503)275-6059. THE ISSUER HEREBY UNDERTAKES TO HONOR ALL DEMANDS FOR PAYMENT MADE IN ACCORDANCE WITH THE TERMS AND CONDITIONS OF THIS CREDIT. ALL REFERENCES IN THE UCP600 TO ISSUING BANK AND TO BANK WHERE THE TERMS INCLUDING AN ISSUING BANK SHALL BE DEEMED TO BE REFERENCES TO THE ISSUER OF THIS CREDIT AND THE ISSUER SHALL HAVE ALL OF THE RIGHTS, DUTIES AND OBLIGATIONS OF AN ISSUING BANK UNDER THE UCP GUIDELINES.
DRAFTS MUST INDICATE LETTER OF CREDIT NOS. 83955729 AND ULCLMW002836.
WE WILL ASSESS A HANDLING CHARGE OF USD75.00 FOR EACH SET OF DOCUMENTS PRESENTED FOR PAYMENT UNDER THIS CREDIT, IN WHICH DISCREPANCIES ARE NOTED AFTER EXAMINATION.

"ADVISE THROUGH"   *57D   : BANK OF CHINA, SHANGHAI BRANCH
20F, BANK FO CHINA TOWER, 200 MID YINCHENG RD,
SHANGHAI CHINA 200120

1. 汇票

BILL OF EXCHANGE

凭　　　　　　　　　　　不可撤销信用证
Drawn under .... Irrevocable L/C No.

支取　　　按......息......付款
Dated .... Payable With interest @ ....%

号码　　　汇票金额
No. .... Exchange for ....

见票　　　日后（本汇票之副本未付）付交　　　　　金额
AT .... sight of this **FIRST** of Exchange （Second of Exchange being unpaid） Pay to the order of .... the sum of ....

此致：
To

2. 商业发票

ISSUER	COMMERCIAL INVOICE	
TO		
	NO.	DATE
TRANSPORT DETAILS	S/C NO.	L/C NO.
	TERMS OF PAYMENT	

Marks and Numbers	Number and kind of package Description of goods	Quantity	Unit Price	Amount
		TOTAL：		
SAY TOTAL：				

3. 装箱单

PACKING LIST

TO:
　　　　　　　　　　　　　　　　　　　　　　　INVOICE NO. _____
　　　　　　　　　　　　　　　　　　　　　　　DATE: _____
　　　　　　　　　　　　　　　　　　　　　　　S/C NO. _____
　　　　　　　　　　　　　　　　　　　　　　　L/C NO. _____

SHIPPING MARKS:

C/NOS.	NOS. & KINDS OF PKGS	QUANTITY	G. W. (KGS)	N. W. (KGS)	MEAS. (M³)
TOTAL					

4. 受益人证明

SHANGHAI TIANSHI TOYS CO., LTD.
NO. 88 HUANGPI N. ROAD   SHANGHAI CHINA
TEL: 0086 - 021 - 84524789

BENEFICIARY'S CERTIFICATE

　　　　　　　　　　　　　　　　　　　　　　　DATE:

TO

　　　　RE: _____   L/C NO.:

　　　　　　　　　　　　　　　　　　　SHANGHAI TIANSHI TOYS CO., LTD.
　　　　　　　　　　　　　　　　　　　　　　　×××

项目五

出口保险单证

实训目标

◆ 了解投保单的概念和作用,掌握投保单的内容以及缮制要求,并学会独立缮制投保单。

◆ 了解保险单的概念和作用,掌握保险单缮制要求,掌握查找保险单错误的方法。

工作任务一 缮制投保单

实训背景

在CIF贸易条件下,由卖方负责办理保险手续,卖方需要向银行提交保险单。单证员王杰在订舱确认后,根据合同和信用证的规定,通过中国人保财险(PICC)公司办理出口货物运输保险手续,填制投保单。

一、实训指南

投保单一般是保险公司根据不同险种事先设计内容格式,由投保人在投保时填写,投保人应根据贸易、运输、货物的实际情况和信用证的要求,明确写出需投保的险别,提出相应的保险要求,并告知货物及装运情况的单据。投保单所写明的事实内容是保险公司据以作为风险衡量、保费计费、出具保险单的依据。各个保险公司投保单的格式不完全一致,但大致内容相同。

二、实训样本

海运出口货物投保单

1) 保险人：　　　　　　　　　　　　　　2) 被保险人：

3) 标记	4) 包装及数量	5) 保险货物项目	6) 保险货物金额
7) 总保险金额：（大写）			

8) 运输工具：　　（船名）　　　　（航次）

9) 装运港：　　　　　　　　　　　　　　10) 目的港：

11) 投保险别：　　　　　　　　　　　　　12) 货物起运日期：

13) 投保日期：　　　　　　　　　　　　　14) 投保人签字：

三、实训缮制要求

投保单是发货人或被保险人在货物发运前,确定装运工具并缮制发票以后,向保险公司(保险人)办理投保手续所填制和提交的单据。投保单由出口公司在投保时填写,其内容应按合同或信用证要求仔细、认真填写,不能有错,保险公司根据投保单的内容来缮制和签发保险单。各保险公司的投保单格式不尽相同,但内容基本一致,主要内容如下:

(1) 保险人。除非信用证有特别规定,一般应为信用证的受益人或合同的卖方即发货人。

(2) 唛头。要求按信用证规定,或与发票等其他单据上的唛头一致。

(3) 数量和保险物资项目。数量即出口货物的总数量,如总重量或总包装件数;保险物资项目即货物的品名或规格,一般按提单的填法,填大类名称或货物的统称,不必详细列明各种规格等细节。

(4) 保险金额。填写计算投保加成后的总保险金额或成交金额,但需标明成交价格条件。

(5) 装运路线。即装于何种运输工具,开航日期即为提单签发日期,运输路线即货物装运地和目的地。

(6) 提单、通知单或邮局收据号次。根据不同的运输方式,填写运单号,如提单号、航空运单号或其他运输单据号。

(7) 保费给付地点及赔款地点。一般在 CIF 条件下,卖方支付保险费,地点为卖方所在地,赔款偿付地点一般为买方所在地。

(8) 保险险别。按合同规定或信用证条款。

(9) 加成。按规定,保险公司一般能接受的最高加成是 30%,超过此比例,保险公司一般不予承保。

(10) 包装情况。集装箱或散货运输。

(11) 保单号次和费率。由保险公司负责填写。

(12) 投保人签章。上述内容填完后投保人须签字盖章才能生效。

除上述的投保单外,有时,出口企业也可用出口货物明细单或发票副本来代替投保单,但必须加注有关的保险项目,如运输工具、开航日期、承保险别、投保金额或投保加成、赔款地和保单份数等要求。

工作任务二 缮制保险单

一、实训指南

(一) 保险单的作用

保险单是保险人(Insurer)根据投保人或被保险人(the Insured)的要求,表示已经承诺保险责任的凭证,也是保险人与投保人之间的正式合同。它由保险公司出具和签署,在被保险货物遭受损失时作为被保险人索赔和保险公司理赔的依据。

(二)信用证中有关保险单据条款举例

(1) INSURANCE POLICIES OR CERTIFICATE IN TWO FOLD PAYABLE TO THE ORDER OF COMMERCIAL BANK OF LONDON LTD. COVERING MARINE INSTITUTE CARGO CLAUSES A (1.1.2009), INSTITUTE STRIKE CLAUSES CARGO(1.1.2009), INSTITUTE WAR CLAUSES CARGO (1.1.2009) FOR INVOICE VALUE PLUS 10% INCLUDING WAREHOUSE TO WAREHOUSE UP TO THE FINAL DESTINATINAT SWISSLAND, MARKED PREMIUM PAID, SHOWING CLAIMS IF ANY, PAYABLE IN SWISS, NAMING SETTLING AGENT IN SWISS.

(保险单或保险凭证一式两份,由伦敦商业银行作记名指示背书,按伦敦保险协会条款(2009年1月1日版)投保ICC(A)、协会罢工险条款(货物)(2009年1月1日版)和协会战争险条款(货物)(2009年1月1日版)投保,按发票金额加10%投保,包括仓至仓条款到达最后目的地SWISSLAND,标明保费已付,在瑞士赔付,同时表明在瑞士理赔代理人的名称。)

(2) INSURANCE POLICY/CERTIFICATE ISSUED TO THE APPLICANT (AS INDICATED ABOVE), COVERING RISKS AS PER INSTITUTE CARGO CLAUSES(A), AND INSTITUTE WAR CLAUSES (CARGO) INCLUDING WAREHOUSE TO WAREHOUSE CLAUSE UP TO FINAL DESTINATION AT SCHOMDORF, FOR AT LEAST 110 PCT OF CIF VALUE, MARKED PREMIUM PAID SHOWING CLAIMS IF ANY PAYABLE IN GERMANY, SHOWING SETTLING AGENT IN GERMANY.

[此保单或保险凭证签发给如上所述的开证申请人,按伦敦保险协会条款投保ICC(A),和协会战争险,包括仓至仓条款到达最后目的地SCHORNDORF,至少按CIF价发票金额110%投保,标明保费已付,注明在德国赔付,同时表明在德国理赔代理人的名称。]

二、实训样本

货物运输保险单

CARGO TRANSPORTATION INSURANCE POLICY

总公司设于北京　　一九四九年创立
Head Office Beijing　　Established in 1949

发票号(INVOICE NO.)123456　　　　　　保单号次
合同号(CONTRACT NO.) ABC234　　　　POLICY NO. HMOP09319089
信用证号(L/C NO.) DT905012
被保险人(INSURED) XYZ TRADING COMPANY

中国人民财产保险股份有限公司(以下简称本公司)根据被保险人的要求,由被保险人向本公司缴付约定的保险费,按照本保险单承保险别和背面所载条款与下列特款承保下述货物运输保险,特立本保险单。

THIS POLICY OF INSURANCE WITNESSES THAT PICC PROPERTY AND CASUALTY COMPANY LIMITED (HEREINAFTER CALLED "THE COMPANY") AT REQUEST OF THE INSURED AND IN CONSIDERATION OF THE AGREED PREMIUM PAID TO THE COMPANY BY THE INSURED, UNDERTAKES TO INSURANCE. THE UNDERMENTIONED GOODS IN TRANSPORTATION SUBJECT TO THE CONDITIONS OF THIS POLICY AS PER THE CLAUSES PRINTED OVERL AND OTHER SPECIAL CLAUSES ATTACHED HEREON.

标记及号码 Marks & Nos.	包装数量 Quantity	保险货物项目 Description of Goods	保险金额 Amount Insured
XYZ 1234567 NEW YORK NOS. 1-500	5 000 PCS	LEATHER BAGS	USD 108 000.00

总保险金额 TOTAL AMOUNT INSURED: <u>US DOLLARS ONE HUNDRED AND EIGHT THOUSAND ONLY</u>

保费：　　　　起运日期：　　　　装载运输工具：
PREMIUM: <u>AS ARRANGED</u>　DATE OF COMMENCEMENT <u>MAY 30,2020</u>　PER CONVEYANCE: <u>"SUN" V. 126</u>
自　　　　经　　　　至
FROM <u>TIANJIN</u> VIA <u>＊＊＊</u> TO <u>LONG BEACH</u>

承保险别：
CONDITIONS
　　COVERING ALL RISKS AS PER CIC OF THE PICCC DATED <u>01/01/2009</u>.

所保货物,如发生保险单项下可能引起索赔的损失或损坏,应立即通知本公司代理人查勘。如有索赔,应向本公司提交保单正本(本保险单共有　　份正本)及有关文件。如一份正本已用于索赔,其余正本自动失效。

IN THE EVENT OF LOSS OR DAMAGE WHICH MAY RESULT IN A CLAIM UNDER THIS POLICY, INNEDIATE NOTICE MUST BE GIVER TO THE COMPANY'S AGENT AS MENTIONED HEREUNDER CLAIMS, IF ANY ONE OF THE ORIGINAL POLICY WHICH HAS BEEN ISSUED IN ORIGINAL TOGETHER WITH THE RELEVENT DOCUMENTS SHALL BE SURRENDERED TO THE COMPANY. IF ONE OF THE ORIGINAL POLICY HAS BEEN ACCOMPLISHED. THE OTHERS TO BE VOID.

中国人民财产保险股份有限公司上海市分公司
赔款偿付地点　　PICC Property and Casualty Company Limited，Shanghai
CLAIM PAYABLE AT/IN <u>LONG BEACH</u> IN <u>USD</u>

出单日期　　　　　　　　　　　　　　　　　×××
ISSUING DATE MAY 16，2020　　　　　　　　GENERAL MANAGER

三、实训缮制要求

各保险公司根据自身印制的保险单固定格式和投保要求,制作保险单,一般包括以下内容。

1. 保险公司名称(Name of Insurance Company)

在保险单顶端已经用中英文印制好保险公司的名称。国际贸易当事人应根据信用证和合同的规定由相应的保险公司办理保险,如信用证规定"INSURANCE POLICY IN TRIPLICATE BY PICC",PICC是指中国人民保险公司,即信用证要求出具由中国人民保险公司出具的保险单。

2. 保险单据名称(Insurance Policy)

在保险人名称下方已经印制好单据名称,需要注意的是,保险单据名称必须与合同和信用证的要求一致。

3. 发票号码(Invoice Number)、合同号(Contract No.)、信用证号(L/C No.)

此处填写发票号码、合同号、信用证号。不是信用证支付,可以不填信用证号。

4. 保险单号码(Policy No.)

填写保险公司编制的保险的保险单号码。

5. 被保险人(Insured)

信用证方式下,如果信用证中未指定被保险人,本栏填受益人。然后交单前背书(如果信用证中没有背书要求,则做空白背书)。如果信用证中已指定,且受益人接受了信用证,则按照信用证要求填写。

托收或其他结算方式下填卖方,交单前背书。

6. 唛头(Marks and Nos)

保险单唛头应与发票、提单等一致,目前保险公司采取打上"AS PER INVOICE NO. ×××"的做法,原因在于办理保险索赔时,必须提供商业发票,在此处打上发票号,便于参照发票进行核对。

7. 包装及数量(Quantity)

填包装种类与包装数量,如"300CTNS"。如果为散装货,则先填货物毛重,接着填"IN BULK"。

8. 保险货物项目(Description of Goods)

和提单一样,一般填货物统称。

9. 保险金额(Amount Insured)

保险金额是保险公司承担赔偿或者给付保险金责任的最高限额,也是保险公司计算保险费的基础。其计算公式如下:

$$保险金额 = CIF 或 CIP 价 \times (1 + 投保加成率)$$

如CIF、CIP价无法确定,则以发票金额加成。

需要注意的是,保险金额一般采用"进一取整"的填法。如,信用证金额为USD 28 567.60,规定"FOR 110% OF FULL INVOICE VALUE",即按发票金额加成10%投保,则

$$保险金额 = 信用证金额 \times (1 + 加成率)$$

$$=USD\ 28\ 567.60\times(1+10\%)$$

$$=USD\ 31\ 424.36$$

进一步取整得 USD 31 425.00。

如果发票金额扣除佣金时,必须以货物总价值为基础来计算保险金额。当保险加成超过20%以上时,需事先征得保险公司同意。

10. 总保险金额(Total Amount Insured)

即保险金额的大写数字,以英文表示,末尾应加"ONLY",以防涂改。此处的大写与上面所述的小写金额和货币必须保持一致。

保险金额使用的货币单位应与信用证中的一致。

11. 保费、费率(Premium, Rate)

一般已由保险公司印就"AS ARRANGED"(按商定)字样。除非信用证另有规定,每笔保费及费率可以不具体表示。

12. 起运日期(Date of Commencement)

一般填"AS PER B/L";陆运填"AS PER CARGO RECEIPT";空运填"AS PER AIRWAY BILL"。也可以填提单等货运单据的签发日期。

13. 装载运输工具(Per Conveyance)

如果为海运方式,本栏目填写船名及航次。

如果涉及转船,填写"一程船名/二程船名"。如二程船名在投保时还不知道,填"一程船名"及"and/or steamer",如:BLUE MOON AND/OR SREAMER。

空运方式下,一般填"by airplane"或"by air"。

14. 起运地和目的地(From To)

此栏填写起运地和目的地名称。当货物经转船到达目的港时,可填写"FROM"装运港"VIA"转运港"TO"目的港。例如:货物由上海经香港运到纽约港。保险单上可打成"FROM SHANGHAI VIA HONGKONG TO NEW YORK"。

有时信用证未明确列明起运港和目的港,如"ANY CHINESE PORT"或"ANY AMERICAN PORT",应根据实际情况选定一个具体的港口,如 GUANGZHOU 或 NEW YORK 等。

15. 承保险别(Conditions)

填写信用证规定的保险险别及相应的保险条款,应注意在文字表述上与信用证严格一致。

根据《2010年国际贸易术语解释通则》,如果双方没有约定保险险别,卖方可以按照最低险别办理保险。

16. 正本份数(Number of Original Policy)

按《UCP600》,如果保险单据表明签发的正本份数超过一份,除非信用证授权,必须提交所有的正本。

17. 理赔代理(Surveying agent)

填保险公司在目的地理赔代理机构的名称及联系方法。

18. 赔付地点和货币(Claim Payable At/In)

如果信用证有规定,则按信用证填写。如果信用证没明确规定,则赔付地点一般填写投保货物的目的地,币种与信用证币种一致。

19. 保单日期(Date)

填写保险单的签发日期。由于保险公司提供仓至仓(Warehouse to Warehouse)服务,所以要求保险手续在货物离开出口方仓库前办理,保险单的日期也应是货物离开出口方仓库前的日期,不晚于提单签发的日期。

根据《UCP600》,除非保险单据表明保险责任最迟已于装船或发运或接受监管之日生效,银行将拒收出单日期迟于运输单据注明的装船或发运或接受监管日期的保险单据。

20. 投保地点(Place)

一般为装运港(地)的名称。

21. 签章(Authorized Signature)

正本保险单必须由保险公司签字或盖章以示保险单正式生效。

22. 背书(Endorsed)

在 CIF 或 CIP 交易中,保险单的被保险人一般为出口商。当出口商向银行交单时必须对保险单据背书,以便将保险单据项下的保险利益,即在货物发生了承保风险造成的损失后能从保险公司获得赔偿的权利,转移给保单的受让人。

保险单的背书必须在正本上。背书的方式主要有:

(1) 空白背书(Blank Endorsed)。若信用证要求"ENDORSED IN BLANK"或"BLANK INDORSED",即要求空白背书。空白背书只需在保险单背面注明被保险人(包括出口商名称 和经办人的名字)名称。

当来证没有规定使用哪一种背书时,也使用空白背书方式。

(2) 记名背书。当来证要求"DELIVERY TO(THE ORDER OF)××× CO. (BANK)"或"ENDORSED IN THE NAME OF ×××",即规定使用记名方式背书。此时,需要在保险单背面注明被保险人的名称和经办人的名字后,打上"DELIVERY TO ××× COMPANY (BANK)"或"IN THE NAME OF ×××"的字样。记名背书在出口业务中较少使用。

单证模拟实训五

一、缮制投保单模拟操作

根据下列资料填写出口投保单和保险单。
SOME MSG FORM L/C

L/C NO. AND DATED: 0120254630 SEP. 18, 2005
BENEFICIARY: NINGBO LIGHT IND. PRODUCTS I/E CORP.
APPLICANT: PROSPERITY INDUSTRIAL CO. LTD 342-3 FLYING BUILDING KINGDOM STREET HONGKONG
GOODS DESCRIPTION: SPORTS GOODS 1125 GROSSES (S/C88G 65) CUR. AND AMT.: USD 57 260.00

DOCUMENTS REQUIRED:

MARINE INSURANCE POLICY OR CERTIFICATE IN DUPLICATE, BLANK ENDORSED, FOR 110% OF INVOICE VALUE STATING CLAIM PAYABLE IN HONGKONG COVERING RISKS AS PER INSTITUTE CARGO CLAUSES (1/1/1982) AND INSTITUTE WAR CLAUSES (CARGO) (1/1/1982) INCLUDING WAREHOUSE TO WAREHOUSE CLAUSE UPTO FINAL DESTINATION AT HONGKONG.

补充资料：
SHIPMENT: FROM NINGBO TO NEWYORK BY DONGFENG V. 32 ON OCT. 5, 2005
VIA HONGKONG
MARKS: KASSAR/NEWYORK/NO. 1-UP
INVOICE NO.: FIN-301
开航日期：OCT. 10, 2005
船名航次：YAXING V. 668

海运出口货物投保单

1) 保险人：　　　　　　　　　　　　　　2) 被保险人：

3) 标记	4) 包装及数量	5) 保险货物项目	6) 保险货物金额

7) 总保险金额：（大写）

8) 运输工具：　　（船名）　　　（航次）

9) 装运港：　　　　　　　　　　　　　　10) 目的港：

11) 投保险别：　　　　　　　　　　　　　12) 货物起运日期：

13) 投保日期：　　　　　　　　　　　　　14) 投保人签字：

二、保险单改错模拟操作

已知资料(1)：

SALES CONTRACT

Contract No.：NJT090218
Date：FEB. 8, 2009
Signed at：Nanjing, China

The Seller：NANJING JINLING TEXTILE CO., LTD.
Address：UNIT A 18/F, JINLING TOWER, NO. 118 JINLING ROAD, NANJING, CHINA
The Buyer：DEXICA SUPERMART S. A.
Address：BOULEVARD PACHECO 44, B-1000 BRUSSELS, BELGIUM

This Sales Contract is made by and between the Sellers and the Buyers, whereby the sellers agree to sell and buyers agree to buy the under-mentioned goods according to the terms and conditions stipulated below：

Commodity and specifications	Quantity	Unit Price	Amount
GIRLS GARMENTS	10 800 PCS	CIF BRUSSELS EUR 5.00/PC	EUR 54 000.00

10% more or less in quantity and amount are acceptable.

Packing：in carton **Shipping Mark**：N/M
Time of Shipment：within 30 days after receipt of L/C.
From NINGBO PORT CHINA to BRUSSELS, BELGIUM.
Transshipment and Partial Shipment：allowed.
Insurance：to be effected by the Seller for 110% of full invoice value covering all risks up to port of destination and war risks included with claim payable at destination.
Terms of Payment：By 100% Irrevocable Letter of Credit in favor of the Sellers to be available by sight draft to be opened and to reach China before APRIL 1, 2009 and to remain valid for negotiation in China until the 21 days after the foresaid Time of Shipment. L/C must mention this contract number L/C advised by BANK OF CHINA JIANGSU BRANCH. ALL banking Charges outside China are for account of the Buyer.

The Seller	The Buyer
NANJING JINLING TEXTILE CO., LTD.	**DEXICA SUPERMART S. A.**
钟山	ALICE

已知资料(2)：

1. 装运信息：指定 APL 承运,装运期 2009 年 4 月 19 日;船名 PRINCESS;航次 V.018。
2. 装箱资料：合计 108 箱,装入 1×20' 集装箱。
3. 商业发票号：NJT090218-09,签发日期 2009 年 4 月 10 日。
4. 信用证号：CMKK9180205。

货物运输保险单
CARGO TRANSPORTATION INSURANCE POLICY

总公司设于北京　　一九四九年创立
Head Office Beijing　　Established in 1949

发票号（INVOICE NO.）NJT090218-09
合同号（CONTRACT NO.）NJT090218　　　　保单号次
信用证号（L/C NO.）CCPIT091810528　　　POLICY NO. PYIE2006080
被保险人（INSURED）XYZ TRADING COMPANY

中国人民财产保险股份有限公司（以下简称本公司）根据被保险人的要求，由被保险人向本公司缴付约定的保险费，按照本保险单承保险别和背面所载条款与下列特款承保下述货物运输保险，特立本保险单。

THIS POLICY OF INSURANCE WITNESSES THAT PICC PROPERTY AND CASUALTY COMPANY LIMITED (HEREINAFTER CALLED "THE COMPANY") AT REQUEST OF THE INSURED AND IN CONSIDERATION OF THE AGREED PREMIUM PAID TO THE COMPANY BY THE INSURED, UNDERTAKES TO INSURANCE. THE UNDERMENTIONED GOODS IN TRANSPORTATION SUBJECT TO THE CONDITIONS OF THIS POLICY AS PER THE CLAUSES PRINTED OVERL AND OTHER SPECIAL CLAUSES ATTACHED HEREON.

标记及号码 Marks & Nos.	包装数量 Quantity	保险货物项目 Description of Goods	保险金额 Amount Insured
DEXICA S/C NJT090218	10 080 DOZEN	LADIES GARMENTS	USD 54 000.00

总保险金额 TOTAL AMOUNT INSURED: US DOLLARS FIFTY FOUR THOUSANDS ONLY
保费：　　　起运日期：　　　装载运输工具：
PREMIUM: AS ARRANGED　DATE OF COMMENCEMENT APR. 9, 2009　PER CONVEYANCE: PRINCESS V. 018
自　　　经　　　至
FROM NANJING PORT CHINA VIA ＊＊＊ TO BRUSSELS, BELGIUM
承保险别：
CONDITIONS
　　COVERING F.P.A. UP TO PORT OF DESTINATION.

所保货物，如发生保险单项下可能引起索赔的损失或损坏，应立即通知本公司代理人查勘。如有索赔，应向本公司提交保单正本（本保险单共有　份正本）及有关文件。如一份正本已用于索赔，其余正本自动失效。
IN THE EVENT OF LOSS OR DAMAGE WHICH MAY RESULT IN A CLAIM UNDER THIS POLICY, INNEDIATE NOTICE MUST BE GIVER TO THE COMPANY'S AGENT AS MENTIONED HEREUNDER CLAIMS, IF ANY ONE OF THE ORIGINAL POLICY WHICH HAS BEEN ISSUED IN ORIGINAL TOGETHER WITH THE RELEVENT DOCUMENTS SHALL BE SURRENDERED TO THE COMPANY. IF ONE OF THE ORIGINAL POLICY HAS BEEN ACCOMPLISHED. THE OTHERS TO BE VOID.

中国人民财产保险股份有限公司江苏省分公司
THE PEOPLE'S INSURANCE COMPANY OF CHINA JIANGSU BRANCH

赔款偿付地点
CLAIM PAYABLE AT/IN Nanjing, China IN USD
出单日期　　　　　　　　　　　　　　×××
ISSUING DATE APR. 20, 2009　　　　　GENERAL MANAGER

项目六

出口运输单证——海运单证

实训目标

- ◆ 掌握集装箱货物托运单的作用和缮制要求,并学会缮制集装箱货物托运单。
- ◆ 掌握海运提单的作用和缮制要求,并学会缮制海运提单。
- ◆ 认识装运通知的作用和缮制要求,了解缮制装运通知的要求。

工作任务一 缮制集装箱货物托运单

实训背景

上海进出口贸易公司与 Brown Brothers 贸易公司会签了出口合同。合同规定,采用 CIF 术语成交、集装箱班轮运输。上海进出口贸易公司的单证员王杰负责向中远集装箱运输有限公司(COSCO CONTAINER LINES)订舱。装船之后,又负责向美国 BROWN BROTHERS TRADING CO. 公司通过传真发送了装船通知(Shipping Advice)。

一、实训指南

现代海上班轮货物运输件杂货所占的比重越来越小,而集装箱货物运输所占的比重越来越高,集装箱运输是以场站收据(Dock Receipt)作为集装箱货物的托运单,该单由发货人或其代理人缮制送交船公司或其代理人订舱,因此,托运单也就相当于订舱单。集装箱货物

托运单通常是由发货人的代理人填写,纸质托运单一式十联:

第一联:集装箱货物托运单(货主留底)(B/N)(现在已不用)。

第二联:集装箱货物托运单(船代留底)(现在已不用)。

第三联:运费通知(1)(现在已不用)。

第四联:运费通知(2)(现在已不用)。

第五联:场站收据(装货单)(S/O)。

第五联附页联:缴纳出口货物港务费申请书(由港区核算应收之港务费用)。

第六联:(浅红色)大副联(场站收据副本)。

第七联:(黄色)场站收据。

第八联:货代留底。

第九联:配舱回单(1)。

第十联:配舱回单(2)。

其中,第五联、第六联、第七联为集装箱托运单的核心单据。第五联是装货单,盖有船公司或其代理人的图章,是船公司发给船上负责人员和集装箱装卸作业区接受装货的指令,报关时海关查核后在此联盖放行章,船方(集装箱装卸作业区)凭以收货装船。第六联供港区在货物装船前交外轮理货公司,当货物装船时与船大副交接。第七联场站收据俗称黄联,在货物装上船后由船大副签字(通常由集装箱码头堆场签章),退回船公司或其代理人,据以签发提单。

集装箱托运流程如下:

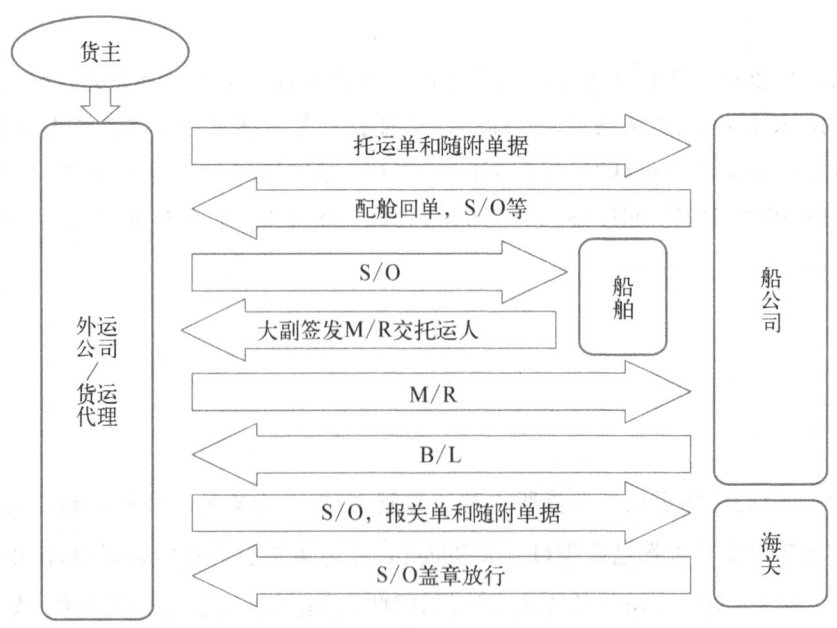

二、实训样本

集装箱货物托运单

Shipper（发货人）		D/R No(编号)
DONGHAI TRADING CO.,LTD. ADD: NO 4516, ZHONG SHAN RD., SHANGHAI, CHINA		

Consignee（收货人）
TO SHIPPER'S ORDER

Notify Party（通知人）	集装箱货物托运单
NIGROS-GENOSSENSCHAFTS-BUND LIMMATSTRASSE 526 POSTEACH 266 CH8031 ZURICH SWITZERLAND	

Pre-carriage by(前程运输)	Place of Receipt（收货地点）	
Vessel(船名) Voy. No.（航次）	Port of Loading（装货港） SHANGHAI	
Port of Discharge（卸货港） HAMBURG	Place of Delivery（交货地点）	Final Destination for the Merchant's Reference(目的地)

Container No.（集装箱号）	Seal No.（封志号） Marks & Nos.（标志与号码） SCHEKERC 06CI-SCH96E HAMBURG C/No.1-300	No. at Containers or Pkgs（箱数或件数） 300 CARTONS	Kind of Packages; Description of Goods（包装种类与货名） STUFFED TOYS	Gross Weight 毛重（千克） 1 527 KGS	Measurement 尺码（立方米） 14.813 CBM

TOTAL NUMBER OF CONTAINERS OR PACKAGES (IN WORDS) 装箱数或件数合计(大写)	SAY THREE HUNDRED AND NINE CARTONS ONLY

FREIGHT & CHARGES（运费与附加费）	Revenue Tons（运费吨）	Rate（运费率）	Per（每）	Prepaid（运费预付）	Collect（到付）
Ex. Rate.（兑换率）	Prepaid at（预付地点）	Payable at（到付地点）		Place of Issue(签发地点) SHANGHAI	
	Total Prepaid（预付总额）	No. of Original B(s)/L（正本提单份数） THREE			

Service Type on Receiving □-CY □-CFS □-DOOR	Service Type on Delivery □-CY □-CFS □-DOOR	Reefer Temperature Required（冷藏温度）		
			°F	°C

TYPE OF GOODS(种类)	Ordinary □（普通）	Reefer □（冷藏）	Dangerous □（危险品）	Auto □（裸装车辆）	危险品	Class: Property: IMDG Code Page UN No.
	Liquid □（液体）	Live Animal □（活动物）	Bulk □（散装）			

可否转船：YES	可否分批：YES
装期：NOV. 31, 2005	效期：DEC. 20, 2005
金额：USD 65 590.00	
制单日期：OCT. 5, 2005	

三、实训缮制要求

1. 托运人(Shipper)

填托运人的全称、街名、城市、国家名称,并填写联系电话、传真号。在信用证结汇方式下,托运人一般按信用证的受益人(Beneficiary)内容填写。

2. 收货人(Consignee)

依据信用证46A对提单的要求,做成如"TO ORDER"或"TO ORDER OF SHIPPER"等凭指示字样。

3. 通知人(Notify Party)

填写通知人的全称、街名、城市、国家名称,并填写联系电话、传真号。在信用证结汇方式下,一般填开证申请人。

4. 装运港(Port of Loading)

填写实际货物被装运上船舶的港口全称,必要时加上港口所在国家(地区)的名称。

5. 卸货港(Port of Discharge)

填写实际货物被卸离船舶的最终港口全称,必要时加上港口所在国家(地区)的名称。

6. 目的地(Final Destination for the Merchant's Reference)

填写货物最终的交货地的城市名称,或地区名称。

7. 货物名称与包装种类(Kind of Packages;Description of Goods)

本栏所填写是符合信用证(45A),与实际货物的名称规格型号成分品牌等相一致的货物名称和包装种类。一般填货物统称。

8. 箱数与件数(No. of Containers or Packages)

此栏填制装入集装箱内货物的外包装件数和集装箱件数。一般要求托运人填写件数的小写在此栏,还要填写件数的大写,防止更改,确保唯一性。例如:小写件数"100 CTNS";大写件数 "SAY ONE HUNDRED CARTONS ONLY "。

9. 封志号、标记与号码(Seal No. & Marks & Nos.)

(1)封志号是发货人装箱完毕后在集装箱门上加封封志的号码,此号码是唯一的。一般在提单上显示封志号,托运单上不填报。收货人提货时应检查封志号,如果实际货箱上封志号与提单载有的封志号相一致,表示该集装箱门未曾被开启。

(2)此栏填报的标记与号码应与实际货物外包装上正面唛头的全部内容完全一致,包括数字、字母和简单图形。

10. 毛重(Gross Weight)

填报实际货物的毛重,以千克为计量单位。

11．体积（Measurement）

填报实际货物的体积，一般以立方米为计量单位。

12．运费的支付（Payment of Freight）

运费是由托运人对承运人安全运送和交付货物，对承运人支付的一种酬劳，也是合同成立的对价条件。因此，有关运费由谁付，何地支付，都应在托运单上注明。一般显示"FREIGHT PREPAID"为托运人支付；显示"FREIGHT COLLECT"为收货人支付。

13．要求签发的提单份数（Number of Original B/Ls）

（1）根据《UCP600》，信用证规定的每种单据须至少提交一份正本。

（2）每份提单具有同等效力。

（3）收货人持凭其中的任一封提单提取货物后，其他各份提单即刻自动失效。

14．要求签发的提单日期和地点（Place and Date of issue）

（1）托运单上一般提出提单签发的时间和签发地点要求，以满足结汇文件的要求。提单的签发日应该是提单上所列货物实际装船完毕的日期，应该与收货单上大副所签的日期是一致的。

（2）提单签发的地点原则上应是装货地点。

15．托运人签字、盖章（Signature）

托运人在完成上述内容的填写后，必须盖章签字，以生效。

工作任务二　缮制海运提单

一、实训指南

海运提单是指船公司或其代理人签发的，证明已收到特定货物，允诺将货物运至特定的目的地，并交付给收货人的凭证。海运提单是收货人在目的港据以向船公司或其代理提取货物的凭证。

从法律规定看，提单的基本作用在于：

（1）提单是海上货物运输合同的证明（Evidence of the Contract Carriage）。

（2）提单是证明货物已由承运人接收或装船的货物收据（Evidence of Receipt for the Cargos）。

（3）提单是承运人保证凭以交付货物的物权凭证（Documents of Title）。

二、实训样本

1. Shipper Insert Name, Address and Phone	B/L No.

中远集装箱运输有限公司
COSCO CONTAINER LINES
TLX: 33057 COSCO CN
FAX: +86(021) 6545 8984

ORIGINAL

BILL OF LADING

2. Consignee Insert Name, Address and Phone

3. Notify Party Insert Name, Address and Phone (It is agreed that no responsibility shall attach to the Carrier or his agents for failure to notify)

RECEIVED in external apparent good order and condition except as other-Wise noted. The total number of packages or unites stuffed in the container, The description of the goods and the weights shown in this Bill of Lading are Furnished by the Merchants, and which the carrier has no reasonable means Of checking and is not a part of this Bill of Lading contract. The carrier has Issued the number of Bills of Lading stated below, all of this tenor and date, One of the original Bills of Lading must be surrendered and endorsed or sig-Ned against the delivery of the shipment and whereupon any other original Bills of Lading shall be void. The Merchants agree to be bound by the terms And conditions of this Bill of Lading as if each had personally signed this Bill of Lading. SEE clause 4 on the back of this Bill of Lading (Terms continued on the back Hereof, please read carefully).

4. Pre-carriage by	5. Place of Receipt
6. Ocean Vessel Voy. No.	7. Port of Loading
8. Port of Discharge	9. Place of Delivery

Marks & Nos. Container/ Seal No.	No. of Containers or Packages	Description of Goods (If Dangerous Goods, See Clause 20)	Gross Weight Kgs	Measurement
		Description of Contents for Shipper's Use Only (Not part of This B/L Contract)		

10. Total Number of containers and/or packages (in words) Subject to Clause 7 Limitation

11. Freight & Charges	Revenue Tons	Rate	Per	Prepaid	Collect
Declared Value Charge					

Ex. Rate:	Prepaid at	Payable at	Place and date of issue
	Total Prepaid	No. of Original B(s)/L	Signed for the Carrier, COSCO CONTAINER LINES

LADEN ON BOARD THE VESSEL   DATE   BY

三、实训缮制要求

1. 托运人(Shipper)

通常是信用证的受益人,即买卖合同中的卖方。但是,根据《UCP600》,除非信用证中另有规定,银行接受以信用证受益人以外的第三方为发货人。

2. 收货人(Consignee)

俗称提单抬头人,信用证下的提单必须严格按照信用证要求操作,其他结算方式下,应该按照合同要求操作。

信用证中对提单收货人的规定一般有:

(1) 指示提单:例如,信用证中46A规定:"Bill of Lading made out to order",则提单收货人栏填"To order"。

(2) 记名提单:例如,信用证中46A规定:"Bill of Lading made out to ABC Co.",则提单收货人栏填"ABC Co."。

3. 被通知人(Notify Party)

如果是记名提单,被通知人一栏不填。

如果不是记名提单:

(1) 信用证下按照信用证(46A)要求填。例如,"… NOTIFY APLLICANT",则填信用证申请人名称、地址。

(2) 托收项下,填合同的买方名称、地址。

4. 收货地(Place of Receipt)

此栏填报实际收货地点,如工厂、仓库等。在一般海运提单中,没有此栏目,但是在多式联运提单中就有此栏目。

5. 装运港(Port of Loading)

必须与信用证规定的装货港一致。

6. 船名(Ocean Vessel Voy. No.)

此栏必须填写船名和航次(Voy. No),如没有航次,允许航次空白。

7. 转运港(Port of Transshipment)

发生转运时,填写转运港名称,必要时加注所在国家名称。

8. 卸货港(Port of Discharge)

信用证规定的卸货港。

9. 交付地(Place of Delivery)

根据实际情况填写具体的交货地名称。如果收货地与交货地都空白,就是海运提单,而不是多式联运提单。

10. 标记与号码,箱号与封号(Marks & Nos,Container/Seal No.)

(1) 提单上的标记、号码应与信用证和其他单据中的唛头一致。若没有唛头时,用"N/M"表示,不得空白。

(2) 托运时,一般箱封号可以不填,但在提单上必须填报每一个集装箱的箱号、封号。

11. 集装箱数量或货物包装件数（No. of Containers or Packages）

填写装运货物的集装箱个数，或货物的总包装件数。

12. 货物描述（Description of Goods）

通常，根据《UCP600》，"除发票外，单据上的货物描述可以用统称"的规定，填写运输货物的统称。

13. 毛重（Gross Weight）

毛重以千克（KGS）为单位。本栏目不可以空白。

14. 体积（Measurement）

体积以立方米（CBM）为单位。本栏目不可以空白。

15. 总箱数/货物总件数（Total Number of Container and/or Packages in Words）

用英文大写字母来填写集装箱的总箱数或货物的总件数。在件数前面须加上"Say"字样，在件数结尾后加上"Only"字样。例：35 CTNS，填："SAY THIRTY FIVE CARTONS ONLY"。

16. 运费的支付（Payment of Freight）

除非信用证规定提单必须显示运费及费用，提单上不必填写详细的运费及费用。一般显示"FREIGHT PREPAID"运费预付；"FREIGHT COLLECT"运费到付。

17. 已装船批注、装船日期、装运日期（Shipped on board the Vessel date、Signature）

根据《UCP600》，通过以下两种方式表明货物已在信用证规定的装货港装上具名船只：

（1）提单上预先印就"已装船"文字或相同意思，如"Shipped on board the vessel named here in apparent good order and condition…"或"Shipped in apparent good order and condition…"，这种提单通常被称为"已装船提单"，不必另行加注"已装船"批注，提单的签发日期就是装船日期和装运日期。

（2）如果提单载有"预期船只"或类似的关于船名的限定语，则需以"已装船"批注明确发运日期以及实际船名。通常这种提单被称为"收妥备运提单"，提单上加注"已装船（On board）"的批注，并在旁边显示装船日期即为发运日期，而提单的签发日期不能视作装船日期和发运日期。

18. 提单的签发日期和地点（Place and Date of issue）

（1）签发地点一般是装货港的所在地，如与该地不一致，银行也可以接受。

（2）每张提单必须有签发日期。

19. 签发的正本提单份数（Number of Original B/Ls）

（1）根据《UCP600》，信用证规定的每一种单据须至少提交一份正本。

（2）如果信用证要求提交单据的副本，提交正本或副本均可。

（3）提单为唯一的正本提单，或如果以多份正本出具，提单中须表明全套正本的份数。

20. 承运人或承运人代理人签字、盖章（Sign or authenticate）

根据《UCP600》，无论名称如何，须表明承运人名称并由下列人员签署证实：

（1）承运人或具名代理人。

（2）船长或具名代理人。

（3）承运人、船长或代理人的任何签字必须标明其承运人、船长或代理人的身份。

(4) 代理人的任何签字必须标明其系代表承运人还是船长签字。

21. 提单编号(B/L No)

提单号一般按装货单上的关单号填写在提单规定的此栏内。

不同船公司有不同的提单号组成规则。通常,提单号由代表船公司名称的英文代码,加上装运港英文代码或目的港英文代码,或加上代表该航次数字和订舱顺序号数字等组成。提单号是查询、报检、报关、跟踪货物、收运杂费、归档等环节中不可缺少的一项重要内容。

工作任务三 缮制装运通知

一、实训指南

装运通知(Shipping Advice)是指出口商向进口商发出货物已于某月某日或将于某月某日装运某船的通知。装运通知的作用在于方便买方购买保险或准备提货手续,其内容通常包括货名、装运数量、船名、装船日期、合同号或信用证号码等。

二、实训样本

装运通知样张如下:

装 运 通 知
Shipping Advice

1. 出口商 Exporter ABC COMPANY, SHANGHAI NO. 11 CHANGCHUN ROAD, SHANGHAI, CHINA	4. 发票号 Invoice No. 123QWE	
	5. 合同号 Contract No. SUM356/09	6. 信用证号 L/C No. KLMU1234
2. 进口商 Importer ALOSMNY INTERNATIONAL TRADE CO. 177 ALHRAM STREET SECOND FLOOR – G102A EGYPT 12111	7. 运输单证号 Transport document No. COSU299120029	
	8. 价值 Value USD 28 820.00	
3. 运输事项 Transport details FROM SHANGHAI TO SAID BY VESSELMOONRIVER V. 987	9. 装运口岸和日期 Port and date of shipment SHANGHAI Aug. 30, 2009	
10. 运输标志和集装箱号 Shipping marks; Container No. A. I. T. C. SUM356/09 SAID C/NO. 1 – 4400 Container NO. PLU6954791	11. 包装种类及件数;商品名称或编码;商品描述 Number and kind of packages; Commodity No. ; Commodity description CANNED ORANGE JAM (MEILING BRAND) PACKED IN SEAWORTHY CARTONS 250 GRAM/CAN 12 CANS/CARTON 52 800 CANS 4 400 CARTONS	
	12. 出口商签章 Exporter stamp and signature ABC COMPANY, SHANGHAI ×××	

三、实训缮制要求

装运通知缮制要求如下:

填 制 栏 目	填制内容和要求
出口商 Exporter	信用证受益人的名称、地址
进口商 Importer	信用证开证申请人的名称、地址
运输事项 Transport details	装货港、卸货港;船名、航次
发票号 Invoice No.	发票号
合同号 Contract No.	合同号
信用证号 L/C No.	信用证号
运输单证号 Transport document No.	提单号
价值 Value	信用证总金额
装运口岸和日期 Port and date of shipment	装货港和装船日期
运输标志和集装箱号 Shipping marks; Container No.	运输标志和集装箱号
包装种类及件数;商品名称或编码;商品描述 Number and kind of packages; Commodity No.; Commodity description	包装种类及件数;商品名称或编码;商品描述
出口商签章 Exporter stamp and signature	出口商名称和盖章

单证模拟实训六

一、缮制海运托运单模拟操作

根据下列信用证资料、外销出仓单资料填制出口托运单。

1. 信用证资料

Applicant: Hanil Synthetic Fiber Co., Ltd.
            Hans Tower 46-5 Guro Dong,
            Guro Gu, Seoul, Korea

Beneficiary: ABC Import and Export Co.

Issuing Bank: To the Order of Industrial Bank of Korea

Port of Shipment: Shanghai, China

Port of Discharge: Busan, Korea

Partial Shipment: Not Allowed

Transshipment: Not Allowed

L/C Number: M04G4410NS00228

Latest Date of Shipment: 20 Nov. 2010

Expiry Date: 25 Nov. 2010

Description of Goods: PP Spunbonded Nonwoven Fabrics

Quantity of Goods: 353 Rolls

Packing: GW 9 000 kgs, Measurement 68 CBM

Number of B/L: Three

Shipping Marks: N/M

2. 外销出仓单资料

GW/NW: 9 000/8 647(KGS)

Volume: 68(CBM)

Shipping Marks: N/M

Quantity of Goods: 353 Rolls

Out Warehouse Date: Nov. 1, 2010

集装箱货物托运单

Shipper（发货人）

D/R No（编号）

Consignee（收货人）

Notify Party（通知人）

集装箱货物托运单

Pre-carriage by（前程运输）	Place of Receipt（收货地点）	
Vessel（船名）Voy. No.（航次）	Port of Loading（装货港）	
Port of Discharge（卸货港）	Place of Delivery（交货地点）	Final Destination for the Merchant's Reference（目的地）

Container No.（集装箱号）	Seal No.（封志号）Marks & Nos.（标志与号码）	No. at Containers or Pkgs（箱数或件数）	Kind of Packages; Description of Goods（包装种类与货名）	Gross Weight 毛重（千克）	Measurement 尺码（立方米）

TOTAL NUMBER OF CONTAINERS OR PACKAGES (IN WORDS) 装箱数或件数合计（大写）					
FREIGHT & CHARGES（运费与附加费）	Revenue Tons（运费吨）	Rate（运费率）	Per（每）	Prepaid（运费预付）	Collect（到付）
Ex. Rate.（兑换率）	Prepaid at（预付地点）	Payable at（到付地点）		Place of Issue（签发地点）SHANGHAI	
	Total Prepaid（预付总额）	No. of Original B(s)/L（正本提单份数）			

Service Type on Receiving ☐- CY ☐- CFS ☐- DOOR	Service Type on Delivery ☐- CY ☐- CFS ☐- DOOR	Reefer Temperature Required（冷藏温度）		℉	℃
TYPE OF GOODS（种类）	Ordinary ☐（普通）	Reefer ☐（冷藏）	Dangerous ☐（危险品）	Auto ☐（裸装车辆）	危险品	Class: Property: IMDG Code Page UN No.
	Liquid ☐（液体）	Live Animal ☐（活动物）	Bulk ☐（散装）			

可否转船：

装期：　　　　　　　　效期：

金额：

制单日期：

二、审核海运提单模拟操作

根据以下资料查找海运提单填制错误模拟操作(共 5 处错误)。

出口货物明细

货 号	数量	计量单位	CIFC2 单价（US$）	包装种类	装箱方式（打/箱）	包装重量(KGS)		包装尺码(CM)		
						毛重	净重	长	宽	高
YW4002	128	打	48.50	纸箱	2	20	18	68	46	62
YW4004	340	打	25.00	纸箱	4	23	21	68	48	45
YW4006	822	打	32.00	纸箱	6	22	20	75	38	32
YW4008	288	打	35.00	纸箱	4	22	20	64	52	52

合同日期　　　　　　合同号码　　　　　　发票日期　　　　　　发票号码
3 - Jan - 08　　　　　SC080103　　　　　　22 - Feb - 08　　　　BB - SC080103

装船日期　　　　　　承运船名　　　　　　航次　　　　　　　　提单号码
10 - Mar - 08　　　　P. LUDER　　　　　　V. 38　　　　　　　　Q65498769353

产地证申请日期　　　产地证号　　　　　　税则号　　　　　　　保单号码
4 - Mar - 08　　　　　834573892　　　　　　9505 9000　　　　　69857540020

运输标记
B. B. TRADING
TIANSHI 649572
LONG BEACH
C/NO. 1 - UP

ADVICE OF A THIRD BANK'S DOCUMENTARY CREDIT

APPLICATION HEADER　　0 710 1229 080117 USBKUS26EHID 7295 3053756 060118 0500 N
　　　　　　　　　　　　＊U. S. BANK
　　　　　　　　　　　　＊PORTLAND, OR
　　　　　　　　　　　　＊(PORTLAND INTERNATIONAL DEPARTMENT)

SEQUENCE OF TOTAL	＊27	: 1/1
FORM OF DOC CREDIT	＊40	: IRREVOCABLE
		WITHOUT OUR CONFIRMATION
DOC DREDIT NUMBER	＊20	: 83955729
DATE OF ISSUE	＊31C	: 080117
EXPIRY	＊31D	: DATE 080328

		PLACE AT BENFICARY'S COUNTRY
ISSUING BANK	*52D	: FIRST NATIONAL BANK OF SAN DIEGO
		410 WEST A STREET
		SAN DIEGO CA 92101
APPLICANT	*50	: BROWN BROTHERS TRADING CO.
		1056 LOMA AVE.
		CORONADO, CA 91228
BENEFICIARY	*59	: SHANGHAI TIANSHI TOYS CO., LTD.
		NO. 88 HUANGPI N. ROAD
		SHANGHAI CHINA
AMOUNT	*32B	: CURRENCY USD AMOUNT 50070, 16
MAX CREDIT AMOUNT	*39B	: NO EXCEEDING
AVAILABLE WITH/BY	*41D	: ANY BANK
		BY NEGOTIATION
DRAFTS AT …	*42C	: SIGHT
DRAWEE	*42A	: FIRST NATIONAL BANK OF SAN DIEGO
		410 WEST A STREET
		SAN DIEGO CA 92101
PARTIAL SHIPMENT	*43P	: ALLOWED
TRANSSHIPMENT	*43T	: ALLOWED
LOADING IN CHARGE	*44A	:
		SHANGHAI, CHINA PORT
FOR TRANSPORT TO	*44B	:
		LONG BEACH CALIFORNIA USA
LATEST DATE OF SHIP	*44C	: 080313
DESCRIP OF GOODS	*45A	
		1578 DOZENS WOODEN TOYS
		AS PER P/O NO. 649672
		SHIPPING TERMS: CIF LONG BEACH CALIFORNIA USA

DOCUMENTS REQUIRED　　*46A

　+ ONE ORIGINAL COMMERCIAL INVOICE MANUALLY SIGNED CERTIFYING THAT MERCHANDISE IS AS PER P/O NO. 649672 AND MUST SHOW THAT LOGOS HAVE BEEN IMPRINTED ON EACH ITEM AS INDICATED BY B. B., AND COPIES IN DUPLICATE

　+ONE ORIGINAL PACKING LIST AND COPIES IN DUPLICATE

+ONE ORIGINAL COUNTRY OF ORIGIN CERTIFICATE ISSUED BY CHAMBER OF COMMERCE AND COPIES IN DUPLICATE

+FULL SET OF CLEAN "ON BOARD" BILLS OF LADING MARKED FREIGHT PREPAID MADE OUT TO THE ORDER OF THE APPLICANT AND NOTIFY APPLICANT AND COPIES IN DUPLICATE

+ORIGINAL INSURANCE POLICY OR CERTIFICATE FOR 120PCT OF THE INVOICE VALUE COVERING: ALL RISKS AND WAR RISKS AND COPIES IN DUPLICATE

ADDITIONAL COND.   *47   : ALL DOCUMENTS MUST INDICATE LETTER OF CREDIT NOS. 83955729 AND ULCLMW002836.

DETAILS OF CHARGES *71B : BENEFICIARY RESPONSIBLE FOR ALL BANKING CHARGES OUTSIDE OF OUR COUNTERS.

PRESENTATION PERIOD *48   : DOCUMENTS TO BE PRESENTED WITHIN 5 DAYS AFTER THE DATE OF SHIPMENT, BUT NOT LATER THAN THE EXPIRY DATE.

CONFIRMATION   *49   : WITHOUT

INSTRUCTIONS   *78   :
THE AMOUNT OF THE DRAFTS MUST BE ENDORSED ON THE REVERSE OF THIS CREDIT. COURIER ALL DOCUMENTS IN ONE MAILING UNDER OUR COVER LETTER FOR PAYMENT TO FIRST NATIONAL BANK OF SAN DIEGO,
111 SW FIFTH AVE., SUITE 500, PORTLAND, OR 97204
PHONE (503) 275-6059. THE ISSUER HEREBY UNDERTAKES TO HONOR ALL DEMANDS FOR PAYMENT MADE IN ACCORDANCE WITH THE TERMS AND CONDITIONS OF THIS CREDIT. ALL REFERENCES IN THE UCP600 TO ISSUING BANK AND TO BANK WHERE THE TERMS INCLUDING AN ISSUING BANK SHALL BE DEEMED TO BE REFERENCES TO THE ISSUER OF THIS CREDIT AND THE ISSUER SHALL HAVE ALL OF THE RIGHTS, DUTIES AND OBLIGATIONS OF AN ISSUING BANK UNDER THE UCP GUIDELINES.
DRAFTS MUST INDICATE LETTER OF CREDIT NOS. 83955729 AND ULCLMW002836.
WE WILL ASSESS A HANDLING CHARGE OF USD 75.00 FOR EACH SET OF DOCUMENTS PRESENTED FOR PAYMENT UNDER THIS CREDIT, IN WHICH DISCREPANCIES ARE NOTED AFTER EXAMINATION.

"ADVISE THROUGH"   *57D : BANK OF CHINA, SHANGHAI BRANCH
                            20F, BANK FO CHINA TOWER, 200 MID YINCHENG RD.,
                            SHANGHAI CHINA 200120

1. Shipper SHANGHAI TIANSHI TOYS CO., LTD. NO. 88 HUANGPI N. ROAD SHANGHAI, CHINA	B/L No. Q65498769353
2. Consignee TO THE ORDER OF THE APPLICANT	中外运集装箱运输有限公司 **SINOTRANS CONTAINER LINES** **BILL OF LADING**

3. Notify Party BROWN BROTHERS TRADING CO. 1 056 LOMA AVE. CORONADO, CA 91228		RECEIVED in external apparent good order and condition except as other-Wise noted. The total number of packages or unites stuffed in the container, The description of the goods and the weights shown in this Bill of Lading are Furnished by the Merchants, and which the carrier has no reasonable means Of checking and is not a part of this Bill of Lading contract. The carrier has Issued the number of Bills of Lading stated below, all of this tenor and date, One of the original Bills of Lading must be surrendered and endorsed or sig-Ned against the delivery of the shipment and whereupon any other original Bills of Lading shall be void. The Merchants agree to be bound by the terms And conditions of this Bill of Lading as if each had personally signed this Bill of Lading. **ORIGINAL**
4. Pre-carriage by	5. Place of Receipt	
6. Vessel & Voyage No. P. LUDER V. 38	7. Port of Loading SHANGHAI, CHINA	
8. Port of Discharge LOS ANGELES CALIFORNIA USA	9. Place of Delivery	

Marks & Nos. Container/Seal No. B. B. TRADING TIANSHI 649572 LONG BEACH C/NO. 1 - UP JEPT3694592/74952	No. of Containers or Packages 358CTNS	Description of Goods (If Dangerous Goods, See Clause 20) WOODEN TOYS FREIGHT PREPAID SHIPPER'S LOAD, COUNT AND SEAL CY/CY	Gross Weight (KGS) 7 833.000	Measurement (CBM) 49.851
		Description of Contents for Shipper's Use Only (Not part of This B/L Contract)		

10. Total Number of containers and/or packages (in words) **SAY ONE FORTY FEET CONTAINER ONLY**
    Subject to Clause 7 Limitation

11. Freight & Charges Declared Value Charge	Revenue Tons	Rate	Per	Prepaid	Collect
Ex. Rate:	Prepaid at	Payable at		Place and date of issue SHANGHAI MAR. 10, 2008	
	Total Prepaid	No. of Original B(s)/L FOUR		Signed for the Carrier, SINOTRANS CONTAINER LINES CHINA MARINE SHIPPING AGENCY SHANGHAI COMPANYLTD 主力 AS AGENT(S) FOR THE CARRIER NAMED ABOVE	

LADEN ON BOARD THE VESSEL
DATE   BY

项目七

出口运输单证——空运单证和其他

实训目标

- ◆ 掌握空运托运单和空运单的用途和缮制要求,并学会缮制空运单和空运托运单。
- ◆ 认识多式联运单据的用途和特点,了解缮制多式联运单据的要求。
- ◆ 了解铁路运单、公路运单、快递收据和邮政收据的用途和缮制要求。

工作任务一 缮制空运托运单

实训背景

钱林在上海进出口贸易公司工作,业务推广中得知韩国客商 KUMHO INDUSTRIAL CO.公司的 KIM,KON 先生,对本公司展览的手工工具很感兴趣,经过磋商,两公司会签了出口合同,规定采用电汇支付方式和航空运输方式。钱林负责这一业务,需要办理相关托运手续,缮制空运托运单。

一、实训指南

空运托运单(Shipping Order,S/O),是空运托运人根据贸易合同和信用证条款内容填制的,向承运人或其代理办理货物托运的单据。空运托运单是出口企业向空运外运公司提供出口货物的必要资料,是空运外运公司定舱配载的依据。它虽然不是出口结汇的正式单据,却是制作提单的主要依据。中国民用航空局制订有统一的国际货物托运书(Shipper's Letter of Instruction),缮制内容与海运托运单大同小异,可按式照填,参照海运托运方法办理托运。

二、实训样本

钱林填制了国际货物托运书(空运托运单),缮制商业发票与装箱单及时向上海客货运

输服务有限公司办理出口货物航空运输手续,以便能在合同规定的装运期内进行交货。缮制空运托运单的依据合同如下:

上 海 进 出 口 贸 易 公 司
SHANGHAI IMPORT & EXPOR TRADE CORPORATIONT
1321 ZHONGSHAN ROAD SHANGHAI CHINA
SALES CONTRACT

Post code: 200032 P/I NO.: 20060228

Fax: (021) 65788876 S/C NO: TXT06081

TEL: (021) 65788877 DATE: AUG.1,2006

TO MESSRS:

KUMHO INDUSTRIAL, CO.

49-1,KWANGCHON SO-GU,KWANGJU,502-210

KOREA

Dear Sirs,

  We hereby confirm having sold to you the following goods on terms and conditions as specified below:

GOODS OF DESCRIPTIONS	QUANTITY	UNIT PRICE	AMOUNT
DOUBLE OPEN END SPANNER 8×10 MM(MTM) 10×12 MM(MTM)	60 000 PCS 80 000 PCS	CPT KWANGJU USD 0.50 USD 0.40	USD 30 000.00 USD 32 000.00

1) SHIPPING MARK: N/M

2) TERMS OF PAYMENT: 30% T/T IN ADVANCE, THE OTHERS 70% T/T AFTER SHIPMENT

3) AIRPORT OF DEPARTURE: PUDONG AIRPORT SHANGHAI, CHINA

4) AIRPORT OF DESTINATION: KWANGJU AIRPORT KOREA

5) LATEST DATE OF SHIPMENT: SEP. 30, 2006

OUR BANK: INFORMATION IS AS BELOW:

BANK NAME: BANK OF CHINA SHANGHAI BRANCH

ACCOUNT NO.: RMB80456861

THE BUYER: THE SELLER:

KUMHO INDUSTRIAL, CO. SHANGHAI IMPORT & EXPOR TRADE

KIM, KON 钱林

钱林缮制空运委托书如下：

上海客货运输服务有限公司
SHANGHAI EXPRESS SERVICE CO., LTD.   IATA

国际货物托运书
SHIPPER'S LETTER OF INSTRUCTION   REF NO.: XY060401

始发站 AIRPORT DEPARTURE SHANGHAI		到达站 AIRPORT OF DESTINATION KWANGJU						供承运人用 FOR CARRIER ONLY	
路线及到达站 ROUTING AND DESTINATION								航班/日期 FRIGHT/DAY	航班/日期 FRIGHT/DAY
至 TO	第一承运人 BY FIRST CARRIER	至 TO	承运人 BY	至 TO	承运人 BY	至 TO	承运人 BY	已预留吨位 DOKKED	
收货人姓名及地址 CONSIGNEE'S NAME AND ADDRESS		KUMHO INDUSTRIAL, CO. KWANGCHON SO-GU, KWANGJU, 502-210, KOREA						运费： CHARGES: FREIGHT: PREPAID	
另行通知 ALSO NOTIFY		SAME AS CONSIGNEE							
托运人账号 SHIPPER'S ACCOUNT NUMBER	045686	托运人姓名及地址 SHIPPER'S NAME & ADDRESS		SHANGHAI IMPORT & EXPORT TRADE CORPORATION 1321ZHONGSHAN ROAD SHANGHAI					
托运人声明的价值 SHIPPER'S DECLARED VALUE NVD		保险金额 AMOUNT OF INSURANCE		所附文件 DOCUMENTS TO ACCOMPANY AIR WAYBILL					
供运输用 FOR CARRIAGE	供海关用 FOR CUSTOMS								
件数 NO. OF PACKAGES	实际毛重 ACTIAL GROSS WEIGHT(KG)	运价类别 RATE CLASS		收费重量 CHARGEABLE WEIGHT		离岸 RATE CHARGE		货物名称及重量（包括体积或尺寸） NATURE AND QUANTITY OF GOODS (INCL DIMENSIONS OF VOLUME)	
1 400 CTNS	3 200							DOUBL EOPENEND PANNER 20 CBM	
在货物不能交于收货人时，托运人指示的处理方法 SHIPPER'S INSTRUCTIONS IN CASE OF INABILITY TO DELIVER SHIPMENT AS CONSIGNED									
处理情况（包括包装方式、货物标志及号码等） HANDLING INFORMATION (INCL METHOD OF PACKING IDENTIFYING MARKS AND NUMBERS, LTC.)									

托运人证实以上所填全部属实并愿遵守托运人的一切载运章程
THE SHIPPER CERTIFIES THAT PARTICALS ON THE FACE HEREOF ARE CORRECT AND AGREES TO THE CONDITIONS OF CARRIAGE OF THE CARRIER

托运人签字　钱林　　日期　2006年9月11日　　经收人　华民彰　　日期　2006年9月11日
SIGNATURE OF SHIPPER　DATE　　　　　　　　　　AGENT　　　　　　　DATE

三、实训缮制要求

空运托运书缮制要求如下：

填 制 栏 目	填制内容和要求
1. AIRPORT DEPARTURE/始发站机场	填写货物始发站的机场的英文名称,不得简写或使用代码
2. AIRPORT OF DESTINATION/目的地机场	填写货物目的地站的机场的英文名称,不得简写或使用代码。如有必要,填写机场所属国家、州的名称或城市的全称
3. FOR CARRIER ONLY/供承运人用	此栏留空,由承运人根据需要填写
4. ROUTING AND DESTINATION/路线及到达站	此栏留空
5. FRIGHT/DAY/航班/日期	填写托运人事先预订的航班/日期
6. CONSIGNEE'S NAME AND ADDRESS/收货人姓名及地址	填写收货人的全称、地址,包括邮政编码和电话号码。此栏内不可填写"TO ORDER"字样
7. ALSO NOTIFY/另行通知	填写 SAME AS CONSIGNEE
8. SHIPPER'S ACCOUNT NUMBER/托运人账号	如果承运人需要,可填写托运人账号
9. SHIPPER'S NAME & ADDRESS/托运人姓名及地址	填写托运人的全称、地址,包括邮政编码和电话号码
10. SHIPPER'S DECLARED VALUE/托运人声明的价值	填写托运人向承运人办理货物声明价值的金额。如托运人未办理货物声明价值,必须填写"NVD"字样
11. CHARGES/运费	填写托运人支付货物运费的方式等项内容
12. AMOUNT OF INSURANCE/保险金额	此栏不填,由中国民航部代理国际货物的保险业务机构填写
13. DOCUMENTS TO ACCOMPANY AIR WAYBIL/所附文件	填写随交承运人有关文件的名称
14. FOR CARRIAGE/供运输用	此栏留空
15. FOR CUSTOMS/供海关用	此栏留空
16. NO. OF PACKAGES/件数	填写货物的包装件数,如果使用不同的货物运价种类,应分别填写,并将总件数填入此
17. ACTIAL GROSS WEIGHT(KG)/实际毛重	填写货物的总毛重
18. RATE CLASS/运价类别	填写所使用的货物运价种类代号,如"M"代表起码运费;"N"代表45千克以下普通货物运价;"Q"代表45千克以上普通货物运价
19. CHARGEABLE WEIGHT/收费重量	此栏留空
20. RATE CHARGE/离岸	此栏留空
21. NATURE AND QUANTITY OF GOODS (INCL DIMENSIONS OF VOLUME)/货物名称及重量(包括体积或尺寸)	填写具体货名与数量。货名不得用统称,危险物品应填写其标准学术名称;外包装要注明尺寸或体积,按长×宽×高×件数的顺序填写
22. SHIPPER'S INSTRUCTIONS IN CASE OF INABILITY TO DELIVER SHIPMENT AS CONSIGNED/在货物不能交于收货人时,托运人指示的处理方法	托运人根据需要作出指示

(续表)

填 制 栏 目	填制内容和要求
23. HANDLING INFORMATION (INCL. METHOD OF PACKING IDENTIFYING MARKS AND NUMBERS, LTC.)/处理情况(包括包装方式、货物标志及号码等)	填写货物在运输、中转、装卸和仓储时需要注意的事项,如货物的包装形式、标志、名称和货物外包装所用的材料,以及写明数量和包装种类
24. SIGNATURE OF SHIPPER, DATE/托运人签字、日期	由托运人或其代理人签字或盖章,并填写托运货物的日期
25. AGENT、DATE/经办人、日期	由承运人或其代理人的经办人签字,并填写收运货物的日期

工作任务二　缮制空运单

实训背景

上海进出口贸易公司的钱林向上海客货运输服务有限公司办理出口货物航空运输手续,在缮制空运托运单之后,以获取上海客货运输服务有限公司签发的空运单。

一、实训指南

（一）空运单介绍

航空运单(Air Way Bill,简称 AWB)是航空运输公司及其代理人即承运人签发给发货人表示已收妥货物并接受托运的货物收据,航空运单也是承运人与托运人之间的运输合同,但它不是物权凭证,既不能背书转让(运单右上方即有"NON NEGOTIABLE"字样),也不能凭以提货。

（二）空运单的分类

航空运单主要分为两大类：

（1）航空主运单(Master Air Waybill，MAWB)。凡由航空运输公司签发的航空运单就称为主运单。航空主运单的当事人双方一方是实际承运人——航空公司,另一方是航空货运代理公司——托运人。

（2）航空分运单(House Air Waybill，HAWB)。集中托运人在办理集中托运业务时签发的航空运单被称作航空分运单。在集中托运的情况下,除了航空运输公司签发主运单外,集中托运人还要签发航空分运单。航空分运单的运输合同当事人双方,一方是航空货运代理公司,另一方则是真正的货主——发货人。

二、实训样本

接任务一的空运托运单缮制后,钱林需获取航空公司签发的空运单。

Shipper' Name and Address	Shipper's Account Number 045686	Not negotiable		
SHANGHAI IMPORT & EXPORT TRADE CORPORATION 1321ZHONGSHAN ROAD SHANGHAI, CHINA		Air Waybill Issued by	中国东方航空公司 CHINA EASTERN AIRLINES 2250 HONGQIAO ROADSHANGHAI CHINA	
Consignee's Name and Address KUMHO INDUSTRIAL, CO. KWANGCHON SO-GU, KWANGJU, 502-210, KOREA	Consignee's Account Number SO099	Copies 1, 2 and 3 this Air Waybill are originals and have the same validity. It is agreed that goods described herein are accepted in apparent good order and condition (except as noted) for carriage SUBJECT TO THE CONDITIONS OF CONTRACT ON THE REVESE HEREOF. ALL GOODS MAY BE CARRIED BY ANY OTHER MEANS INCLUDING ROAD OR ANY OTHER CARRIER UNLESS SPECIFIC CONTRARY INSRUCTIONS ARE GIVEN HEREON BY THE SHIPPER, AND SHIPPER AGREES THAT THE SHIPPMENT MAY BE CARRIED VIA INTERMEDIATE STOPPING PLACES WHICH THE CARRIER DEEMS APPROPRIATE. THE SHIPPER'S ATTENTION IS DRAWN TO THE NOTICE CONCERNING CARRIER'S LIMIATION OF LIABILITY. Shipper may increase such limitation of limitation of liability by declaring a higher value for carriage and paying a supplemental charge if required.		
Issuing Carrier's Agent Name and City FUKANGWA EX3(030-424) SEMARANG EXPRESS CO., LTD.		Accounting Information FREIGHT: PREPAID		
Agents IATA Code 08321550	Account No.	D = 34 (20 CBM)		

Airport of Departure (Addr. Of First Carrier) and Requested Routing

To	By First Carrier	Routing and Destination	To	By	To	By	Currency USD	Chgs Code	WT/VAL PPD / COLL ××	Other PPD / COLL ××	Declared Value for Carrier N.V.D	Declared Value for Customs

Airport of Destination	Requested Flight/Date MU0514/02	Amount of Insurance	If shipper requests insurance in accordance with the conditions thereof indicate amount to be insures in figures in box marked "Amount of Insurance".

Handing Information
AS PER REF NO: XY050401

No. of Place RCP	Gross Weight	kg lb	Rate Class Commodity Item No.	Chargeable Weight	Rate / Charge	Total	Nature and Quantity of Goods (Incl. Dimensions or Volume)
1	400	K	S		1.50	2 400.00	DOUBLEOPENEND PANNER 20 CMB

Prepaid / Weight Charge / Collect	Other Charges		
Valuation Charge	AWB FEE: 200.00		
Tax			
Total other Charges Due Agent 200.00	Shipper certifies that particular's on the face hereof are correct and agrees THE CONDITIONS ON REVERSE HEREOF: PUDONG / AIR EXPORT 华民彰		
Total other Charges Due Carrier	Signature Shipper or his Agent		
Total Prepaid 2 200.00	Total Collect	Carrier certifies that the goods described hereon are accepted for carriage subject to THE CONDITION OF CONTRACT ON THE REVERSE HEREOF. The goods then being in apparent good order and condition except as noted hereon. SEP.20, 2006 SHANGHAI, CHINA	AIRLINES
Currency Conversion Rate	CC Charges in Dest., Currency	Executed on(date) at(place)	Signature of issuing Carrier
For Carriers Use only at Destination	Charges at Destination	Total Collect Charges	789-3905 0933

三、实训缮制要求

空运单缮制要求如下：

1	(1)栏空运单左上角居中的地方：填写始发站机场的 IATA 三字代码,由承运人填写。如果没有机场的 IATA 三字代码,可以填写机场所在城市的 IATA 三字代码 (1A)栏空运单左上角、右上角和右下角的地方：印制或者电脑打制承运人的票证注册代号 (1B)栏货运单左上角、右上角和右下角的地方：货运单号码由八位数字组成,前七位为顺序号,第八位为检查号 (1C)栏货运单"Air Waybill"右边填写所属航空公司名称及总部所在地址。此处还印有航空公司的标志
2	(2)栏(Shipper's Name and Address)：托运人姓名和地址。此栏填制托运人姓名（名称）、详细地址、国家（或国家两字代号）以及托运人的电话、传真号码
3	(3)栏(Shipper's Account Number)：托运人账号。此栏不需填写,除非承运人另有要求
4	(4)栏(Consignee's Name and Address)：收货人姓名和地址。填制收货人姓名（名称）、详细地址、国家（或国家两字代号）以及收货人的电话、传真号码
5	(5)栏(consignee's Account Number)：收货人账号。此栏仅供承运人使用,一般不需填写,除非最后的承运人另有要求
6	(6)栏(Issuing Carrier's Agent Name and City)：出票航空公司货运代理人名称和城市。此栏填制向出票航空公司收取佣金的国际航协代理人的名称和所在机场或城市
7	(7)栏(Agent's IATA Code)：国际航协代号。航空公司为便于内部系统管理,要求其代理人在此处填制相应数字代码。采用货物财务结算系统(CASS — Cargo Accounts Settlement System)清算的代理人按规定填入相应代号
8	(8)栏(Account No.)：账号。本栏一般不需填写,除非承运人另有需要
9	(9)栏(Airport Of Departure and Requested Routing)：始发站机场和要求的运输路线。此栏填制运输始发站机场或所在城市（始发地机场与所在城市使用相同代码）的全称,以及所要求的运输路线
10	(10)栏(Accounting Information)：相关财务信息。此栏填制有关财务说明事项,如：付款方式：现金支票或其他方式。作为货物运输的行李使用MCO付款时,此栏应填制MCO号码、换取服务金额以及旅客客票号码、航班号、日期及航程 如因货物无法交付需要退运时填开的货运单,应将原始货运单号码填入本栏内
11	(11A～11F)栏(Routing and Destination)：运输路线和目的站 (11A)to (by first carrier)至（第一承运人） 填制目的地机场或第一个转运点的 IATA 三字代码（当该城市有多个机场,不知道机场名称时,可用城市代号） (11B)by first carrier 由第一承运人 填制第一承运人的名称（全称与IATA两字代号皆可） (11C)to (by second carrier)至（第二承运人） 填制目的地机场或第二个转运点的 IATA 三字代码（当该城市有多个机场,不知道机场名称时,可用城市代号） (11D)by second carrier 由第二承运人 填制第二承运人的名称（全称与IATA两字代号皆可）

（续表）

11	(11E)to（by third carrier）至(第三承运人) 填制目的地机场或第三个转运点的 IATA 三字代号(当该城市有多个机场,不知道机场名称时,可用城市代号) (11F)by third carrier 由第三承运人 填制第三承运人的名称(全称与 IATA 两字代号皆可)
12	(12)栏(Currency)：货币。填制运输始发地货币代号(统一采用国际标准化组织——ISO 的货币代号)。 注：运输始发地货币指运输始发地运价资料所公布的货币 除(33A)栏~(33D)栏外,货运单上所列明的费用金额均按上述货币表示
13	(13)栏(CHGS Code)：付款方式(填写货物运费的支付方式)
14	(14A)(14B)货物运费、声明价值费栏 "WT/VAL"表示货物航空运费、声明价值附加费的预付(14A)或到付(14B) 有关费用预付(PPD)或到付(COLL),分别用字母"PP"、"CC"在货运单上表示,或在相关栏目内用"×"表示 注：货运单上(24A)、(25A)或(24B)、(25B)两项费用必须全部预付或全部到付
15	(15A)(15B)：其他费用付款方式栏,"Other"表示其他费用预付(15A)或到付(15B) 有关费用预付(PPD)或到付(COLL),分别用字母"PP"、"CC"在货运单上表示,或在相关栏目内用"×"表示 货运单上(27A)、(28A)或(27B)、(28B)两项费用必须全部预付或全部到付
16	(16)栏(Declared Value for Carriage)：运输声明价值。填制托运人关于货物运输声明价值的金额。如果托运人没有运输声明价值,此栏不可以空着,必须填制"NVD"字样(NVD — No Value Declared,没有声明价值)
17	(17)栏(Declared Value for Customs)：供海关用声明价值。填制货物过海关时海关需要的货物商业价值金额。如果货物没有商业价值,或海关不要求声明,此栏必须打印"NCV"字样(NCV—NO Commercial Value or NO Customs Value,没有商业价值。)
18	(18)栏(Airport of Destination)：目的站机场。填制最后承运人的目的地机场全称
19	(19A)(19B)栏(Flight/Date)：航班/日期。仅供承运人使用
20	(20)栏(Amount of Insurance)：保险金额。如果承运人向托运人提供代办货物保险业务时,此栏打印托运人货物投保的金额。如果承运人不提供此项服务或托运人不要求投保时此栏内必须打印"×××"符号
21	(21)栏(Handling Information)：运输处理注意事项 (21A)SCI,海关信息：填写海关信息,仅在欧盟国家之间运输货物时使用
22	(22A)至(22L)货物运价及细目。一票货物中如含有两种或两种以上不同运价类别计费的货物应分别填写,每填写一项另起一行,如果含有危险品,则该危险货物应列在第一项 (22A)栏(NO. of Pieces RCP)货物件数/运价组合点。运价组合点是指如果使用分段相加运价计算运费时,在件数的下面应打印运价组合点城市的 IATA 三字代码 (22B)栏(Gross Weight)：毛重。填入货物实际毛重(以千克为单位时可保留至小数点一位) (22C)栏(Kg/Lb)：重量单位千克或磅。以千克为单位用代号"K";以磅为单位用代号"L" (22D)栏(Rate Class)：运价等级

(续表)

22	(22E)栏(Commodity Item NO.)商品品名编号。运输指定商品,货物运费使用指定商品运价计费时,此栏打印指定商品品名代号(打印位置应与运价代号 C 保持水平);运输等级货物,使用等级货物运价计费时,此栏打印附加或附减运价的比例(百分比);如果是集装货物,打印集装货物运价等级 (22F)栏(Chargeable Weight):计费重量。填入计算货物运费适用的计费重量 (22G)栏(Rate/Charge):运价/运费。当使用最低运费时,此栏与运价代号"M"对应打印最低运费。填入与运价代号"N"、"Q"、"C"等相应的运价。当货物为等级货物时,此栏与运价代号"S"(表示附加等级运价)或"R"(表示附减等级运价)对应打印附加或附减后的运价 (22H)栏(Total):总计。填入计费重量与适用运价相乘后的运费金额;如果是最低运费或集装货物基本运费时,本栏与(22G)内金额相同 (22I)栏(Nature and Quantity of Goods):货物品名和数量。 (22J)、(22K)、(22L)分别为货物总件数、总毛重、总运费
23	(23)栏(Other charges):其他费用。其他费用种类用下列两字代码表示,以下为部分其他费用两字代码: AC——Animal Container 动物容器租费 AS——Assembly Service Fee 集中货物服务费 AT——Attendant 押运员服务费 AW——Air Waybill 货运单工本费 DB——Disbursement Fee 代垫付款手续费 FC——Charges Collect Fee 运费到付手续费 LA——Live Animals 动物处理费 RA——Dangerous Goods Surcharge 危险品处理费 SD——Surface Charge Destination 目的站地面运输费 SU——Surface Charge 地面运输费 注:此栏中任一费用均需用三个字母表示;前两个字母表示费用种类,第三个字母表示费用归属。承运人收取的其他费用"C"表示,代理人收取的其他费用"A"表示。如"AWC",属于出票航空公司收取的货运单工本费。"AWA",为代理人收取的货运单工本费
24	(24A)(24B)栏(Weight Charge):航空运费。此栏填入航空运费计算栏(22)栏计算所得的航空运费总数。如果航空运费预付,填入(24A),航空运费到付,则填入(24B)
25	(25A)(25B)栏(Valuation Charge):声明价值费 当托运人声明货物运输声明价值时,此栏填入声明价值附加费金额。该费用必须与航空运费同步付款;同时预付或同时到付。声明价值附加费预付填入(25A),到付填入(25B)
26	(26A)(26B)Tax 税款:填写按规定收取的税款额,可以预付或者到付,根据付款方式分别填写,但是,必须同(24A)和(25A)或(24B)和(25B)同时全部预付或者同时全部到付
27	(27A)(27B)(Total Other Charges Due Agent):由代理人收取的其他费用总额。预付填入(27A),到付填入(27B)
28	(28A)(28B)(Total Other Charges Due Carrier):由出票航空公司收取的其他费用总额。预付填入(28A),到付填入(28B)
29	(29A)栏:无名称阴影栏目。本栏不需打印,除非承运人需要
30	(30A)(30B):预付和到付费用总额 (30A)填入(24A)(25A)(26A)(27A)(28A)等栏有关预付款项之和 (30B)填入(24B)(25B)(26B)(27B)(28A)等栏有关预付款项之和

（续表）

31	（31）栏：托运人证明栏。填制托运人名称，并由托运人或其代理人在本栏内签字或盖章
32	（32A）（32B）（32C）：承运人填写栏。将填开货运单日期、地点、所在机场或城市的全称或缩写分别填入（32A）、（32B）、（32C）。填开日期采用按日、月、年的顺序。（32C）要求填开货运单的承运人或其代理人在本栏内签字
33	（33A）（33B）（33C）（33D）栏：仅供有关承运人在目的地机场等目的站使用。收货人用目的地国家货币付费 （33A）栏（Currency Conversion Rate）：货币兑换比价，填入将运输始发地货币换算成目的地国家货币的比价（银行卖出价） （33B）栏（CC Charges in Destination Currency）：用目的地国家货币表示的付费金额 （33C）栏（Charges at Destination）：目的站费用。最后一个承运人将目的站发生费用金额填制在本栏中 （33D）栏（Total Collect Charges）：到付费用总额
34	（34）栏仅供承运人在目的站使用（For Carrier's Use Only at Destination）仅限在目的站由承运人填写

工作任务三　缮制多式联运单据

实训背景

上海进出口贸易公司的钱林遇到新的运输业务办理，公司交给他一项办理多式联运运输的工作任务，对于这一新业务，钱林从认识国际多式联运、国际多式联运单据的相关知识开始接触这一工作任务。

一、实训指南

国际多式联运是指按照国际多式联运规则，以两种或两种以上不同的运输方式，由多式联运经营人将货物从一国境内接管货物的地点运至另一国境内指定交付货物的地点，多式联运经营人为发货人，签发多式联运提单，供发货人按照信用证的要求结汇，提供"一票到底，全程负责"的服务。

多式联运单据（Combined Transport Documents，简称 CTD 或 Multimodal Transport Document，简称 MTD）是证明国际多式联运合同成立及证明多式联运经营人接管货物，并负责按照多式联运合同条款支付货物的单据。

二、实训样本

钱林找到 COSCO 公司的多式联运单据，认真研究其填制内容。多式联运单据的样本如下：

Shipper Insert Name, Address and Phone		B/L No.	
		中远集装箱运输有限公司 COSCO CONTAINER LINES TLX: 33057 COSCO CN FAX: +86(021) 6545 8984 **ORIGINAL**	
Consignee Insert Name, Address and Phone			
Notify Party Insert Name, Address and Phone (It is agreed that no responsibility shall attach to the Carrier or his agents for failure to notify)		Port-to-Port or Combined Transport **BILL OF LADING** RECEIVED in external apparent good order and condition except as otherwise noted. The total number of packages or unites stuffed in the container, The description of the goods and the weights shown in this Bill of Lading are furnished by the Merchants, and which the carrier has no reasonable means of checking and is not a part of this Bill of Lading contract. The carrier has issued the number of Bills of Lading stated below, all of this tenor and date, one of the original Bills of Lading must be surrendered and endorsed or signed against the delivery of the shipment and whereupon any other original Bills of Lading shall be void. The Merchants agree to be bound by the terms and conditions of this Bill of Lading as if each had personally signed this Bill of Lading. SEE clause 4 on the back of this Bill of Lading (Terms continued on the back Hereof, please read carefully). * Applicable Only When Document Used as a Combined Transport Bill of Lading.	
Combined Transport *	Combined Transport *		
Pre-carriage by	Place of Receipt		
Ocean Vessel Voy. No.	Port of Loading		
Port of Discharge	Combined Transport *		
	Place of Delivery		

Container/ Seal No.	Marks & Nos.	No. of Containers or Packages	Description of Goods	Gross Weight (Kgs)	Measurement (M³)

Total Number of containers and/or packages (in words)

Freight & Charges	Revenue Tons	Rate	Per	Prepaid	Collect

Ex. Rate	Prepaid at	Payable at	Place and Date of Issue
	Total Prepaid	No. of Original B(s)/L	Signed for the Carrier, COSCO CONTAINER LINES

LADEN ON BOARD THE VESSEL

Date		By	

三、实训缮制要求

填 制 栏 目	填制内容和要求
1. 单据名称(Title)	多式联运单据
2. 收货地和目的地(Place of Receipt and Place of Delivery)	根据《UCP600》,通过事先印就的文字,或者表明货物已经被发送、接管或装运日期的印戳或批注,都表明货物已经在信用证规定的地点发送、接管或已装运
3. 预期船只和预期港口(Intended Vessel and Intended Port)	在多式联运单据中允许载有"预期船只"、"预期装货港"或"预期卸货港",或类似于关于船只、装货港或卸货港的限定语,只要表明信用证规定的发送、接管或发运地点,以及最终目的地,可接受。无须像海运提单那样再加上"已装船"批注和船名或港口名
4. 转运条款(Transshipment Terms)	根据《UCP600》,运输单据可以表明货物将要或可能被转运,只要全程运输由同一运输单据涵盖。即使信用证禁止转运,注明将要或者可能发生转运的运输单据仍可接受
5. 承运条款(Shipment Terms)	根据《UCP600》,载有承运条款和条件,或提示承运条款和条件参见别处(简式/背面空白的运输单据),银行将不审核承运条款和条件的内容
6. 出具日期和发运日期(Issuing Date And Shipment Date)	根据《UCP600》,多式联运单据的出具日期将被视为发送、接管或装运的日期,也即发运的日期。然而如单据以印戳或批注的方式表明了发送、接管或装运日期,该日期将被视为发运日期
7. 签发或证实(Sign or Authenticate)	根据《UCP600》,多式联运单据,必须表明承运人名称并由以下人员签署或证实:承运人或其具名代理人,或船长或其具名代理人
8. 更正处(Correction)	多式联运单据的更正处必须有承运人、船长或其具名代理人的证实或小签

工作任务四 了解铁路运单、公路运单、快递单据及邮政收据

实训背景

> 上海进出口贸易公司的钱林积极学习新的运输业务的办理,公司交给他办理铁路运输、公路运输、邮政运输和快递运输的工作任务,对于这些新业务,钱林积极学习相关运输方式的单证知识。

一、实训指南

(一)铁路运单

铁路运输单据(Railway Bill)简称铁路运单,是铁路运输当局向托运人签发的承运货物

的收据。我国对外贸易铁路运输按营运方式分为国际铁路联运和国内铁路承运,其铁路运单分别采用国际货协运单和承运货物收据。

1. 国际铁路货物联运运单

国际铁路货物联运运单是参加国际货协各成员国之间办理铁路联运时所使用的运输单据。它是承运人向托运人出具的货物收据,具有合同性质。运单上载明的栏目一般包括经由路线及到达站、收货人及发货人名称地址、发货的特别声明、货物名称、数量、唛头、包装、价格、运费、海关记载和车辆记载等。

2. 承运货物收据

我国由国内铁路运输经深圳运往港澳地区的货物,都委托中国对外贸易运输公司办理。该公司将各出口企业委托发运的货物装上火车后,即签发一份"承运货物收据"(Cargo Receipt)给托运人,供托运人办理收汇。承运货物收据既是承运人的货物收据,也是承运人与托运人之间的运输合同。

(二)公路运单

公路货物运单是公路货物运输及运输代理的合同凭证,是运输经营者接受货物并在运输期间负责保管和据以交付的凭证,也是记录车辆运行和行业统计的原始凭证。公路运单必须标明承运人名称,并由承运人或其具名代理人签署,或以签字、印戳或批注表明货物收讫、接管并承运,以及据以保证交付货物的单据。它是一份运输合同的证明,是承运人收到货物的初步证据和交货凭证。

(三)快递单据和邮政收据

1. 快递收据

快递收据(Courier Receipt)是由快递公司出具表明货物收讫待运的收据凭证。它的正面内容相当于空运分单,且增加了收货人签收栏,因此,是一种简单的买卖双方对物品交货和收货凭证。

2. 邮政收据

邮政收据(Post Receipt)是邮政运输的主要单据,它既是邮局收到寄件人的邮包后所签发的凭证,也是收件人凭以提取邮件的凭证,当邮包发生损坏或丢失时,它还可以作为索赔和理赔的依据。

《UCP600》规定:银行接受邮政收据、专递和快递机构的运输收据,但这些收据必须显示邮费已付或预付。邮戳日期即作为装运日期,邮戳日期不能晚于装运日期。

二、实训样本

(一)铁路运单

承运货物收据样张如下:

中国对外贸易运输公司上海分公司

承运货物收据 运输 NO. _____
CARGO RECEIPT 发票 NO. _____
第一联（凭提货物） 合约 NO. _____

委托人： Shipper		收货人： Consignee 通知 Notify

自 From 上海 Shanghai　　　　至 To

发运
　　日期　　　　车号：Car No.
装车

标记 Marks & Nos.	件数 Package	货物名称 Description of Goods	标记 Remarks

全程运费在上海付讫
Freight Prepaid at

请向下列地点接洽提货
For Delivery Apply to

中国对外贸易公司上海分公司
押汇银行
Bank's Endorsement

收货人签收
Consignee's signature

（二）邮政收据

邮政收据样张如下：

上海市邮政局
国际大宗包裹、小包、挂号印刷、函件执据

寄件人姓名：_____ 详细地址：

序 号	收件人姓名、地址	挂号号码	重量（千克）	资 费
1				￥
2				
3				
4				
5				
6				
7				
8				
9				
10				

共计： 件

签署_____

三、实训缮制要求

（一）铁路运单和公路运单

填制栏目	填制内容和要求
1. 单据名称（Title）	铁路运单或公路运单
2. 发货地和目的地（Place of Receipt and Place of Delivery）	根据《UCP600》，铁路运单和公路运单，必须表明信用证规定的发运地和目的地
3. 收货人（Consignee）	如果信用证没有特殊规定，这类单据必须制成记名抬头，不允许指示抬头或空白抬头
4. 转运条款（Transshipment Terms）	根据《UCP600》，只要全程运输由同一运输单据涵盖，铁路运单可以注明货物将要或可能被转运。即使信用证禁止转运，注明将要或者可能发生转运的铁路运单仍可接受
5. 正本（Original）	根据《UCP600》，铁路运输单据、公路运输单据必须看似为开给发货人或托运人的正本，或没有任何标记表明单据开给何人

(续表)

填 制 栏 目	填制内容和要求
6. 出具日期和发运日期（Issuing Date and Shipment Date）	根据《UCP600》,铁路运单和公路运单的出具日期将被视为发运日期,除非运输单据上盖有带日期的收货印戳,或注明了收货日期或发运日期
7. 签发或证实（Sign or Authenticate）	根据《UCP600》,铁路运单和公路运单,表明承运人名称并由以下人员签署：承运人或其具名代理人,或承运人或其具名代理人以签字、印戳或批注表明货物收讫
8. 更正处（Correction）	铁路运单和公路运单的更正处必须有承运人或其具名代理人的证实或小签

（二）快递单据和邮政收据

根据《UCP600》和相关机构的有关规定,快递收据、邮政收据使用事项如下：

填 制 栏 目	填制内容和要求
1. 单据名称（Title）	快递收据或邮政收据
2. 机构名称（Name of Courier or Post Company）	必须表明机构名称,并在信用证规定的货物发运地点由该具名机构盖章或签字
3. 收件人（Receiver）	收件人必须是记名收件人,须显示详细的收件人名称、国家、城市、街道、电话和传真
4. 发运日（Shipment Date）	根据《UCP600》,快递收据须表明取件或收件的日期或类似词语。该日期将被视为发运日期。邮政收据须在信用证规定的货物发运地点或签署并注明日期,该日期将被视为发运日期
5. 签发人（Signer）	根据《UCP600》,快递收据和邮政单据必须表明快递机构和邮政机构名称
6. 费用（Change）	单据上可以以印戳或其他方式提及运费或运费之外的费用
7. 更正处（Correction）	单据上如果有更改之处,应有出具单据人的小签或印章
8. 部分发运（Partial Shipment）	在同一发货地,同一天内多次快递或投递,将不视为部分发运

单证模拟实训七

一、缮制空运委托书模拟操作

上海进出口贸易公司业务员黄源在春季华交会上,遇到对该公司展览的上海牌26英寸和28英寸山地自行车很感兴趣的日本客商 Fujiyama Trading Corporation 的山本先生。随后,双方签订了销售确认书。合同签订后,黄源委托上海国际货代公司办理货物运输手续。为此,黄源缮制装箱单,填写国际货物托运书。

缮制资料合同如下:

上 海 进 出 口 贸 易 公 司
SHANGHAI IMPORT & EXPORT TRADE CORPORATION
1321 ZHONGSHAN ROAD SHANGHAI CHINA

SALES CONFIRMATION

Post code: 200032　　　　　　　　　　　　　S/C NO: TXT06081
Fax: (021) 65788876　　　　　　　　　　　　DATE: SEP. 10, 2007
TEL: (021) 65788877
TO MESSRS:
FUJIYAMA TRADING CORPORATION
121, KAWARA MACH OSAKA, JAPAN

Dear Sirs,
　　We hereby confirm having sold to you the following goods on terms and conditions as specified below:

SHIPPING MARK	GOODS OF DESCRIPTIONS	QUANTITY	UNIT PRICE	AMOUNT
PT TXT06081 OSAKA C/NO. 1 – UP	SHANGHAI COUNTRY BICYCLE ART SH28INCH ART SH26INCH	300 PCS 400 PCS	CPT OSAKA USD 100.00 USD　80.00	USD 30 000.00 USD 32 000.00

　　1) TERMS OF PAYMENT: 30% T/T IN ADVANCE, THE OTHERS 70% T/T AFTER SHIPMENT
　　2) AIRPORT OF DEPARTURE:　　PUDONG AIRPORT SHANGHAI, CHINA
　　3) AIRPORT OF DESTINATION:　　OSAKA AIRPORT JAPAN
　　4) LATEST DATE OF SHIPMENT: DEC. 20, 2007

5) PACKED IN 1 CARTON OF 10 SET EACH
OUR BANK INFORMATION IS AS BELOW:
BANK NAME: BANK OF CHINA SHANGHAI BRANCH
ACCOUNT NO.: RMB80456861

THE BUYER: FUJIYAMA TRADING CORPORATION 山本   THE SELLER 上海进出口贸易公司 合同专用章 黄源

黄源缮制装箱单：

上海进出口贸易公司

SHANGHAI IMPORT & EXPORT TRADE CORPORATION
1321 ZHONGSHAN ROAD SHANGHAI CHINA
PACKING LIST

TEL: 0512-6578876   INVOICE NO: XH051111
FAX: 0512-6578877   DATE: DEC.2,2007
E-mail: LUZHENSH@163.COM   S/C NO: TXT07081
TO: FUJIYAMA TRADING CORPORATION   SHIPPING MARK
121,KAWARA MACH OSAKA, JAPAN   N/M

CASE NO	GOODS DESCRIPTION & PACKING	QUANTITY (PCS)	G.W (KGS)	N.W (KGS)	MEAS (M^3)
1-30 31-70	SHANGHAI COUNTRY BICYCLE ART SH28INCH ART SH26INCH PACKED IN 1 CARTON OF 10 SET EACH	300 PCS 400 PCS	300 430	260 390	14 17
TOTAL:		140 000	730	650	31

SAY TOTAL: ONE THOUSAND FOUR HUNDRED CARTONS ONLY.

SHANGHAI IMPORT & EXPORT TRADING CORPORATION
黄源

黄源填制国际货物托运书：

上海客货运输服务有限公司
SHANGHAI EXPRESS SERVICE CO., LTD.　　　　*IATA*

国际货物托运书
SHIPPER'S LETTER OF INSTRUCTION　　REF NO: XY050401

始发站 AIRPORT DEPARTURE			到达站 AIRPORT OF DESTINATION				供承运人用 FOR CARRIER ONLY	
路线及到达站 ROUTING AND DESTINATION							航班/日期 FRIGHT/DAY	航班/日期 FRIGHT/DAY
至 TO	第一承运人 BY FIRST CARRIER	至 TO	承运人 BY	至 TO	承运人 BY	至 TO	承运人 BY	已预留吨位 DOKKED
收货人姓名及地址							运费: CHARGES: FREIGHT:	
另行通知 ALSO NOTIFY								
托运人账号 SHIPPER'S ACCOUNT NUMBER				托运人姓名及地址 SHIPPER'S NAME & ADDRESS				
托运人声明的价值 SHIPPER'S DECLARED VALUE NVD			保险金额 AMOUNT OF INSURANCE	所附文件 DOCUMENTS TO ACCOMPANY AIR WAYBILL				
供运输用 FOR CARRIAGE	供海关用 FOR CUSTOMS							
件数 NO. OF PACKAGES	实际毛重 ACTIAL GROSS WEIGHT(KG)	运价类别 RATE CLASS	收费重量 CHARGEABLE WEIGHT	离岸 RATE CHARGE		货物名称及重量(包括体积或尺寸) NATURE AND QUANTITY OF GOODS (INCL DIMENSIONS OF VOLUME)		
在货物不能交于收货人时,托运人指示的处理方法 SHIPPER'S INSTRUCTIONS IN CASE OF INABILITY TO DELIVER SHIPMENT AS CONSIGNED								
处理情况(包括包装方式、货物标志及号码等) HANDLING INFORMATION (INCL METHOD OF PACKING IDENTIFYING MARKS AND NUMBERS. LTC.)								

托运人证实以上所填全部属实并愿遵守托运人的一切载运章程
THE SHIPPER CERTIFIES THAT PARTICALS ON THE FACE HEREOF ARE CORRECT AND AGREES TO THE CONDITIONS OF CARRIAGE OF THE CARRIER

托运人签字:　　　　　日期:　　　　　经收人:　　　　　日期:
SIGNATURE OF SHIPPER　　DATE　　　　AGENT　　　　DATE

二、缮制空运单模拟操作

　　航空公司签发空运单如下:

Shipper's Name and Address	Shipper's Account Number 045686	Not negotiable		
		Air Waybill 中国东方航空公司 Issued by CHINA EASTERN AIRLINES 2250 HONGQIAO ROAD SHANGHAI, CHINA		
Consignee's Name and Address KUMHO INDUSTRIAL, CO. KWANGCHON SO-GU, KWANGJU, 502-210, KOREA	Consignee's Account Number SO099	Copies 1,2 and 3 this Air Waybill are originals and have the same validity. It is agreed that goods described herein are accepted in apparent good order and condition (except as noted) for carriage SUBJECT TO THE CONDITIONS OF CONTRACT ON THE REVESE HEREOF. ALL GOODS MAY BE CARRIED BY ANY OTHER MEANS INCLUDING ROAD OR ANY OTHER CARRIER UNLESS SPECIFIC CONTRARY INSRUCTIONS ARE GIVEN HEREON BY THE SHIPPER, AND SHIPPER AGREES THAT THE SHIPPMENT MAY BE CARRIED VIA INTERMEDIATE STOPPING PLACES WHICH THE CARRIER DEEMS APPROPRIATE. THE SHIPPER'S ATTENTION IS DRAWN TO THE NOTICE CONCERNING CARRIER'S LIMIATION OF LIABILITY. Shipper may increase such limitation of limitation of liability by declaring a higher value for carriage and paying a supplemental charge if required.		
Issuing Carrier's Agent Name and City		Accounting Information		
Agents IATA Code 08321550	Account No.			

Airport of Departure (Addr. Of First Carrier) and Requested Routing												
To	By First Carrier Routing and Destination	To	By	To	By	Currency USD	Chgs Code	WT/VAL PPD / COLL ××		Other PPD / COLL ××	Declared Value for Carrier N.V.D	Declared Value for Customs
Airport of Destination	Requested Flight/Date MU0514/02					Amount of Insurance					If shipper requests insurance in accordance with the conditions thereof indicate amount to be insures in figures in box marked "Amount of Insurance".	

Handing Information
AS PER REF NO: XY050401

No. of Place RCP	Gross Weight	kg lb	Rate Class Commodity Item No.	Chargeable Weight	Rate / Charge	Total	Nature and Quantity of Goods (Incl. Dimensions or Volume)
		K	Q				

Prepaid / Weight Charge / Collect	Other Charges		
Valuation Charge	AWB FEE:		
Tax			
Total other Charges Due Agent	Shipper certifies that particular's on the face hereof are correct and agrees THE CONDITIONS ON REVERSE HEREOF: PUDONG / AIR EXPORT 华氏韵		
Total other Charges Due Carrier	......................Signature Shipper or his Agent......................		
Total Prepaid / Total Collect	Carrier certifies that the goods described hereon are accepted for carriage subject to THE CONDITION OF CONTRACT ON THE REVERSE HEREOF. The goods then being in apparent good order and condition except as noted hereon.		
Currency Conversion Rate / CC Charges in Dest., Currency	DEC.20,2007 SHANGHAI,CHINA Executed on(date) at(place)		AIRLINES Signature of issuing Carrier
For Carriers Use only at Destination	Charges at Destination	Total Collect Charges	789-3905 0933

项目八

出口官方单证——原产地和报检单证

实训目标

◆ 了解一般原产地证书申请书和一般原产地证书缮制要求，学会缮制原产地证书申请书和原产地证书。

◆ 了解普惠制原产地证书申请书和普惠制原产地证书缮制要求，学会缮制普惠制原产地证书申请书和普惠制原产地证书。

◆ 了解出口货物报检单和出口货物通关单的缮制要求，学会填制出口货物报检单和出口货物通关单。了解检验证书的种类和缮制方法。

工作任务一 缮制申请书和一般原产地证书

实训背景

钱林从某高职院校国际商务专业毕业后，进入上海进出口贸易公司工作，业务推广中得知韩国客商 Kumho Industrial 公司的 Kim，Kon 先生，对本公司展览的手工工具很感兴趣，经过磋商，上海进出口贸易公司与 Kumho Industrial 公司会签了出口合同。目前，钱林需要办理相关的申请一般原产地证书的手续，缮制申请书和一般原产地证书。

一、实训指南

（一）原产地证书概述

原产地证书简称产地证，是由出口国政府有关机构签发的一种证明货物的原产地或制造地的文件。它主要用于进口国海关实行差别关税,实施进口限制、不同进口税率和不同进口配额等不同国别政策的书面依据。

原产地证主要分为一般原产地证书、普惠制原产地证书、输欧盟纺织品产地证、对美国出口的原产地声明书以及区域性经济集团互惠原产地证书等。

由于一般原产地证书和普惠制原产地证书格式 A 在实践中使用最多,因此,我们主要介绍这两种原产地证明书。

(二) 一般原产地证明书(C/O,Certificate of Origin)

1. 定义

一般原产地证明书又称为普通产地证书,是证明本批出口商品的生产或制造符合《中华人民共和国出口货物原产地规则》的一种法律文件。

2. 四种形式

(1) 检验检疫局(CIQ)出具的《中华人民共和国原产地证书》。

(2) 贸促会(CCPIT)出具的《中华人民共和国原产地证书》。

(3) 出口商出具的《原产地证书》。

(4) 生产厂家出具的《原产地证书》。

3. 申领所需要的文件

(1) 提供规定格式并已制作的《一般原产地证明书申请单》一份。

(2) 提供制作完毕的《中华人民共和国原产地证明书》一套(一正三副)。

(3) 提供出口商业发票正本一份。

(4) 发证机构所需的其他证明文件,如"加工工序清单"等。

4. 申领产地证的时间

根据我国有关规定,出口企业最迟于货物出运前 3 天,持签证机构规定的正本文件,向签证机构申请办理产地证书。特殊情况应在出货后 1 个月内办理,并提供提单或其他运输单据复印件。出货 1 个月来办理的,还需提交企业出具的情况说明,若超过 3 个月,则不予办理。

二、实训样本

(一) 一般原产地证书申请书

钱林缮制《原产地证明书申请书》与《原产地证明书》,并随附商业发票一份向上海出入境检验检疫局主管部门申请签发。

合同如下:

上海进出口贸易公司
SHANGHAI IMPORT & EXPORT TRADE CORPORATION
1321 ZHONGSHAN ROAD SHANGHAI, CHINA

SALES CONTRACT

Post code: 200032
Fax: (021) 65788876
TEL: (021) 65788877

P/I NO.: 20060228
S/C No: TXT06081
DATE: AUG.1,2006

TO MESSRS:

KUMHO INDUSTRIAL CO.

49 - 1, KWANGCHON SO - GU, KWANGJU, 502 - 210

KOREA

Dear Sirs,

We hereby confirm having sold to you the following goods on terms and conditions as specified below:

GOODS OF DESCRIPTIONS	QUANTITY	UNIT PRICE	AMOUNT
DOUBLE OPEN END SPANNER 8×10 MM(MTM) 10×12 MM(MTM)	60 000 PCS 80 000 PCS	CPT KWANGJU USD 0.50 USD 0.40	USD 30 000.00 USD 32 000.00

1) SHIPPING MARK: N/M

2) TERMS OF PAYMENT: 30% T/T IN ADVANCE, THE OTHERS 70% T/T AFTER SHIPMENT.

3) AIRPORT OF DEPARTURE: PUDONG AIRPORT SHANGHAI, CHINA

4) AIRPORT OF DESTINATION: KWANGJU AIRPORT KOREA

5) LATEST DATE OF SHIPMENT: SEP. 30, 2006

OUR BANK: INFORMATION IS AS BELOW:

BANK NAME: BANK OF CHINA SHANGHAI BRANCH

ACCOUNT NO.: RMB80456861

THE BUYER:
KUMHO INDUSTRIAL, CO.
KIM, KON

THE SELLER:
SHANGHAI IMPORT & EXPORT TRADE
钱林

填制一般原产地证书申请书如下：

一般原产地证明书/加工装配证明书

申 请 书

申请单位注册号：866742Q 　　　　　　　　　　　　　证书号：

申请人郑重申明：

本人被正式授权代表本企业办理和签署本申请书。

本申请书及一般原产地证明书/加工装配证明书所列内容正确无误，如发现弄虚作假，冒充证书所列货物，擅改证书，自愿接受签发机构的处罚并承担法律责任，现将有关情况申报如下：

企 业 名 称	上海进出口贸易公司	发 票 号		XH061111
商 品 名 称	活络扳手	H.S.编码（六位数）		8204.11
商品FOB总值（以美元计）	USD 59 600.00	最终目的地国家/地区		韩国
拟出运日期	2006.9.20	转口国（地区）		* * *
贸易方式和企业性质（请在适用处划"√"）				
一般贸易√		三来一补		其他贸易方式
国有企业	三资企业	国有企业	三资企业	国有企业　　三资企业
√				
包装数量或毛重或其他数量	1 400箱			
证书种类（划"√"）	一般原产地证明书√			加工装配证明书

现提交中国出口货物商业发票副本一份，一般原产地证明书/加工装配证明书一正三副，以及其他附件　　份，请予审核签证。

申请单位盖章　　　　　　　　　　　　　　　　申请人（签名）钱林
　　　　　　　　　　　　　　　　　　　　　　电话：65788888
　　　　　　　　　　　　　　　　　　　　　　日期：2006年9月12日

商 检 局 联 系 记 录

(二)一般原产地证书

根据以上情况,上海出入境检验检疫局主管部门签发一般原产地证书如下:

1. Exporter (full name and address) SHANGHAI IMPORT & EXPORT TRADE CORPORATION 1321 ZHONGSHAN ROAD SHANGHAI, CHINA			CERTIFICATE No.: 500511266 CERTIFICATE OF ORIGIN OF THE PEOPLE'S REPUBLIC OF CHINA	
2. Consignee (full name, address, country) KUMHO INDUSTRIAL CO. 49-1, KWANGCHON SO-GU, KWANGJU, 502-210 KOREA				
3. Means of transport and route FROM SHANGHAI TO SEMARANG BY AIR			5. For certifying authority use only	
4. Country/Region Of Destination KOREA				
6. Marks and numbers of packages N/M	7. Description of goods; number and kind of packages DOUBL EOPENEND PANNER ONE THOUSAND FOUR HUNDRED (1 400) CARTONS **********************	8. H. S. Code 8 204.11	9. Quantity or weight 140 000 PCS	10. Number and date of invoice XH061111 SEP. 11, 2006
11. Declaration by the exporter 　The undersigned hereby declares that the above details and statements are correct; that all the goods were produced in China and that they comply with the Rules of Origin of the People's Republic of China SHANGHAI SEP. 12, 2006···　　　钱林 Place and date. signature and stamp of authorized signatory			12. Certification 　It is hereby certified that the declaration by the exporter is correct. SHANGHAI SEP. 15, 2006···　　　丁毅 Place and date. signature and stamp of certifying authority	

三、实训缮制要求

(一) 一般原产地证书申请书的缮制

填 写 栏 目	填制内容和要求
1. 申请单位注册号	填写申请单位在检验检疫局产地证签证部门注册的注册号
2. 证书号	根据签证机构的编号规则,对应于每批审证货物的编号,不得重号或跳号
3. 企业名称	申请原产地证的出口企业
4. 发票号	填写正式出口发票的号码,并与随附发票相一致
5. 商品名称	填写商品品名的中英文,并且与发票证书的商品名称一致
6. H.S.税目号	商品的 H.S.六位数编码,海关统计编码前六位
7. 商品 FOB 总值	根据申报的出口货物出口发票上所列的金额以 FOB 价格,填写(以美元计)
8. 最终目的地国家/地区	即货物即将运抵的最终销售国
9. 拟出运日期	如实准确填写货物离开起运口岸的当天日期(年、月、日)
10. 转口国(地区)	填写本批货物的转口国家,无转运港的填"＊＊＊"
11. 贸易方式和企业性质	根据实际情况选择划"√"
12. 包装数量,毛重或其他数量	填写该批出口货物的箱数、毛重或个数等
13. 证书种类	在此证书种类栏划"√"
14. 申请单位盖章	申请原产地证的出口企业盖章
15. 领证人	填写领证人姓名及日期

(二) 一般原产地证书的缮制

填 写 栏 目	填制内容和要求
1. Exporter(出口商名称)	填报出口商的企业全称、详细地址
2. Consignee(收货人名称)	填报本批货物最终目的地收货人名称、地址、国家全称。通常,收货人是外贸合同的买方或信用证规定的提单通知人
3. Means of Transport and Route(运输方式和路线)	填报装运港、目的港、中转港的名称,并说明运输方式
4. Country/Region of Destination(运抵国/地区)	按信用证或合同规定的目的港和国家,填报港口名称和国家或地区名称。提示:在转口贸易时,一般不能填报转口商的国家,而填报最终进口国的国名或地区
5. For certifying authority use only(供签证机构使用)	本栏供签证机构对后发证书、补发证书、签发副本或其他事项加注声明时使用,证书申领单位应将此栏留空

(续表)

填 写 栏 目	填制内容和要求
6. Marks and numbers（唛头和包装号）	填报的唛头应按信用证或合同中的规定填写,且与商业发票和提单的同项内容有一致图案、文字、数字和包装号
7. Number & Kind of packages; description of goods（商品名称、包装件数和种类）	填报的商品名称应系发票中所描述的货物,但可用与其他单据无矛盾的统称。包装件数和种类分外包装数量及包装种类。若散装货物,用"In Bulk"表示
8. H.S. Code（商品编码）	按照商务部和海关总署根据 H.S. 分类编制了《中华人民共和国进出口商品的目录对照表》,填报实际商品名称和不同商品的编码
9. Quantity or Weight（毛重或其他数量）	依据发票和货运单据的有关毛重、数量、正常计量单位来填报
10. Number and date of Invoice（发票号码及日期）	填报实际发票号码及日期
11. Declaration by the exporter（出口商声明）	填制申报地点、申报日期
12. Certification（签证机构证明）	签证机构证明已事先印制,签证机构在此加盖签证机构印章并由授权人签名,两者不能重叠。注明签发地点和签发日期

工作任务二　缮制申请书和普惠制原产地证书

实训背景

上海进出口贸易公司与日本高田商会经过磋商,签了出口合同。合同规定,采用信用证支付方式。上海进出口贸易公司的王莉负责这一业务,需要办理相关申请普惠制原产地证书手续,缮制申请书和普惠制原产地证书。

一、实训指南

（一）普惠制产地证（FORM A）定义

普惠制产地证简称GSP产地证,又称FORM A,是发达国家对发展中国家出口的制成品和半制成品给予普遍的、非歧视性的、非互惠的一种关税制度,并由受惠国有关机构就本国出口商品向给惠国出口受惠商品而签发的用以证明原产地证明的一种文件。在我国,由出入境检验检疫局办理签证。

(二) 申领时间和要求

根据我国检验检疫局有关规定,出口企业最迟于货物出运前 5 天,持签证机构规定的正本文件,向签证机构申请办理普惠制产地证书。

外贸公司在对给惠国出口"可受惠商品"时,不管信用证是否要求提供 GSP 产地证,都应申领此证交收货人,使其能享受普惠制的待遇。

(三) 申领所需要的文件

(1) 提供规定格式并已缮制的《普惠制原产地证明书申请单》一份。
(2) 提供制作完毕的《普惠制原产地证明书 FORM A》一套(一正三副)。
(3) 提供出口商业发票正本一份。
(4) 发证机构所需的其他证明文件,如"加工工序清单"等。
(5) 如果出口商品含有进口成分,还应提供《含进口成分受惠商品成本明细单》一式两份。

(四) 普惠制产地证三种格式

普惠制产地证主要有三种格式:普惠制产地证格式 A、普惠制产地证格式 59A 和普惠制产地证格式 APR,其中格式 A(FORM A)使用范围最广。需要说明的是在给惠国中,有两个国家例外:新西兰采用 Form59A;澳大利亚则不用任何规定的格式,只需在商业发票上加注指定声明文句即可。

二、实训样本

(一) 普惠制原产地证书申请书

王莉开始运作这一业务,她填制了普惠制原产地证书申请书,向上海出入境检验检疫局主管部门申请签发普惠制原产地证书。缮制依据的信用证如下:

IRREVOCABLE DOCUMENTARY CREDIT

SEQUENCE OF TOTAL	*27	: 1/1
FORM OF DOC, CREDIT	*40 A	: IRREVOCABLE
DOC. CREDIT NUMBER	*20	: XT173
DATE OF ISSUE	31 C	: 060510
DATE AND PLACE OF EXPIRY	*31 D	: DATE 060630 PLACE CHINA
APPLICANT	*50	: TKAMLA CORPORATION
		6-7, KAWARA MACH OSAKA
		JAPAN
ISSUING BANK	52A	: FUJI BANK
		1013, SAKULA OTOLIKINGZA MACHI OSAKA
		JAPAN
BENEFICIARY	*59	: SHANGHAI IMPORT & EXPORT TRADE

		CORPORATION 1321 ZHONGSHAN ROAD SHANGHAI, CHINA
AMOUNT	*32 B	: CURRENCY USD AMOUNT 32 800.00
AVAILABLE WITH/BY	*41 D	: OSAKA BANK NEW YORK BRANCH BY NEGOTIATION
DRAFTS AT ···	42 C	: DRAFTS AT SIGHT FOR FULL INVOICE COST
DRAWEE	42 A	: FUJI BANK
PARTIAL SHIPMENTS	43 P	: ALLOWED
TRANSSHIPMENT	43 T	: ALLOWED
LOADING ON BOARD	44 A	: SHANGHAI PORT
FOR TRANSPORTATION TO ···	44 B	: OSAKA PORT
LATEST DATE OF SHIPMENT	44 C	: 060620
DESCRIPT OF GOODS	45 A	: CHINESE GREEN TEA AS PER S/C NO. TXT264 CIF OSAKA
DOCUMENTS REQUIRED	46 A:	

+ SIGNED COMMERCIAL INVOICE, 2 ORIGINAL AND 4 COPIES.

+ PACKING LIST, 1 ORIGINAL AND 4 COPIES.

+ CERTIFICATE OF ORIGIN GSP CHINA FORM A, ISSUED BY THE CHAMBER OF COMMERCE OR OTHER AUTHORITY DULY ENTITLED FOR THIS PURPOSE.

+ FULL SET OF NEGOTIABLE INSURANCE POLICY OR CERTIFICATE BLANK ENDORSED FOR 110 PERCENT OF THE INVOICE VALUE COVERING ALL RISKS

+ FULL SET OF B/L, (3 ORIGINAL AND 5 COPIES) CLEAN ON BOARD, MADE OUT TO ORDER OF SHIPPER AND BLANK ENDORSED AND MARKED " FREIGHT PREPAID " AND NOTIFY APPLICANT.

+ QUALITY CERTIFICATE IS ISSUED BY CHINA EXIT & ENTRY INSPECTION & QUARANTINE BUREAU.

CHARGES	71B	: ALL BANKING CHARGES OUTSIDE JAPAN ARE FOR ACCOUNT OF BENEFICIARY.
PERIOD FOR PRESENTATION	48	: DOCUMENTS MUST BE PRESENTED WITHIN 15 DAYS AFTER THE DATE OF SHIPMENT BUT WITHIN THE VALIDITY OF THE CREDIT.

普惠制产地证申请书

普惠制产地证明书申请书

申请单位(加盖公章): [上海进出口贸易公司印章]

申请人郑重申明:

本人被正式授权代表本企业办理和签署本申请书的。

本申请书及普惠制产地证明书格式A所列内容正确无误,如发现弄虚作假,冒充格式A所列货物,擅改证书,自愿接受签发机构的处罚并承担法律责任。现将有关情况申报如下:

证书号: ……………………
注册号: 88559966

生产单位	苏州茶叶厂	生产单位联系人电话		24788853
商品名称 (中英文)	中国绿茶 CHINESE GREEN TEA	H.S.税目号 (以六位数码计)		0902.10
商品FOB总值(以美元计)		31 001.00 美元	发票号	TX0622
最终销售国	日本	证书种类"√"	加急证书	普通证书√
货物拟出运日期		2006.6.10		

贸易方式和企业性质(请在适用处划"√")

正常贸易 C	来进料加工 L	补偿贸易 B	中外合资 H	中外合作 Z	外商独资 D	零售 Y	展卖 M
√							

包装数量或毛重或其他数量	330箱

原产地标准:
本项商品系在中国生产,完全符合该给惠国给惠方案规定,其原产地情况符合以下第(1)条:
(1) "P"(完全国产,未使用任何进口原材料);
(2) "W"其H.S.税目号为 _____ (含进口成分);
(3) "F"(对加拿大出口产品,其进口成分不超过产品出厂价值的40%)。
本批产品系: 1.直接运输从 上海 到 大阪 ;
            2.转口运输从 _____ 中转国(地区) _____ 到 _____ 。

申请人说明	领证人(签名)王 莉 电话: 日期:2006年6月2日

现提交中国出口商业发票副本一份,普惠制产地证明书格式A(FORM A)一正两副,以及其他附件 _____ 份,请予审核签证。
注:凡有进口成分的商品,必须要求提交《含进口成分受惠商品成本明细单》。

商 检 局 联 系 记 录

(二)普惠制原产地证书

根据以上情况,上海出入境检验检疫局主管部门签发普惠制原产地证书样本如下:

1. Goods consigned from (Exporter's business name, address, country) SHANGHAI IMPORT & EXPORT CORPORATION 1321 ZHONGSHAN ROAD SHANGHAI, CHINA	Reference No.:20060606 GENERALIZED SYSTEM OF PREFERENCES CERTIFICATE OF ORIGIN (COMBINED DECLARATION AND CERTIFICATE)
2. Goods consigned to (Consignee's name, address, country) TKAMLA CORPORATION 6-7, KAWARA OSAKA JAPAN	**FORM A** ISSUED IN THE PEOPLE'S REPUBLIC OF CHINA (COUNTRY) SEE NOTES OVERLEAF
3. Means of transport and route (as far as known) FROM SHANGHAI TO OSAKA BY S.S	4. For official use

5. Item number	6. Marks and numbers of packages	7. Number and kind of packages; description of goods	8. Origin criterion (see notes overleaf)	9. Gross weight or other quantity	10. Number and date of invoices
1	T.C TXT264 OSAKA C/NO. 1-66	CHINESE GREEN TEA SAY TOTAL SIXTY SIX (66) CARTONS ONLY ************************	"P"	G.W. 416 KGS	TX0622 JUN. 1, 2006

11. Certification is hereby certified, on the basis of control carried out, that the declaration by the exporter is correct SHANHGHAI JUN. 5, 2006 丁毅 Place and date, signature and stamp of certifying authority	12. Declaration by the exporter The undersigned hereby declares that the above details and statements are correct; that all the goods were produced in <u>**CHINA**</u> (country) and that they comply with the origin requirements specified for those goods in the Generalized System of Preference for goods exported to <u>JAPAN</u> (importing country) SHANHGHAI JUN. 2, 2006 王莉 Place and date, signature of authorized signatory

三、实训缮制要求

(一)普惠制原产地证书格式 A 申请书的缮制

填 制 栏 目	填制内容和要求
1. 申请单位(盖章)栏	申请原产地证的出口企业并加盖申请单位公章
2. 注册号	填写申请单位在检验检疫局产地证签证部门注册的注册号。如:14G001
3. 证书号	根据签证机构的编号规则,对应于每批审证货物的编号。不得重号或跳号
4. 生产单位	填写该批出口货物的生产企业全称
5. 生产单位联系人电话	填写该批出口货物生产企业的联系电话
6. 商品名称	填写商品品名的中英文,并且与发票证书的商品名称一致
7. H.S.税目号	商品的 H.S.六位数编码,海关统计编码前六位
8. FOB 总值	根据申报的出口货物出口发票上所列的金额以 FOB 价格填写(以美元计),如出口货物不是以 FOB 价格成交,应换算成 FOB 价格
9. 发票号	填写正式出口发票的号码,并与随附发票相一致
10. 最终销售国	即货物即将运抵的最终销售国
11. 证书种类	在此证书种类栏划"√"
12. 拟出运日期	如实准确填写货物离开起运口岸的当天日期(年、月、日)
13. 贸易方式和企业性质	根据实际情况选择划"√"
14. 包装数量,毛重或其他数量	填写该批出口货物的箱数、毛重或个数等
15. 原产地标准	根据提示及货物实际情况选择 1~4 项如实填写
16. 本项商品系	根据货物运输路线的起运港、中转港及目的港填写本批商品运输路线,无转运港的填写"＊＊＊"
17. 申请人说明	填写具体说明,如果没有则填"＊＊＊"
18. 领证人	填写领证人姓名及日期

(二)普惠制产地证格式 A 的缮制

填 制 栏 目	填制内容和要求
1. 出口商名称、地址、国家(GOODS CONSIGNED FROM)	此栏带有强制性,应填明详细地址,包括街道名、门牌号码等
2. 收货人的名称、地址、国家(GOODS CONSIGNED TO)	该栏应填给惠国最终收货人名称。如最终收货人不明确,可填发票抬头人。但不可填中间转口商的名称
3. 运输方式及路线(MEANS OF TRANSPORT AND ROUTE)	一般应填装货、到货地点(始运港、目的港)及运输方式(如海运、陆运、空运)

(续表)

填制栏目	填制内容和要求
4. 供官方使用(FOR OFFICAL USE)	此栏由签证当局填写,申请签证的单位应将此栏留空。正常情况下此栏空白
5. 商品顺序号(ITEM NUMBER)	如同批出口货物有不同品种,则按不同品种、发票号等分列"1","2","3",…,以此类推。单项商品,此栏填"1"
6. 唛头及包装号(MARKS AND NUMBERS OF PACKAGES)	唛头应与货物外包装上的及发票上的唛头一致
7. 包装件数量及种类,商品的名称(NUMBER AND KIND OF PACKAGES, DESCRIPTION OF GOODS)	包装件数量必须用英文和阿拉伯数字同时表示
8. 原产地标准(ORIGIN CRITERION)	此栏填写该栏原产地标准符号,例如: (1) 完全原产品,不含任何进口成分,出口到所有给惠国,填"P" (2) 含有进口成分的产品,出口到欧盟、挪威、瑞士和日本,填"W",其后加上出口产品的 H.S. 税目号,如"W"42.02
9. 毛重或其他数量(GROSS WEIGHT OR OTHER QUANTITY)	此栏应以商品的正常计量单位填,如"只"、"件"、"双"、"台"、"打"等。以重量计算的则填毛重,只有净重的,填净重亦可,但要标上 N.W.（NET WEIGHT）
10. 发票号码及日期(NUMBER AND DATE OF INVOICE)	此栏不得留空
11. 签证当局的证明(CERTIFICATE)	此栏填打检验检疫局的签证地点、日期
12. 栏目出口商的申明(DECLARATION BY THE EXPORTER)	此栏在生产国横线上填英文的"中国"(CHINA)。进口国横线上填最终进口国,进口国必须与目的港的国别一致。申请单位应授权专人在此栏手签,标上申报地点、日期,并加盖申请单位中英文印章
13. 证书号码(REFERENCE NO.)	此栏不得留空,否则,证书无效

工作任务三 缮制出口货物报检单

实训背景

王莉办理好相关申请普惠制原产地证书手续,上海进出口贸易公司还须根据我国有关检验检疫法规的规定,需要向上海出入境检验检疫局办理出口货物报检,填制报检单。

一、实训指南

商检机构在对每一批出口商品进行检验之前,报检人填写《出境货物报验单》,向检验检疫机构申请报检。报验人必须按报验单的要求详细填写,每份《出境货物报验单》仅限填报一个合同、一份信用证的商品。对同一合同、同一信用证,但标记号码不同者,应分别填写报检单。报验申请一般在发运前7天提出。

二、实例样本

根据上面的背景,王莉可缮制出口报检单如下:

中华人民共和国出入境检验检疫
出境货物报检单

报检单位(加盖公章): 上海进出口贸易公司(印章)　　　　*编　号: 896541231

报检单位登记号: 12345Q　　联系人: 王莉　　电话: 65788877　　报检日期: 2006年6月3日

发货人	(中文)上海进出口贸易公司
	(外文)SHANGHA IMPORT & EXPORT TRADE CORPORATION
收货人	(中文)
	(外文)TKAMLA CORPORATION

货物名称(中/外文)	H.S.编码	产地	数/重量	货物总值	包装种类及数量
中国绿茶 CHINESE GREEN TEA	0902.1090	中国 上海	毛重416千克 净重330千克	32 800美元	66箱

运输工具名称号码	PUDONG V.503	贸易方式	一般贸易	货物存放地点	逸仙路9号
合同号	TXT264	信用证号	XT173	用途	自营内销
发货日期	2006.06.10	输往国家(地区)	日本	许可证/审批证	06AB122433
起运地	上海	到达口岸	大阪	生产单位注册号	

集装箱规格、数量及号码	1×20' 拼箱 GATU0506118

合同、信用证订立的检验 检疫条款或特殊要求	标记及号码	随附单据(划"√"或补填)	
	T.C. TXT264 OSAKA C/NO.1-66	☑ 合同 ☑ 信用证 ☑ 发票 ☑ 换证凭单 ☑ 装箱单 ☐ 厂检单	☐ 包装性能结果单 ☑ 许可/审批文件 ☐ ☐ ☐ ☐

需要证单名称(划"√"或补填)		*检验检疫费
☐ 品质证书　__正__副 ☑ 重量证书　1正2副 ☐ 数量证书　__正__副 ☐ 兽医卫生证书　__正__副 ☐ 健康证书　__正__副 ☐ 卫生证书　__正__副 ☐ 动物卫生证书　__正__副	☐ 植物检疫证书　__正__副 ☐ 熏蒸/消毒证书　__正__副 ☐ 出境货物换证凭单　__正__副	总金额 (人民币元) 计费人 收费人

报检人郑重声明: 1. 本人被授权报检。 2. 上列填写内容正确属实,货物无伪造或冒用他人的厂名、标志、认证标志,并承担货物质量责任。 签名: 王莉	领取证单
	日期 签名

注:有"*"号栏由出入境检验检疫机关填写　　◆ 国家出入境检验检疫局制

三、实训缮制要求

出境货物报检单所列各栏必须填写完整、准确、清晰,栏目内容确实无法填写的,以"＊＊＊"表示,不得留空。

填 制 栏 目	填制内容和要求
1. 报检单位	本栏填报报检单位的中文名称,并加盖与名称一致的公章
2. 报检单位登记号	指在检验检疫机构的报检注册登记号。本栏填10位数登记证号码。联系人:填报检人员姓名;电话号:填报检人员的联系电话
3. 联系人、电话	填写申请报检人的姓名和联系电话
4. 编号	由检验检疫机构受理人指定
5. 报检日期	填写实际报检的日期。指检验检疫机构接受报检当天的日期。本栏填制的报检日期统一用阿拉伯数字来表示,而不用英文等表示
6. 发货人	指本批货物的贸易合同中卖方名称或信用证中的受益人的名称,发货人应与提单上的托运人一致
7. 收货人	填写信用证的实际收货人,如果中间商需要转让,写成"TO WHOM IT MAY CONCERN"或"TO ORDER"。证书中不要求打上收货人的,可留空
8. 商品名称及规格	此栏用中英文对照填写商品名称,该名称应与国家检验检疫机构制定公布的《检验检疫商品目录》所列的货物名称相符合
9. H.S.编码	指货物对应的海关《商品分类及编码协调制度》中的代码
10. 产地	填写货物的生产/加工的省(自治区、直辖市)以及地区(市)名称
11. 数/重量	填写报检货物的数量和重量,重量一般以净重填写,如果填写毛重,或以毛作净,需注明。有多个H.S.编码的,要根据每个H.S.编码填写对应数/重量
12. 货物总值	按本批货物合同或发票上所列的总值填写(以美元计),有多个H.S.编码的,要根据每个H.S.编码对应填写金额、币种
13. 包装种类及数量	填写货物的外包装种类(如纸箱、木箱等)及包装种类代码和具体的件数;有多个H.S.编码的,要根据每个H.S.编码对应填写包装种类及数量
14. 运输工具名称号码	填写货物实际装载的运输工具类别名称(如飞机、火车、轮船、货柜车、邮包等)和运输工具编号。报检时,未能确定运输工具编号的,可只填写运输工具类别
15. 贸易方式	填写成交条件,主要有一般贸易、三来一补、边境贸易、进料加工、其他贸易等几种
16. 货物存放的地点	指本批货物存放的地点,该地点应该详细具体

(续表)

填制栏目	填制内容和要求
17. 合同号	填写本批货物贸易合同编号
18. 信用证号	填写本批货物所对应的信用证编号,没有的可留空
19. 用途	填写本批货物出境用途,从以下九个选项中选择符合实际出境货物用途来填报:种用或繁殖、食用、奶用、观赏或演艺、伴侣动物、试验、药用、饲用、其他
20. 发货日期	按本批货物信用证或由所列的出境日期填写实际装运日期或大约装运日期。因为商品检验必须在发货前办理,所以此栏一般都是预计的大约日期
21. 输往国家地区	指贸易合同中买方所在国家或地区。本栏填报输往国家(地区)的中文名称
22. 许可证/审批号	如果该批货物出口需要提供出口许可证或出口审批文件,应填写其号码,不需质量许可证或卫生注册证或出口审批的货物可留空
23. 起运地	本栏填报出境货物最后离境的口岸或所在地的中文名称
24. 到达口岸	填写本批货物预定最后抵达的交货港(地)
25. 生产单位注册号	填写生产该批货物的单位在检验检疫机构的注册登记编号
26. 集装箱规格、数量及号码	填写装载本批货物的集装箱规格(如40英尺、20英尺等)以及对应的数量和集装箱号码。如果集装箱太多,可用附页形式填报。不用集装箱运输的,此栏可留空
27. 合同、信用证订立的检验检疫条款或特殊要求	填写合同或信用证中双方对本批货物特别约定的质量、卫生等条款和报检单位对本批货物的检验检疫的其他特别要求,例如环保测试等。没有要求的可留空
28. 标记及号码	按出境货物实际运输包装标填写,如没有标记及号码,填写 N/M 或 NO MARKS,并注明裸装或散装
29. 随附单据	按实际向检验检疫机构提供的单据,在对应的"□"打"√"。对报检单上未标出的,自行填写提供的单据名称
30. 需要证单名称	按需要检验检疫机构出具的证单,在对应的窗口打"√",并在相应栏目注明所需证单的正副本的数量,对报检单上未标出的证单,则须将所需提供的单据名称及正副本份数补填在空白处
31. 检验检疫费	此栏留空,由检验检疫局填写
32. 报检人郑重声明	必须有报检人的亲笔签名。说明未尽事宜的按国家出入境检验检疫局发布的有关规定办理
33. 领取证单日期、签名	由出口企业报检员在领取证单时填写领取证单的日期并签名

工作任务四 缮制出口货物通关单

实训背景

王莉办理好相关申请普惠制原产地证书手续,填制上交报检单后,上海出入境检验检疫局签发出境货物通关单。

一、实训指南

出境货物通关单是国家质量监督检验总局授权的出入境检验检疫机构依法对列入《出入境检验检疫机构实施检验检疫的进出境商品目录》(简称《检验检疫法检目录》)以及虽未列入《检验检疫法检目录》,但国家有关法律、行政法规明确由出入境检验检疫机构实施检验检疫的出境货物及特殊物品等签发的出口货物发货人或其代理人已办理报检手续的证明文书。

二、实训样本

经过工作任务二,王莉获取出境货物通关单如下:

中华人民共和国出入境检验检疫
出境货物通关单

编号:060688

1. 收货人 TKAMLA CORPORATION			5. 标记及唛码 T.C. TXT264 OSAKA C/NO.1-66
2. 发货人 上海进出口贸易公司			
3. 合同/提(运)单号 TXT264	4. 输出国家或地区 日本		
6. 运输工具名称及号码 PUDONG V.503	7. 目的地 大阪		8. 集装箱规格及数量 1×20'
9. 货物名称及规格 CHINESE GREEN TEA ART NO.555 ART NO.666 ART NO.777	10. H.S.编码 0902.1090	11. 申报总值 32 800.00 美元	12. 数/重量、包装数量及种类 330 千克 66 箱
13. 证明 　　　　　上述货物业已报检/申报,请海关予以放行。 　　　　　本通关单有效期至 2006 年 7 月 4 日 签字:丁毅　　　　　　　　　　　　　　　日期:2006 年 6 月 4 日			
14. 备注			

三、实训缮制要求

填 制 栏 目	填制内容和要求
1. 收/发货人	通关单的经营单位与报检单的收/发货人一致
2. 输出国家或地区	通关单的起运国与报检单的输出国家或地区一致,通关单的运抵国与报检单的输往国家或地区一致
3. 法检商品的项数和次序	通关单上法检商品的项数和次序与报检单上货物的项数和次序一致
4. 法检商品 H.S.编码	通关单上法检商品与报检单上对应商品的 H.S.编码一致
5. 商品的数量/重量	与报检单上对应商品的数量/重量一致
6. 有效期	出口货物通关单上有效期要考虑报关单的申报日期
7. 出口口岸和运输方式	与报检单上对应商品的数量/重量一致

工作任务五 缮制检验证书

实训背景

王莉向上海出入境检验检疫局办理出口货物报检后,获取出境货物通关单,并获取了检验检疫证书。

一、实训指南

检验证书(Inspection Certificate)是各种进出口商品检验证书、鉴定证书和其他证明书的统称,是对外贸易有关各方履行契约义务、处理索赔争议和仲裁、诉讼举证,具有法律依据的有效证件,也是海关验放、征收关税和优惠减免关税的必要证明。

根据进出境货物不同的检验检疫要求、鉴定项目和不同作用,我国检验检疫机构签发不同的检验检疫证书、凭单、监管类证单、报告单和记录报告,共有85种以上。常见的有以下几种:

(1)出入境检验检疫品质证书(Quality Certificate)。

(2)出入境检验检疫数量检验证书(Quantity Certificate)。

(3)出入境检验检疫植物检疫证书(Phytosanitary Certificate)。

(4)出入境检验检疫动物检疫证书(Animal Health Certificate)。

(5)出入境检验检疫卫生证书(Sanitary Certificate)。

(6)熏蒸/消毒证书(Fumigation/Disinfection Certificate)。

二、实训样本

以数量检验证书为例,根据以上情况缮制数量证书如下:

中 华 人 民 共 和 国 出 入 境 检 验 检 疫
ENTRY-EXIT INSPECTION AND QUARANTINEOF THE PEOPLE'S REPUBLIC OF DHINA

数量检验证书
QUANTITY CERTIFICAT

编号
No.:060697

发货人:SHANGHA IMPORT & EXPORT TRADE CORPORATION SHANGHAI BRANCH
Consignor

收货人:TKAMLA CORPORATION
Consignee

品 名:CHINESE GREEN TEA
Description of Goods

报验数量/重量:33 000 DOZS
Quantity Weight Declared

包装种类及数量:330 CARTONS
Number and Type of Packages

运输工具:PUDONG V.503
Means of Conveyance

标记及号码
Mark & No.
T.C.
TXT264
OSAKA
C/NO.1-66

检验结果:
Results of Inspection
  CHINESE GREEN TEA
   ART NO.555
   ART NO.666
   ART NO.777
PACKED IN 66 CARTONS OF 5 KGS EACH
TOTAL:330 KGS
TOTAL:66 CARTONS

  我们已尽所知和最大能力实施上述检验,不能因我们签发本证书而免除卖方或其他方面根据合同和法律所承担的产品质量责任和其他责任。

  All inspections are carried out conscientiously to the best of our knowledge and ability. This certificate does not in any respect absolve the seller and other related parties from his contractual and legal obligations especially when product quality is concerned.

印章 Stamp Official	签证地点 SHANGHAI Place of Issue	签证日期 JUN.7, 2006 Date of Issue	签名 丁毅 Signature

三、实训缮制要求

填 制 栏 目	填制内容和要求
1. 证书名称	除非信用证另有规定,检验、检疫证明书的名称应符合合同或信用证的规定
2. 品名、数量、重量、包装种类及数量、口岸、运输工具和唛头等	应与商业发票和提单上所描述的内容完全一致
3. 收货人	一般填写"＊＊＊",也可填"To whom it may concern"或"To order"
4. 检验结果	此栏中记载报验货物经检验的状况,是证明货物是否符合合同或信用证要求的关键所在,也是交接货物或索赔、理赔的证明文件
5. 出证机关、地点	可由我国质检局/商会出具,亦可由外国公证行、公证人、鉴定人签发。出证地点通常在装运口岸
6. 证书的日期	在提单之前或与之同日;证书日也不可过分早于提单日(比如鲜活商品),根据ISBP规定,分析证、检验证、装船前检验证上注明的日期可以晚于提单日期
7. 单证的份数	检验、检疫证份数通常一正三副
8. 签字盖章	一般而言,盖章与签字一样有效。但是有的国家则要求出具的检验证书一定要经手签,在这种情况下,只有盖章而无签字的检验证明书则被视作无效

单证模拟实训八

一、缮制原产地证书申请书和原产地证书模拟操作

上海进出口贸易公司和 FUJIYAMA 公司签订了进出口销售合同,上海进出口贸易公司收到日商 30% 电汇货款后,通知宁波兴旺工具厂(宁波市木行路 302 号)开始着手备货,并根据 FUJIYAMA 公司提供一般原产地证书的要求向中国贸易促进委员会上海分会主管部门申请签发。对此,钱林按照规定缮制《一般原产地证明书申请书》、《一般原产地证书》。

上海进出口贸易公司
SHANGHAI IMPORT & EXPORT TRADE CORPORATION
1321 ZHONGSHAN ROAD SHANGHAI, CHINA

SALES CONFIRMATION

Post code: 200032　　　　　　　　　　　　　　　　S/C No.: TXT07081
Fax: (021) 65788876　　　　　　　　　　　　　　　DATE: SEPT. 10, 2007
TEL: (021) 65788877
TO　MESSRS:
FUJIYAMA TRADING CORPORATION
121, KAWARA MACH OSAKA, JAPAN

Dear Sirs,
　　We hereby confirm having sold to you the following goods on terms and conditions as specified below:

GOODS OF DESCRIPTIONS	QUANTITY	UNIT PRICE	AMOUNT
DOUBLE OPEN END SPANNER 8×10 MM (MTM) 10×12 MM (MTM)	60 000 PCS 80 000 PCS	CPT OSAKA USD 0.50 USD 0.60	USD 30 000.00 USD 48 000.00

1) TERMS OF PAYMENT: 30% T/T IN ADVANCE, THE OTHERS 70% T/T AFTER SHIPMENT.
2) AIRPORT OF DEPARTURE:　PUDONG AIRPORT SHANGHAI, CHINA.
3) AIRPORT OF DESTINATION:　OSAKA AIRPORT JAPAN.
4) LATEST DATE OF SHIPMENT:　DEC. 20, 2007.
5) PACKED IN 1 400 CARTONS OF 100 PCS EACH.
OUR BANK INFORMATION IS AS BELOW:
BANK NAME: BANK OF CHINA SHANGHAI BRANCH.
ACCOUNT NO.:　RMB80456861

THE BUYER: [FUJIYAMA TRADING CORPORATION]　　　　　THE SELLER [上海进出口贸易公司 合同专用章]
　　　　　　　山本　　　　　　　　　　　　　　　　　　　　　　　钱林

钱林填制一般原产地证明书申请书：

中国贸促会上海分会

中国国际商会分会

一般原产地证明书/加工装配证明书

申 请 书

申请单位注册号：866742Q	证书号：_____	全部国产填上 P
申请人郑重申明：	发票号：_____	含进口成分填上 W

本人被正式授权代表本企业办理和签署本申请书。

本申请书及一般原产地证明书/加工装配证明书所列内容正确无误，如发现弄虚作假，冒充证书所列货物，擅改证书，愿按《中华人民共和国出口货物原产地规则》有关规定受惩处并承担法律责任。现将有关情况申报如下：

商品名称		H.S.编码（八位数）	
商品生产、制造、加工单位、地点			
含进口成分产品主要制造加工工序			
商品 FOB 总值（以美元计）		最终目的地国家/地区	
拟出运日期		转口国（地区）	
包装数量或毛重或其他数量			
贸易方式和企业性质			
贸 易 方 式		企 业 性 质	

现提交中国出口货物商业发票副本一份，报关单一份或合同/信用证影印件，一般原产地证明书/加工装配证明书　正　副，以及其他附件　份，请予审核签证。

申领人（签名）：

电话：

申请单位盖章：　　　　　　　　　　　　　　　　日期：　年　月　日

签发一般原产地证明书：

1. Exporter (Full Name and Address)	CERTIFICATE No.：500511266
	CERTIFICATE OF ORIGIN
	OF
2. Consignee (Full name, Address, Country)	THE PEOPLE'S REPUBLIC OF CHINA
3. Means of Transport and Route	5. For Certifying Authority Use Only
4. Country/Region Of Destination	

6. Marks and Numbers of Packages	7. Description of Goods; Number and Kind of Packages	8. H. S. Code	9. Quantity or Weight	10. Number and Date of Invoice

11. Declaration by the Exporter 　　The undersigned hereby declares that the above details and statements are correct; that all the goods were produced in China and that they comply with the Rules of Origin of the People's Republic of China	12. Certification 　　It is hereby certified that the declaration by the exporter is correct.
Place and date. signature and stamp of authorized signatory	Place and date. signature and stamp of certifying authority

二、缮制普惠制原产地证书模拟操作

上海隆达进出口公司与 MANDARS IMPORTS CO., LTD. 就弹力牛仔女裙交易条件达成一致。上海隆达进出口公司申请签发普惠制原产地证书,陆炎先生根据有关规定填写《普惠制原产地证书申请书》、《普惠制原产地证书》并随附商业发票等单据向出入境检验检疫局办理申请签发《普惠制原产地证书》。

上海隆达进出口公司
SHANGHAI LONGDA IMP. & EXP. CO.
21 WEST ZHONGSHAN ROAD SHANGHAI CHINA
售货确认书

POST CODE:200031
FAX: (021) 64500002
TEL:(021) 64500003
To Messrs:
MANDARS IMPORTS CO., LTD.
38 QUEENSWAY,2008 UK

S/C No.:TXT200710
DATE:MAR. 15,2007

敬启者:兹确认售予你方下列货品,其成交条款如下:
Dear Sirs,
　　We hereby confirm having sold to you the following goods on terms and conditions as specified below:

唛 头 SHIPPING MARK	商品名称、规格及包装 NAME OF COMMODITY AND SPECIFICATIONS, PACKING	数 量 QUANTITY	单 价 UNIT PRICE	总 值 TOTAL AMOUNT
MANDARS TXT200710 LONDON C/NO.:1-UP	LADIES DENIM SKIRT FABRIC:99% COTTON 1% ELASTIC AS PER SAMPLE PACKING: FLAT PACK WITHOUT FOLDING 6 PIECES ASSORTED SIZES PER POLYBAG, 3 POLYBAGS IN A MASTER POLYBAG AND THEN INTO AN EXPORT CARTON	18 000 PCS	CIF LONDON USD 7.00	USD 126 000.00

装运港: SHANGHAI
LOADING PORT:
目的港: LONDON
DESTINATION:
装运期限: LATEST DATE OF SHIPMENT 070530
TIME OF SHIPMENT:
分批装运: ALLOWED
PARTIAL SHIPMENT:
转 船: ALLOWED
TRANSHIPMEN:T

保　险： FOR 110 PERCENT OF THE INVOICE VALUE COVERING ALL RISKS AND WAR RISK INSURANCE；
付款条件： BY L/C AT 60 DAYS SIGHT AFTER B/L
TERMS OF PAYMENT：

唛头：☑由卖方指定。□由买方指定，须在信用证开出前__天提出并经卖方同意，否则由卖方指定。
Shipping mark： ☑ To be designated by the sellers.　In case the buyers desire to designate their own shipping mark, the buyers shall advise the sellers __days before opening L/C, and the sellers' consent must be obtained, otherwise the shipping mark will be designated by the sellers.

买方须于2007年5月10日前开出本批交易的信用证（或通知售方进口许可证号码），否则，售方有权不经过通知取消本确认书，或向买方提出索赔。
The Buyer shall establish the covering Letter of Credit (or notify the Import License Number) before May. 10, 2007, falling which the Seller reserves the right to rescind without further notice, or to accept whole or any part of this Sales Confirmation non-fulfilled by the Buyer, or, to lodge claim for direct losses sustained, if any.

凡以CIF条件成交的业务，保额为发票价的110%，投保险别以售货确认书中所列的为限，买方如果要求增加保额或保险范围，应于装船前经卖方同意，因此而增加的保险费由买方负责。
For transactions conclude on CIF basis, it is understood that the insurance amount will be for 110% of the invoice value against the risks specified in Sales Confirmation. If additional insurance amount or coverage is required, the buyer must have consent of the Seller before Shipment, and the additional premium is to be borne by the Buyer.

装运单据：卖方应向议付行提供下列单据：
Shipping documents： The sellers shall present the following documents to the negotiating bank for payment：

(1) 全套清洁已装船空白抬头空白背书提单，注明运费已付。
Full set clean on board of shipped Bills of Lading made out to order and blank endorsed, mark "Freight Prepaid".

(2) 商业发票__6__份。
Commercial invoice in __6__ copies.

(3) 装箱单或重量单__5__份。
The packing list or weight list in 5 copies.

(4) 可转让的保险单或保险凭证正本一份及副本__2__份。
One original and 2 duplicate copies of the transferable insurance policy or insurance certificate.

(5) 买方指定的机构签发的品质、重量/数量检验证书正本一份，副本__2__份。
One original and 2 duplicate copies of inspection certificate of quality, quantity/weight issued by The Inspecting Agency Designated By The Buyer.

(6) 中国商会签发的原产地证明书正本一份，副本__1__份。
One original and __1__ duplicate copies of the Certificate of origin issued by The Chamber Of Commerce Or Other Authority Duly Entitled For This Purpose.

品质/数量异议：如买方提出索赔，凡属品质异议须于货到目的口岸之__60__日内提出，凡属数量异议须于货到目的口岸之__30__日内提出，对所装货物所提任何异议属于保险公司、轮船公司等其他有关运输或邮递机构，卖方不负任何责任。
QUALITY/QUANTITY DISCREPANCY： In case of quality discrepancy, claim should be filed by the Buyer within __60__ days after the arrival of the goods at port of destination; while for quantity discrepancy, claim should be filed by the Buyer within __30__ days after the arrival of the goods at port of destination. It is understood that the seller shall not be liable for any discrepancy of the goods shipped due to causes for which the Insurance Company, Shipped Company other transportation organization/or Post Office are liable.

买 方：Peter　　　　　　　　　　　　　　　卖 方：陆炎
THE BUYER：　　　　　　　　　　　　　　　THE SELLERS：

陆炎先生填制普惠制产地证书申请书：

普惠制产地证明书申请书

申请单位(加盖公章)：　　　　　　　　　　　　　　证书号：..................
申请人郑重申明：　　　　　　　　　　　　　　　　　注册号：88559966
本人被正式授权代表本企业办理和签署本申请书的。
本申请书及普惠制产地证明书格式 A 所列内容正确无误，如发现弄虚作假，冒充格式 A 所列货物，擅改证书，自愿接受签发机构的处罚并承担法律责任。现将有关情况申报如下：

生产单位		生产单位联系人电话	
商品名称 (中英文)		H.S.税目号 (以六位数码计)	

商品 FOB 总值(以美元计)			发票号		
最终销售国		证书种类"√"		加急证书	普通证书
货物拟出运日期					

贸易方式和企业性质(请在适用处划"√")						
正常贸易 C	来进料加工 L	补偿贸易 B	中外合资 H	中外合作 Z	外商独资 D	零售 Y	展卖 M

包装数量或毛重或其他数量	

原产地标准：
本项商品系在中国生产，完全符合该给惠国给惠方案规定，其原产地情况符合以下第(　)条：
　(1) "P"(完全国产，未使用任何进口原材料)；
　(2) "W"其 H.S.税目号为 _____ (含进口成分)；
　(3) "F"(对加拿大出口产品，其进口成分不超过产品出厂价值的40%)。
本批产品系：1. 直接运输从 ___上海___ 到 ___伦敦___ ；
　　　　　　2. 转口运输从 _____ 中转国(地区) _____ 到 _____ 。

申请人说明　　　　　　　　　　　　　　　领证人(签名)
　　　　　　　　　　　　　　　　　　　　　电话：
　　　　　　　　　　　　　　　　　　　　　日期：

现提交中国出口商业发票副本一份，普惠制产地证明书格式 A（FORM A）一正两副，以及其他附件一份，请予审核签证。
注：凡有进口成分的商品，必须要求提交《含进口成分受惠商品成本明细单》。

商 检 局 联 系 记 录

陆炎先生填制普惠制产地证书：

1. Goods consigned from (Exporter's business name, address, country)	Reference No.: GENERALIZED SYSTEM OF PREFERENCES CERTIFICATE OF ORIGIN (COMBINED DECLARATION AND CERTIFICATE) **FORM A** ISSUED IN THE PEOPLE'S REPUBLIC OF CHINA (COUNTRY) SEE NOTES OVERLEAF
2. Goods consigned to (Consignee's name, address, country)	
3. Means of transport and route (as far as known)	4. For official use

5. Item number	6. Marks and numbers of packages	7. Number and kind of packages; description of goods	8. Origin criterion (see notes overleaf)	9. Gross weight or other quantity	10. Number and date of invoices

11. Certification is hereby certified, on the basis of control carried out, that the declaration by the exporter is correct	12. Declaration by the exporter The undersigned hereby declares that the above details and statements are correct; that all the goods were produced in **CHINA** (country) and that they comply with the origin requirements specified for those goods in the Generalized System of Preference for goods exported to ＿＿＿＿＿＿＿＿＿ (importing country)
Place and date, signature and stamp of certifying authority	Place and date, signature of authorized signatory

三、缮制出口报检单和出口通关单模拟操作

根据模拟操作一中的情境缮制报检单和通关单。上海进出口贸易公司钱林在货物装运前一周，缮制报检单，并随附商业发票、装箱单、合同等有关单据向出境口岸上海出入境检验检疫机构报检。出入境检验检疫机构经对货物扳手检验合格后，签发出境货物通关单。

钱林填写出境货物报检单：

中华人民共和国出入境检验检疫
出境货物报检单

报检单位（加盖公章）：   *编   号：_____

报检单位登记号：   联系人：   电话：   报检日期：

发货人	（中文）
	（外文）
收货人	（中文）
	（外文）

货物名称（中/外文）	H.S.编码	产地	数/重量	货物总值	包装种类及数量

运输工具名称号码		贸易方式		货物存放地点	
合同号		信用证号		用途	
发货日期		输往国家（地区）		许可证/审批证	
起运地		到达口岸		生产单位注册号	
集装箱规格、数量及号码					

合同、信用证订立的检验检疫条款或特殊要求	标记及号码	随附单据（划"√"或补填）
		☐ 合同 ☐ 包装性能结果单 ☐ 信用证 ☐ 许可/审批文件 ☐ 发票 ☐ ☐ 换证凭单 ☐ ☐ 装箱单 ☐ ☐ 厂检单 ☐

需要证单名称（划"√"或补填）		*检验检疫费	
☑ 品质证书 __正__副 ☐ 重量证书 __正__副 ☐ 数量证书 __正__副	☐ 植物检疫证书 __正__副 ☐ 熏蒸/消毒证书 __正__副 ☐ 出境货物换证凭单 __正__副	总金额 （人民币元）	
☐ 兽医卫生证书 __正__副 ☐ 健康证书 __正__副 ☐ 卫生证书 __正__副 ☐ 动物卫生证书 __正__副		计费人	
		收费人	

报检人郑重声明：
  1. 本人被授权报检。
  2. 上列填写内容正确属实，货物无伪造或冒用他人的厂名、标志、认证标志，并承担货物质量责任。
                                签名：_____
	领 取 证 单	

	日期	
	签名	

注：有"*"号栏由出入境检验检疫机关填写   ◆ 国家出入境检验检疫局制

中华人民共和国出入境检验检疫
出境货物通关单

编号：070688

1. 收货人		5. 标记及唛码 TXT264
2. 发货人		
3. 合同/提(运)单号	4. 输出国家或地区	
6. 运输工具名称及号码	7. 目的地	8. 集装箱规格及数量
9. 货物名称及规格	10. H.S.编码　　　11. 申报总值	12. 数/重量、包装数量及种类

13. 证明

　　　　上述货物业已报检/申报，请海关予以放行。
　　　　本通关单有效期至　　年　月　日

签字：　　　　　　　　　　　　　　　　日期：　年　月　日

14. 备注

项目九

出口官方单证——报关及其他单证

实训目标

- ◆ 了解出口货物报关单的缮制要求,掌握缮制出口货物报关单的方法。
- ◆ 掌握出口收汇核销单的作用和缮制要求,并学会缮制出口收汇核销单。
- ◆ 掌握出口退税单证的作用和缮制要求,并学会缮制出口货物退税汇总申报表。

工作任务一 缮制出口货物报关单

实训背景

王杰在办理订舱、投保手续后,根据我国《海关法》规定,出口货物在运抵海关监管区后,装货的24小时以前,需要办理相应的出口货物报关手续。

一、实训指南

出口货物报关单是指出口货物的发货人或其代理人,按照海关规定的格式对出口货物的实际情况作出的书面声明,以此要求海关对货物按适用的海关制度办理报关手续的法律文书。

二、实训样本

中华人民共和国海关出口货物报关单

预录入编号：　　　　　　　　海关编号：

出口口岸		备案号		出口日期		申报日期	
经营单位		运输方式		运输工具名称		提运单号	
发货单位		贸易方式		征免性质		结汇方式	
许可证号		运抵国（地区）		指运港		境内货源地	
批准文号		成交方式		运费		保费	杂费
合同协议号		件数		包装种类		毛重（千克）	净重（千克）
集装箱号		随附单据				生产厂家	
标记唛码及备注							

项号	商品编号	商品名称、规格型号	数量及单位	最终目的国（地区）	单价	总价	币制	征免

税费征收情况

录入员　　　　录入单位	兹声明以上申报无讹并承担法律责任	海关审单批注及放行日期（签章）	
报关员		审单	审价
单位地址	申报单位（签章）	征税	统计
邮编　　　电话　　　填制日期		查验	放行

三、出口货物报关单的内容及缮制要点

1. 出口口岸

货物申报出境的口岸海关名称。本栏目应根据货物实际出口的口岸海关选择填报《关区代码表》中相应的口岸海关名称及代码。

2. 备案号

备案号是指出口企业在海关办理加工贸易合同备案或征减、免税审批备案等手续时,海关给予《登记手册》《征免税证明》或其他有关备案审批文件的编号。

一份报关单只允许填报一个备案号。无备案审批文件的报关单,本栏目免予填报。

首位代码	备案审批文件
B	加工贸易手册(来料加工)
C	加工贸易手册(进料加工)
E	加工贸易电子账册
Y	原产地证书
Z	征免税证明

备案号首位	贸易方式	征免性质	用途	征免
B	来料加工(0214)	来料加工(502)	加工返销	全免
C	进料对口(0615)	进料加工(503)	加工返销	全免
Z	一般贸易	科教用品 鼓励项目 自有资金	企业自用	全免

3. 出口日期

出口日期是指运载所申报货物的运输工具办结出境手续的日期。出口日期供海关打印报关单证明联用,免于填报。

4. 申报日期

海关接受出口货物的发货人或受其委托的报关企业向海关申报的日期。本栏目在申报时免于填报。

5. 经营单位

经营单位是指对外签订并执行出口贸易合同的中国境内企业、单位或者个人。必须填报经营单位名称和10位编码。

6. 运输方式

载运货物出关境所使用的运输工具的分类,即海关规定的运输方式。

常见运输方式及代码

代　码	运输方式名称	备　　注
2	水路运输	BILL OF LADING(B/L)(提单)；(Ocean)Vessel(船名)；Steam ship(S/S,轮船)表示为水路运输
3	铁路运输	
4	汽车运输	
5	航空运输	Air Way Bill(AWB空运单)；Flight No.(航班号)；By Air 表示航空运输
9	其他运输	人扛、驮畜、输水管道、输油管道、输电网等方式

7. 运输工具名称

运输工具名称是指载运货物出境的运输工具的名称或运输工具编号。一份报关单只允许填报一个运输工具名称。水路运输填报船名(Vessel)(来往我国港、澳地区小型船舶为监管簿编号)＋"/"＋航次号(voyage No.)。航空运输填报航班号。

8. 提运单号

提运单号是指出口货物提单或运单的编号，编号必须与运输部门向海关提供的载货清单所列相应内容一致。一份报关单只允许填报一个提运单号。

运输方式	填　制　要　求	备　　注
水路运输	进口提单号； 有分提单的填写：进口提单号＋"＊"＋分提单号	(B/L NO.)
航空运输	填报总运单号＋"－"＋分运单号，无分运单的填报总运单号	MAWB NO.(总运单) HAWB NO.(分运单)

9. 发货单位

发货单位是出口货物在境内的生产或销售单位。必须填写中文名称及编码，无编码填中文名称。

10. 贸易方式(海关监管方式)

贸易方式(海关监管方式)是指以国际贸易中出口货物的交易方式为基础，结合海关对出口货物监督管理综合设定的对出口货物的管理方式。一份报关单只允许填报一种贸易方式。

常见贸易方式及代码

代　　码	简　　称	备　　注
0110	一般贸易	
0214	来料加工	无须付汇进口,B手册

(续表)

代 码	简 称	备 注
0255	来料深加工	
0615	进料对口	须付汇进口，C手册
0654	进料深加工	
2025	合资合作设备	经营单位编码第6位是2或3，Z证明
2225	外资设备物品	经营单位编码第6位是4，Z证明
2600	暂时进口货物	
3010	货样广告品A	有出口经营权的企业出口
3100	无代价抵偿	
3339	其他出口免费	
4500	直接退运	

11. 征免性质

征免性质是指海关根据有关的法律法规对出口货物实施的征免税管理的性质类别。一份报关单只允许填报一种征免性质。

常见征免性质

代 码	简 称	范 围
101	一般征税	包括除其他征税性质另有规定者外的一般照（包括按照公开暂定税率）征税或补税的出口货物
299	其他法定	对除无偿援助出口物资外的其他实行法定减免税费的出口货物以及其他非按全额货值征税的部分出口货物
401	科教用品	大专院校及科研机构进口科教用品
501	加工设备	适用于加工贸易经营单位按照有关征减免税政策进口的外商免费（即不需经营单位付汇，也不需用加工费和差价偿还）提供的加工生产所需设备
502	来料加工	适用于来料加工装配和补偿贸易进口所需的料件等，以及经加工后出口的成品、半成品
503	进料加工	适用于为生产外销产品用外汇购买进口的料件以及加工后返销出口的成品、半成品
601	中外合资	适用于中外合资企业自产的出口产品
602	中外合作	适用于中外合作企业自产的出口产品
603	外资企业	适用于外商独资企业自产的出口产品

(续表)

代码	简称	范围
789	鼓励项目	适用于按规定程序审批的国家鼓励发展的国内投资和外商投资项目在投资总额内按照有关征减免税政策进口的,以及1998年后利用外国政府和国际金融组织贷款项目进口的设备、技术等
799	自有资金	适用于鼓励类外商投资企业、外商投资研究开发中心、先进技术型和产品出口型外商投资企业以及符合中西部利用外资优势产业和优势项目目录的项目,利用投资总额外的自有资金,按照有关征减免税政策进口的设备、技术等

12. 结汇方式

结汇方式是指出口货物的发货人或其代理人收结外汇的方式。出口报关单栏不得为空,填写结汇方式的名称或代码。出口货物不需结汇的,应填报"其他"。

结汇方式代码表

代码	方式	英文缩写	英文名称
6	信用证	L/C	Letter of Credit
5	承兑交单	D/A	Document Against Acceptance
4	付款交单	D/P	Document Against Payment
3	票汇	D/D	Remittance by Banker's Demand Draft
2	电汇	T/T	Telegraph Transfer
1	信汇	M/T	Mail Transfer

13. 许可证号

许可证号是指商务部及其授权发证机关签发的出口货物许可证的编号。填报长度为10位字符的出口货物许可证编号。一份报关单只允许填报一个许可证号。

14. 运抵国(地区)

运抵国(地区)是指出口货物离开我国关境直接运抵或者在运输中转(地区)未发生任何商业性交易的情况下最后运抵的国家(地区)。

(1) 直接运抵:货物运抵的国家(地区)为运抵国。例:上海某公司出口货物去日本,从上海直接运抵大阪,则运抵国为日本。

(2) 只有运输中转,未进行中间交易,运抵国(地区)不变,仍然是最后运抵的国家(地区)。例:上海某公司出口货物去日本,在中国香港中转,但未进行中间交易,则运抵国为日本。

(3) 既有运输中转又发生了买卖关系,则以中转地为运抵国(地区)。例:上海某公司出口货物去日本,在中国香港中转并进行中间交易,则运抵国中国香港。

主要国别代码表

国别代码	中文名(简称)	英文名(简称)
110	中国香港	Hong Kong
116	日本	Japan
142	中国	China
143	中国台澎金马关税区	Taiwan Prov.
303	英国	United Kingdom
304	德国	Germany
305	法国	France
344	俄罗斯联邦	Russia
502	美国	United States
701	国(地)别不详的	Countries(reg.) Unknown

15. 指运港

指运港是指出口货物运往境外的最终目的港。应填中文名称,非中文名称应翻译成中文。

16. 境内货源地

境内货源地是指已知的出口货物在境内的生产地或原始发货地(包括供货地点)。"境内货源地"栏均按《国内地区代码表》选择国内地区名称或代码填报,代码含义与经营单位代码前5位的定义相同。

17. 批准文号

批准文号是指出口收汇核销单上的编号。

18. 成交方式

成交方式也称贸易术语,在我国习惯称为价格条件。报关单中 CIF\CFR\FOB 可以用于任何运输方式。"成交方式"栏应根据实际成交价格条款,按海关规定的《成交方式代码表》选择填报相应的成交方式名称或代码。

实际成交方式与报关单的成交方式的关系

实际成交方式	报关单上的成交方式	代码	备注
EXW、FCA、FAS、FOB	FOB	3	若实际成交时使用的贸易术语不是列在海关的成交方式代码表中的,应该根据对应的关系选择适用报单填写的成交方式
CFR、CPT	CFR	2	
CIF、CIP、DDP、DAT、DAP	CIF	1	

19. 运费

运费是指出口货物从始发地至目的地的国际运输所需要的各种费用。

"运费"栏不同的运费标记填报如下:
(1) 运费率:直接填报运费率的数值,如:5%的运费率填报为"5/1"。
(2) 运费单价:填报运费币值代码+"/"+运费单价的数值+"/"+运费单价标记。
如:24美元的运费单价填报为"502/24/2"。
(3) 运费总价:填报运费币值代码+"/"+运费总价的数值+"/"+运费总价标记。

"成交方式"和"运费"、"保险费"填报与否的对应关系

	成 交 方 式	运 费	保 险 费
出 口	CIF(1)	填	填
	CFR(2)	填	不填
	FOB(3)	不填	不填

20. 保险费

保险费是指在国际运输过程中,由被保险人付给保险人的保险费用。

"保费"栏不同的保费标记填报如下:
(1) 保费率:直接填报保费率的数值,如,3‰的保险费率填报为"0.3/1"。
(2) 保费总价:填报保费币值代码+"/"+保费总价的数值+"/"+保费总价标记,如:10 000港元保险费总价填报为"110/10000/3"。

21. 杂费

杂费是指成交价格以外的,应计入货物价格或应从货物价格中扣除的费用,如手续费、佣金、折扣等。

22. 合同协议号

在原始单据(发票)上合同协议号一般表示为"Contract No.;Sales confirmation No. (S/C NO.);Order No."等。

23. 件数

件数是指有外包装的单件出口货物的实际件数。

24. 包装种类

包装种类是指包裹和捆扎货物用的内部或外部包装和捆扎物的总称。原始单据(装箱单或提运单据)上件数和包装种类一般表示为"No. Of PKGS",其后数字即表示应填报的件数;或"TOTAL PACKED IN ×××CARTONS ONLY";或"TOTAL ××× WOODEN CASES ONLY"。

常见包装种类

名 称	英 文
木箱	(Wooden)case
纸箱	Cartons/CTNS

(续表)

名 称	英 文
桶装	Drum/Barrel
散装	Bulk
托盘	Pallet
包	Bale

25. 毛重

毛重(Gross Weight,G.W.)是指商品的重量加上商品的外包装物料的重量。

(1)"毛重"栏填报出口货物实际毛重,以千克(公斤)计,不足1千克的填报为1。例:0.9千克,"毛重"栏的正确内容为:1。

(2)如货物的毛重在1千克以上且非整数,其小数点后保留4位,第五位及以后略去。例:毛重9.567 89千克,该栏应填9.567 8;毛重123 456.789千克,应填:123 456.789。

(3)报关单的"毛重"栏不得为空,毛重应大于或等于1。

26. 净重

净重(Net Weight, N.W.)是指货物的毛重扣除外包装材料后所表现出来的纯商品重量。

27. 集装箱号

集装箱号的组成规则是:箱主代号(3位字母)+设备识别号"U"+顺序号(6位数字)+校验码(1位数字),例如:EASU9809490。

(1)在填制纸质报关单时,集装箱号以"集装箱号"+"/"+"规格"+"/"+"自重"的方式填报,例如:20' Container No:TEXU3605231, Tare weight:2275KG,则填写为:TEXU3605231/20/2275

(2)多个集装箱的,第一个集装箱号填报在"集装箱号"栏中,其余的依次填报在"标记唛码及备注"栏中。

(3)非集装箱货物,填报为"0"。

28. 随附单据

随附单据是指随进(出)口货物报关单一并向海关递交的单证或文件。

(1)合同、发票、装箱单、许可证等随附单证不在"随附单据"栏填报。

(2)填报纸质报关单时,本栏目填报监管证件的代码及编号,格式为:监管证件的代码+":"+监管证件编号。

(3)所申报货物涉及多个监管证件代码和编号填报在"随附单据"栏,其余监管证件代码和编号填报在"标记唛码及备注"栏中。

常见监管证件代码表

代　　码	监　管　证　件　名　称
1	进口许可证
4	出口许可证
7	自动进口许可证
O	自动进口许可证（新旧机电产品）
V	自动进口许可证（加工贸易）
A	入境货物通关单
B	出境货物通关单
Y	原产地证明
5	纺织品临时出口许可证
P	固体废物进口许可证
E	濒危物种允许出口证明书
F	濒危物种允许进口证明书

29. 生产厂家

生产厂家是指出口货物的境内生产企业的名称。

30. 标记唛码及备注

货物的运输标志。标记唛码英文表述为：Marks、Marking、MKS、Marks & No.、Shipping Marks等。

31. 项号

项号是指申报货物在报关单中的商品排列序号。

（1）第一行填报商品在报关单中的商品排列序号。

（2）第二行用于加工贸易等已经备案的货物，即加工贸易项下的货物有两个项号。

例如：进口某加工贸易料件，该货物列加工贸易手册第5项，则项号应该填报为：01（第一行），05（第二行）。

32. 商品编号

商品编码也称商品编号，是按《关税税则》确定的出口货物的8位税则号列。

33. 商品名称、规格型号

商品名称是指出口货物规范的中文名称。商品的规格型号是指反映商品性能、品质和规格的一系列指标，如品牌、等级、成分、含量、纯度、大小、长短、粗细等。一般商品名称即型号都在发票的"Description of Goods"、"Product and Description"、"Goods Description"、"Quantities and Description"栏有具体的描述。

"商品名称及规格型号"栏分两行填报：

（1）第一行，填出口货物规范的中文名称。如发票中不是中文名的，应翻译成规范的中文名称填报。

(2) 第二行,填报规格型号。

例如:氨纶弹力丝(第一行,规范的中文名称),40 DENIER TYPE 149B MERGE 17124 5 KG TUBE(第二行,规格型号)。

34. 数量及单位

出口商品的实际数量和计量单位填列要求如下:

出口货物必须按海关法定计量单位和成交计量单位填报。

"数量及单位"栏分三行填报:

(1) 法定第一计量单位及数量应填报在本栏目第一行。

(2) 凡列明海关第二法定计量单位的,必须填报第一及第二法定计量单位及数量,第二法定计量单位填在第二行,无第二法定计量单位本栏为空。

(3) 以成交计量单位申报的,须填报海关法定计量单位转换后的数量,同时还需将成交计量单位及数量填报在本栏第三行。如成交计量单位与海关法定计量单位一致时,本栏为空。

35. 最终目的国(地区)

最终目的国(地区)是指已知出口货物最后交付、实际消费、使用或作进一步加工制造的国家或地区。应该按照"国别(地区)代码"表选择填报相应的国家(地区)中文名称或者代码。

36. 单价、总价、币制

单价是指商品的一个计量单位以某一种货币表示的价格。总价是指出口货物实际成交的商品总价。币制是指出口货物实际成交价格的计价货币。

常见货币代码表

币制代码	币制符号	币制名称	币制代码	币制符号	币制名称	币制代码	币制符号	币制名称
110	HKD	港币	116	JPY	日元	132	SGD	新加坡元
142	CNY	人民币	133	KRW	韩国元	300	EUR	欧元
302	DKK	丹麦克朗	303	GBP	英镑	330	SEK	瑞典克朗
331	CHF	瑞士法郎	344	SUR	俄罗斯卢布	501	CAD	加拿大元
502	USD	美元	601	AUD	澳大利亚元	609	NZD	新西兰元

37. 征免

征免是指海关依照《海关法》、《出口关税条例》及其他法律、行政法规,对出口货物进行征税、减税、免税或特案处理的实际操作方式。同一份报关单上可以有不同的征免税方式。

项目九 出口官方单证——报关及其他单证

征免方式代码表

代 码	名 称	代 码	名 称
1	照章征税	6	保证金
2	折半征税	7	保函
3	全免	8	折半补税
4	特案	9	全额退税
5	随征免性质		

工作任务二　缮制出口收汇核销单

实训背景

上海进出口贸易公司出口了一批全棉弹力牛仔女裙（Ladies Denim Skirt）。上海进出口贸易公司根据《出口收结汇联网核查办法》的规定，在银行开立出口收汇核销待查账户，得知本批货款到达账户后，向国家外汇管理局领取出口收汇核销单，按照合同、发票的有关内容进行填制，并持该笔业务的有关单据向国家外汇管理局办理核销手续。

一、实训指南

出口收汇核销单是我国特有的国际商务单据。主要当事人包括出口企业、海关、外汇管理部门和指定外汇银行。外汇核销单的基本操作流程如下：

（1）出口企业凭有关单证，向外汇管理局申请领有编号，并加盖"国家外汇管理局监制章"的核销单。

（2）出口企业凭已缮制的核销单、注明核销单编号的出口报关单和其他有关单据，向海关报关。

（3）海关核准无误后，在核销单"海关签注栏"处加盖"验讫章"，退还出口企业。

（4）出口企业在出口企业于报关后 90 天内，将出口报关单、出口收汇核销单存根和发票交外汇管理局备案。

（5）出口企业在汇票和发票上注明核销单编号，持全套结汇单据向银行办理托收或议付。

（6）银行结汇后，交出口企业。

（7）出口企业持经海关签章的收汇核销单及其他有关文件，到外汇管理局办理核销。

（8）外汇管理局在核销单上加盖"已核销"章后，将核销单和报关单（出口退税专用）给出口企业。

（9）出口企业向税务机关申请办理退税手续。

(10) 税务机关核准后,向出口企业退税。

二、实训样本

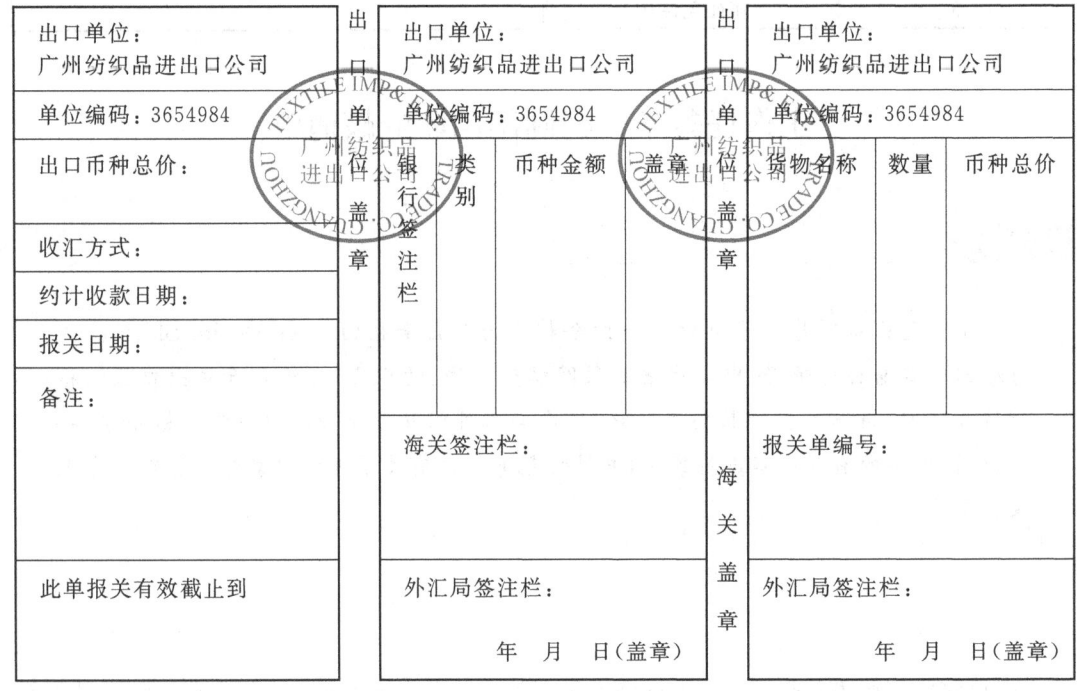

三、实训缮制要求

核销单分成存根、正文、出口退税专用三个部分。出口企业应该按照栏目要求,如实正确填写。

(1) 存根部分:

栏　　目	填　报　要　求
1. 出口单位名称	填签订并执行合同的出口企业名称,必须包括国家质检总局签章的组织代码证上注明的十位数代码
2. 出口货币	总价:按发票金额填,应为收汇原币金额,应与报关单一致
3. 收汇方式	按实际填信用证、托收、T/T等方式中的一种,如远期收汇,还须列明相应的远期收汇天数
4. 预计收款日期	根据交易中的具体情况填写
5. 报关日期	填实际报关放行日期
6. 备注	可写出合同号,出口发票号等须附加说明的内容,原来的出口商品如发生变更填写原出口商品核销单的编号等情况

(2) 正文：

栏　　目	填　报　要　求
1. 编号	已由外汇管理部门预先编印
2. 出口单位	单位编码，参照存根
3. 银行单位	现在一般不填
4. 海关备注栏	海关加盖报关验讫章
5. 外管局备注栏	由外管局填

(3) 出口退税专用：

栏　　目	填　报　要　求
1. 单位代码	填十位数代码
2. 货物名称	按实际品名填写，与发票、报关单一致
3. 数量	按外包装数或件数填写，与报关单、发票一致
4. 币种总价	按发票上金额币制填写，与左边存根一致
5. 报关单编号	按实际情况填写
6. 外汇局签注栏	由外管局盖核销章并填日期

工作任务三　缮制出口退税单证

实训背景

上海进出口贸易公司向国家外汇管理局办理好出口收汇核销后，王杰持该笔出口业务的外销发票、增值税专用发票、出口货物报关单（出口退税专用）、核销单（出口退税专用）等全套出口退税单证及时到国家税务局主管退税机关办理出口退税申报手续，获取出口退税金额，加快企业资金的周转。

一、实训指南

出口退税是指已报关离境的商品，由税务机关将其出口前在生产和流通各环节中已缴纳的国内税收款退还给已出口企业，使出口产品以无税成本进入国际市场，加强其市场竞争力，扩大产品出口。目前，出口退税已成为各国政府普遍采用的国际惯例，它体现了自由竞争、公平税负，不将本国税收转嫁给他国消费者的课税原则。

二、实训样本

外贸企业出口货物退税汇总申报表
(适用于增值税一般纳税人)

申报年月: 　年　月　　　　　　申报批次:

纳税人识别号:

海关代码:

纳税人名称(公章):　　　申报日期:　年　月　日　　金额单位:元至角分、美元

出口企业申报		主管退税机关审核	
出口退税出口明细申报表　份,记录　条		审单情况	机审情况
出口发票	张,出口额　　美元	本次机审通过退增值税额　　元	
出口报关单	张,	其中:上期结转疑点退增值税　元	
代理出口货物证明	张,	本期申报数据退增值税　元	
收汇核销单	张,收汇额　美元	本次机审通过退消费税额　元	
远期收汇证明	张,其他凭证　张	其中:上期结转疑点退消费税　元	
出口退税进货明细申报表　份,记录　条		本期申报数据退消费税　元	
增值税专用发票	张,其中非税控专用发票　张	本次机审通过退消费税额　元	
普通发票	张,专用税票　　张	结余疑点数据退增值税　元	
其他凭证	张,总进货金额　元	结余疑点数据退消费税　元	
总进货税额	元,		
其中:增值税	元,消费税　　元		
本月申报退税额	元,		
其中:增值税	元,消费税　　元		
进料应抵扣税额	元,	授权人申明	
申请开具单证		(如果你已委托代理申报人,请填写以下资料)	
代理出口货物证明	份,记录　　条	为代理出口货物退税申报事宜,现授权为本纳税人的代理申报人,任何与本申报表有关的往来文件都可寄与此人。	
代理进口货物证明	份,记录　　条		
进料加工免税证明	份,记录　　条		
来料加工免税证明	份,记录　　条		
出口货物转内销证明	份,记录　　条		
补办报关单证明	份,记录　　条		
补办收汇核销单证明	份,记录　　条	授权人签字(盖章)	
补办代理出口证明	份,记录　　条		
内销抵扣专用发票　张,其他非退税专用发票　张		审单人:	审核人: 　年　月　日
申报人声明			
此表各栏目填报内容是真实、合法的,与实际出口货物情况相符。此次申报的出口业务不属于"四自三不见"等违背正常出口经营程序的出口业务。否则,本企业愿承担由此产生的相关责任。 　　企业填表人: 　　财务负责人:　　　　(公章) 　　企业负责人:　　　　年　月　日		签批人: (公章) 　　　　　　　　　　年　月　日	

受理人:　　　　　受理日期:　年　月　日　　　　受理税务机关(签章):

三、实训缮制要求

填 制 栏 目	填制内容和要求
1. 申报年月	填外贸企业出口退税申报的时间
2. 申报批次	填外贸企业出口退税申报所属时间内第几次申报
3. 纳税人识别号	填税务登记证号码
4. 海关代码	填外贸企业在海关的注册编号
5. 纳税人名称	填写纳税人单位名称全称,不得填写简称
6. 申报日期	填外贸企业向主管退税机关申报退税的日期

上海进出口公司向国家外汇管理局办理好出口收汇核销后,王杰持该笔出口业务的外销发票、增值税专用发票、出口货物报关单(出口退税专用)、核销单(出口退税专用)等全套出口退税单证及时到国家税务局主管退税机关办理出口退税申报手续,获取出口退税金额。

(1)办理增值税专用发票认证。

上海市增值税专用发票
抵扣联

开票日期:2010年5月5日　　　　　　　　　　　　　　　　　　　NO. 06053011

购货单位	名称	上海进出口公司					密码区		
	纳税人识别号	3101466775532							
	地址、电话	上海市中山路1321号 025-23501111							
	开户银行及账号	中国银行上海分行 SZR80066686							
货物或应税劳务名称	规格型号	单位(件)	数量	单价	金额	税率	税额		
电动钻头			1 800	¥10.00	¥18 000.00	17%	¥3 060.00		
合　计			1 800		¥18 000.00	17%	¥3 060.00		
价税合计(大写)	贰万壹仟零陆拾元整								
销货单位	名称	上海电动工具公司					备注		
	纳税人识别码	310457654221							
	地址、电话	上海市人民路11号							
	开户银行及账号	上海市工商银行人民支行 0086132733658							

注:纳税人识别号即纳税人登记号。

中华人民共和国
税收(出口货物专用)缴款书

编号：060510号

填发日期 2010年5月10日

征收机关：上海市国税局

经济类型：国营经济

缴款单位	税务登记号	0	3	2	0	4	8	6	5	1	2		预算科目	款		
	全称	上海电动工具公司												项		
	开户银行	上海市工商银行人民支行												级次		
	账号	00861327 3658											收款国库	市金库		
购货企业	全称	上海进出口公司														
	税务登记号	0	2	4	3	5	6	8	8	1	5		销货发票号码	06053011		
	海关代码	0487124888														

税款所属时期	2010年5月30日			税款限缴日期	2010年5月30日		
货物名称	课税数量	单位价格	计税金额	法定税率(额)	征税率	实缴税额	
电动钻头	1 800件	¥10.00	¥18 000.00	17%	17%	¥3 060.00	

金额合计	(大写)贰万壹仟零陆拾元整	¥21 060.00	备注

缴款单位 (盖章) 上海电动工具公司 经办人：王工	税务机关 (盖章) 上海税务局 填票人：张言	上列款项已收妥并划转收款单位账户 国库(银行)盖章 2010年5月30日 上海市工商银行人民支行

第二联(收据乙)国库(经收处)收款盖章后退缴款单位转交购货企业，逾期不缴按税法规定加收滞纳金

(2) 王杰填制并提交出口货物退税汇总申报表

外贸企业出口货物退税汇总申报表
(适用于增值税一般纳税人)

申报年月:2010 年 7 月　　　　　　　　申报批次:1

纳税人识别号:02435688□□

海关代码:0387124666

纳税人名称(公章):　　　申报日期:2010 年 7 月 31 日　　　金额单位:元至角分、美元

出口企业申报		主管退税机关审核	
出口退税出口明细申报表　1 份,记录 25 条		审单情况	机审情况
出口发票　　1 张,出口额　7 200.00 美元		本次机审通过退增值税额　　　元	
出口报关单　　　1 张,		其中:上期结转疑点退增值税　　元	
代理出口货物证明　　　张,		本期申报数据退增值税　　元	
收汇核销单　　1 张,收汇额 7 200.00 美元		本次机审通过退消费税额　　　元	
远期收汇证明　　　张,其他凭证　　　张		其中:上期结转疑点退消费税　　元	
出口退税进货明细申报表　1 份,记录 24 条		本期申报数据退消费税　　元	
增值税专用发票　1 张,其中非税控专用发票　张		本次机审通过退消费税额　　　元	
普通发票　　1 张,专用税票　　　张		结余疑点数据退增值税　　　　元	
其他凭证　　　张,总进货金额　　　元		结余疑点数据退消费税　　　　元	
总进货税额　　3 060.00 元,				
其中:增值税　　3 060.00 元,消费税　　元				
本月申报退税额　　3 060.00 元,				
其中:增值税　　3 060.00 元,消费税　　元				
进料应抵扣税额　　　元,		授权人申明	
申请开具单证		(如果你已委托代理申报人,请填写以下资料)	
代理出口货物证明　　　份,记录　　条		:::
代理进口货物证明　　　份,记录　　条		为代理出口货物退税申报事宜,现授权为本纳税人的代理申报人,任何与本申报表有关的往来文件都可寄与此人。	
进料加工免税证明　　　份,记录　　条		
来料加工免税证明　　　份,记录　　条		
出口货物转内销证明　　份,记录　　条		
补办报关单证明　　　份,记录　　条		
补办收汇核销单证明　　份,记录　　条		授权人签字(盖章)	
补办代理出口证明　　　份,记录　　条		
内销抵扣专用发票 1 张,其他非退税专用发票　张		审核人:	
申报人声明		审单人:	年　月　日
此表各栏目填报内容是真实、合法的,与实际出口货物情况相符。此次申报的出口业务不属于"四自三不见"等违背正常出口经营程序的出口业务。否则本企业愿承担由此产生的相关责任。 企业填表人:徐永发 财务负责人:岷山 企业负责人:王杰　　2010 年 7 月 31 日		签批人: (公章) 　　　　年　月　日	

受理人:　　　　　　受理日期:　　年　月　日　　　　　受理税务机关(签章):

单证模拟实训九

一、缮制出口货物退税汇总申报表模拟操作

卖　方：广州拉科进出口公司
　　　　广州北京路 530 号
　　　　TEL：(020)64043030　FAX：(020)64043031
单位代码：3654984
企业组织机构代码：2313294132
买　方：OLEARA IMPORT & EXPORT CORPORATION
　　　　310-224 HOLA STREET MARSEILLE FRANCE
　　　　TEL：491-38241234
合同号：ST071032
开证银行：CITY BANK MARSEILLE BRANCH（地址：1025 WEST GEORGIA STREET, MARSEILLE FRANCE）
信用证号：07/CB4578
开证日期：2010 年 6 月 20 日
支付方式：不可撤销跟单即期信用证
信用证金额：40 500.00 美元
货　名：男式衬衫 Art No.88（蓝色）、Art No.44（黑色）
数　量：Art No.88（蓝色）3 000 件、Art No.44（黑色）3 000 件
发票号码：GZT00021
报关单编号：GZ43920565
包　装：每 20 件装入一出口纸箱
支付方式：BY L/C AT SIGHT
外汇账号：Y4321337235
人民币结算单位账号：R123668645
报关日期：2010 年 7 月 26 日
此单报关有效期截止到：2010 年 7 月 31 日
贸易方式：一般贸易
申报年月：2010 年 8 月
申报批次：1 次
纳税人识别号：3456756881
海关代码：3048712481
申报日期：2010 年 8 月 31 日
出口退税出口明细申报表：1 份（其中记录 25 条）
出口发票：1 张（出口额 40 500.00 美元）
出口报关单：1 张
总进货税额：20 655.00 元（其中增值税为 20 655.000 元）
本月申报退税额：20 655.00 元（其中增值税为 20 655.00 元）
内销抵扣专用发票：1 张

请你以广州拉科进出口公司业务员王伟的身份,根据上述资料、销售合同书和信用证的有关内容填写外贸企业出口货物退税汇总申报表。

外贸企业出口货物退税汇总申报表
(适用于增值税一般纳税人)

申报年月:　　年　月　　　　　　申报批次:
纳税人识别号:
海关代码:
纳税人名称(公章):　　　　申报日期:　年　月　日　　　　金额单位:元至角分、美元

出口企业申报		主管退税机关审核	
		审单情况	机审情况
出口退税出口明细申报表　份,记录　条			
出口发票　　　　张,出口额　　　美元		本次机审通过退增值税额　　　　　元	
出口报关单　　　张,		其中:上期结转疑点退增值税　　　　元	
代理出口货物证明　张,		本期申报数据退增值税　　　　元	
收汇核销单　　　张,收汇额　　　美元		本次机审通过退消费税额　　　　　元	
远期收汇证明　　张,其他凭证　　张		其中:上期结转疑点退消费税　　　　元	
出口退税进货明细申报表　份,记录　条		本期申报数据退消费税　　　　元	
增值税专用发票　张,其中非税控专用发票　张		本次机审通过退消费税额　　　　　元	
普通发票　　　张,专用税票　　　　张		结余疑点数据退增值税　　　　　　元	
其他凭证　　　张,总进货金额　　　元		结余疑点数据退消费税　　　　　　元	
总进货税额　　　　　　元,			
其中:增值税　　　元,消费税　　　元			
本月申报退税额　　　元,			
其中:增值税　　　元,消费税　　　元			
进料应抵扣税额　　　元,		授权人申明	
申请开具单证		(如果你已委托代理申报人,请填写以下资料)	
代理出口货物证明　　份,记录　　条			
代理进口货物证明　　份,记录　　条		为代理出口货物退税申报事宜,现授权为本纳税人的代理申报人,任何与本申报表有关的往来文件都可寄与此人。	
进料加工免税证明　　份,记录　　条			
来料加工免税证明　　份,记录　　条			
出口货物转内销证明　份,记录　　条			
补办报关单证明　　　份,记录　　条			
补办收汇核销单证明　份,记录　　条		授权人签字(盖章)	
补办代理出口证明　　份,记录　　条			
内销抵扣专用发票　张,其他非退税专用发票　张		审单人:　　　　审核人:　　　　年　月　日	
申报人声明			
此表各栏目填报内容是真实、合法的,与实际出口货物情况相符。此次申报的出口业务不属于"四自三不见"等违背正常出口经营程序的出口业务。否则,本企业愿承担由此产生的相关责任。 　企业填表人: 　财务负责人:　　　　　　(公章) 　企业负责人:　　　　　年　月　日		签批人: (公章) 　　　　　　　　　　　年　月　日	

受理人:　　　　受理日期:　年　月　日　　　　受理税务机关(签章):

二、缮制出口收汇核销单模拟操作

(一) 信用证资料

From of Doc. Credit	*40A	:	IRREVOCABLE
Doc. Credit Number	*20	:	LC-320-0254771
Date of Issue	31C	:	060922
Expiry	*31D	:	Date 061222 Place CHINA
Applicant	*50	:	MARCONO CORPORATION RM1001, STAR BLDG. TOKYO, JAPAN
Beneficiary	*59	:	QINGDAO(SHANDONG) HUARUI CO. NO. 35 WUYI ROAD QINGDAO, CHINA
Amount	*32B	:	CURRENCY USD AMOUNT 70 000.00
Pos./Neg. Tol. (%)	39A	:	5/5
Available with/by	*41D	:	ANY BANK BY NEGOTIATION
Draft at …	42C	:	DRAFTS AT SIGHT FOR FULL INVOICE VALUE
Drawee	42A	:	ROYAL BANK LTD., TOKYO
Partial Shipments	43P	:	ALLOWED
Transshipment	43T	:	NOT ALLOWED
Loading in Charge	44A	:	SHIPMENT FROM CHINESE MAIN PORT
For Transport to	44B	:	OSAKA, JAPAN
Latest Date of Ship	44C	:	061210
Descript. of Goods	45A	:	

HALF DRIED PRUNE 2005 CROP

GRADE	SPEC		QNTY (CASE)	UNIT PRICE (USD/CASE)	
A	L: 500 CASE	M: 500 CASE	1 000	22.0	CFR OSAKA
B	L: 1 200 CASA	M: 1 200 CASE	2 400	20.0	CFR OSAKA

PACKING: IN WOODEN CASE, 12 KGS PER CASE
TRADE TERMS: CFR OSAKA

Documents required 46A:
+FULL SET OF CLEAN ON BOARD OCEAN BILLS OF LADING MADE OUT TO ORDER OF SHIPPER AND BLANK ENDORSED AND MARKED "FREIGHT PREPAID" AND "NOTIFY MARCONO CORPORATION. RM1001, STAR BLDG. TOKYO, JAPAN"
+MANUALLY SIGNED COMMERCIAL INVOICE IN TRIPLICATE (3) INDICATING APPLICANT'S REF. NO. SCLI-98-0474.
+PACKING LIST IN TRIPLICATE (3).

Details of Charges 71B: ALL BANKING CHARGES OUTSIDE JAPAN ARE FOR ACCOUNT OF BENEFICIARY

Presentation Period 48 : DOCUMENTS TO BE PRESENTED WITHIN 15 DAYS AFTER THE DATE OF SHIPMENT, BUT WITHIN THE VALIDITY OF THE CREDIT.

(二)补充资料

发票号码：76IN-C001　　　　　　发票日期：2006年9月8日
提单号码：NSD220055　　　　　　提单日期：2006年12月5日
船名：FENGLEI V.66026H　　　　装运港：青岛港
集装箱：2×20'FCL CY/CY　　　　出口口岸：青岛海关
　　　TRIU 1764332 SEAL 05003　合同号：HA1101
　　　KHLU1766888 SEAL 05004　SHIPPING MARKS（唛头）
出口商：青岛华瑞贸易公司　　　　MQ
净重：12.00 KGS/CASE　　　　　 HA1101
毛重：14.00 KGS/CAES　　　　　 OSAKA
尺码：(20×10×10) CM/CASE　　　NOS1-3400

根据所给资料缮制出口收汇核销单：

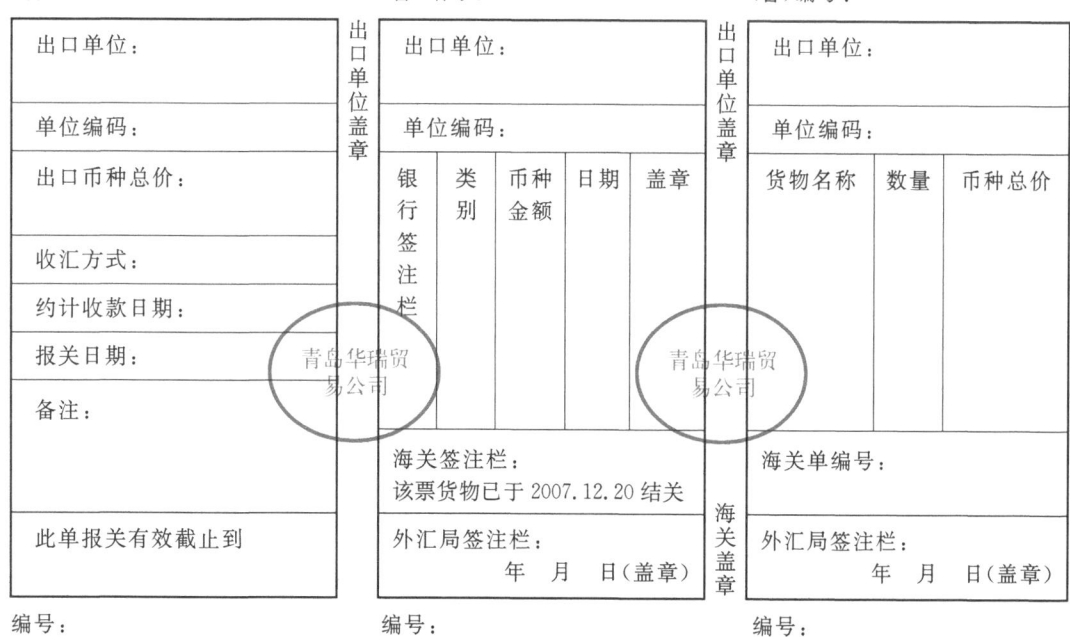

三、缮制出口货物报关单模拟操作

广州天马自行车公司（企业代码为440913333）出口货物一批，该货物于2004年10月26日向广州新风窖心海关申报。经营单位与发货单位相同。生产厂家为星辉儿童车专业厂。

《检验检疫出境货物通关单》代码及编号：B:440300201016448　　商品编号：9501.0000

法定计量单位：辆　　VESSEL VOYAGE NO.：FEIDA/5386　　B/L NO.：GZXF010382
收汇方式：电汇　　装运港：广州　　目的港：仁川
出口收汇核销单号：44E818954　　合同号：2004GBE2-88A
商品：儿童三轮车 AA087 30辆，每辆20美元，每辆装在一个纸箱中，装在一个20英尺的集装箱中，集装箱号为 TEXU2326802，自重5 560 KGS　　G.W.：7 154 KG　　N.W.：6 570 KG

中华人民共和国海关出口货物报关单

预录入编号：　　　　　　　　海关编号：

出口口岸		备案号	出口日期	申报日期
经营单位		运输方式	运输工具名称	提运单号
发货单位		贸易方式	征免性质	结汇方式
许可证号	运抵国(地区)		指运港	境内货源地
批准文号	成交方式	运费	保费	杂费
合同协议号	件数	包装种类	毛重(千克)	净重(千克)
集装箱号	随附单据		生产厂家	
标记唛码及备注				

项号　商品编号　商品名称、规格型号　数量及单位　最终目的国(地区)单价　总价　币制　征免

税费征收情况			
录入员　　录入单位	兹声明以上申报无讹并承担法律责任	海关审单批注及放行日期(签章)	
报关员		审单	审价
单位地址	申报单位(签章)	征税	统计
邮编　　电话	填制日期	查验	放行

项目十

进口单证——汇款和开证申请书

实训目标

- ◆ 了解购买外汇申请书的内容以及缮制要求,并学会独立缮制购买外汇申请书。
- ◆ 了解汇款申请书的内容以及缮制要求,并学会独立缮制汇款申请书。
- ◆ 了解开证申请书的格式及内容,并学会独立缮制开证申请书。

工作任务一 缮制购买外汇申请书

实训背景

上海进出口贸易公司与 TAKAMRA TRADING CORPORATION 进行洽谈,签订了购货合同书,采取电汇支付方式:30% T/T IN ADVANCE,70% T/T AFTER CUSTOMS CLEARANCE。上海进出口贸易公司的刘进开始准备缮制购买外汇申请书。

一、实训指南

外汇管理是指政府制定外汇管理法令及相应的制度,对境内外汇买卖,国际结算和外汇汇率所实施的管理。我国的外汇管理机关是国务院外汇管理部门及其分支机构。

外汇银行对企业购汇实行售汇制。售汇制是指外汇银行受理企业提供国家认可的进口用汇有效凭证,用人民币办理购买及对外支付外汇的制度。

外贸企业需要购汇时,必须提供贸易合同、正本提单、发票、费用收据、进口许可证、进口登记表等与支付方式相适应的有效商业单据和凭证。如果采取信用证结算方式,还需提供开证申请书;如果采取进口托收结算方式,还需提供有关付款通知单;如果采取进口汇款结算方式,还需提供汇款申请书。

二、实训样本

刘进根据合同缮制购买外汇申请书。

SHANGHAI IMPORT & EXPORT TRADE CORPORATION
1321 ZHONGSHAN ROAD SHANGHAI, CHINA
PURCHASE CONTRACT

TEL: 021-65788877　　　　　　　　　　　　P/C NO.: TX201023
FAX: 021-65788876　　　　　　　　　　　　DATE: Aug. 10, 2010

The Buyer: SHANGHAI IMPORT & EXPORT TRADE CORPORATION
1321 ZHONGSHAN ROAD SHANGHAI, CHINA

The Seller: TAKAMRA TRADING CORPORATION
　　　　　　82-324 OTOLI MACHI TOKYO, JAPAN
　　　　　TEL: 028-548-742　FAX: 028-548-743

Dear Sir or Madam:
We have faxed to you order for 89 books before. As follows are the terms details of the books.

Order No	Description	Quantity	Amount
SK0626215	EDUCATIONAL BOOKS	89 SET	CIP SHANGHAI USD 5 030.51

PACKING: Packed In 26 Cartons
AIRPORT OF DEPARTURE: Osaka Airport
AIRPORT OF DESTINATION: Pudong Airport Shanghai, China
PARTIAL SHIPMENT: Not Allowed
TRANSHIPMENT: Not Allowed
TIME OF SHIPMENT: Latest Date Of Shipment 100930
TERMS OF PAYMENT: 100% T/T In Advance
INSURANCE: For 110 Percent Of The Invoice Value Covering W.P.A. By The Seller
DOCUMENTS: The Seller Shall Present The Following Documents.
1) Two Air Waybill
2) Three Copies Of Signed Commercial Invoice Indicating Contract Number.
3) Three Copies Of Packing List.
4) Two Copies Of Certificate Of Quality Issued By Manufacture.
5) Insurance Policy In 2 Copies.

THE BUYER: 　　　　　　THE SELLER: TAKAMRA TRADING CORPORATION 高田

缮制如下：

中国银行上海市分行

购 买 外 汇 申 请 书

中国银行　　上海黄浦　　分（支）行：

　　我公司为执行第　TX201023　号合同项下对外支付，需向贵行购汇。现按外汇局有关规定向贵行提出下述内容及所附文件，请审核并按实际付汇日牌价办理售汇。所需人民币资金从我公司在贵行账户　　SZR80066686　　中支付。

1. 购汇金额：
2. 用　　途：☑进口商品　　□从附费用　　□索退赔款　　□其他
3. 支付方式：□信用证　　□代收　　☑汇款　　（□货到付款　　☑预付货款）
4. 商品名称：教育图书
5. 数量：89套
6. 合同号：TX201023　　　　金额：USD 5 030.51
7. 发票号：IN05791　　　　　金额：USD 5 030.51
8. ☑一般进口商品，无须批文
    □控制进口商品，批文随附如下：
    　　　　□进口证明　　□许可证　　□登记证明　　□其他批文
    　　　　批文号码：　　　　　批文有效期：
9. 附件：□批文　　☑合同/协议　　☑发票　　☑正本运单
    　　　☑报关单　　□运费单/收据　　□保险费收据
    　　　□佣金单　　□关税证明　　□仓单　　□其他
10. □请于开证时立即售汇，转存保证金专用户。

　　　　　　　　　　　　　　　　　　　申请单位刘进易公司　（盖章）
　　　　　　　　　　　　　　　　　　　（上海进出口公司印章）

银行审核意见：
　　上述内容与随附文件/凭证描述相符，拟按申请书要求办理售汇。
　　经办人：中迎　　　　复核人：张立　　　　核准人：兰兰
　　售汇日期：2010.8.12　　　　　　　　　　经办人：
　　（加盖售汇专用章）　　售汇专用章（黄浦）

三、实训缮制要求

购买外汇申请书比较简单,可参照各银行填制提示缮制。

工作任务二　缮制汇款申请书

一、实训指南

汇款申请书是合同双方确定使用汇付时采用的一种支付单证。以中国银行为例,中国银行全球汇款提供多种货币的电汇(T/T)和票汇(D/D)服务。电汇速度较快,但收费较票汇高,如汇款金额较大或急于用款时,可采用电汇;在汇款金额较小、短期出境或不急于用款时,可采用票汇。

1. 电汇

办理电汇需填写电汇申请书,必须以英文填写,在办理业务前,需要提供如下信息:

(1) 汇款货币及金额。

(2) 收款人姓名及地址。

(3) 收款人在开户银行的账号。

(4) 收款人开户银行名称、SWIFT 代码(SWIFT CODE)或地址。

2. 票汇

办理票汇需填写汇票汇款申请书,以英文填写(汇往中国港澳台地区可以中文填写),需要提供如下信息:

(1) 汇款货币及金额。

(2) 收款人姓名及地址。

二、实训缮制要求

填 制 栏 目	填制内容和要求
1. 选择汇款方式	包括电汇(T/T)和票汇(D/D)两种
2. 日期	申请日期
3. 户名	汇款人名称及地址
4. 账号	汇款人账户
5. 汇款币种及金额小写	汇款金额小写
6. 汇款金额大写	汇款金额大写,如"壹佰玖拾玖元整"

（续表）

填 制 栏 目	填制内容和要求
7. 收款人名称及地址	第一行写收款人，第二行写地址
8. 收款人所在地银行	收款人开户银行名称及地址
9. 收款人常驻国家(地区)名称及代码	如：美国 840
10. 汇款附言	自行填写，限 140 个字位
11. 国内外费用承担（"费用负担"方式）	包括共同 SHA、收款人 BEN、汇款人 OUR 三种
12. 付款单位银行盖章	付款银行（汇款人开户行）盖章
13. 复核、经办	复核人、经办人签章

工作任务三　缮制开证申请书

实训背景

上海进出口贸易公司从日本 Tokyo Import & Export Corporation 进口扳手。上海进出口贸易公司陈冲根据合同规定的开证时间向中国银行上海分行办理开证。陈冲填写好开证申请书后，通知财务部将 30% 的保证金转账到公司的保证金账户。开证行根据开证申请书的要求开出不可撤销的即期信用证，副本交给开证人，正本寄送通知行。

一、实训指南

当进出口双方在贸易合同中确立以信用证方式结算后，进口方即可按贸易合同规定向当地银行申请开立信用证，填写开证申请书（Application for Irrevocable Documentary Credit）。这样，进口商即成为开证申请人，开证申请书是银行开具信用证的依据。银行按照开证申请书开立信用证后，在法律上就与进口商构成了开立信用证的权利与义务的关系，两者之间的契约就是开证申请书。

二、实训样本

上海进出口贸易公司从日本 TOKYO IMPORT & EXPORT CORPORATION 进口扳手。合同资料如下：

上海进出口贸易公司

SHANGHAI IMPORT & EXPORT TRADE CORPORATION

1321 ZHONGSHAN ROAD SHANGHAI, CHINA

PURCHASE CONTRACT

TEL: 021-56082266
FAX: 021-56082265

P/C NO.: TX200923
DATE: AUG. 20, 2020

买 方:
The Buyer: SHANGHAI IMPORT & EXPORT TRADE CORPORATION
1321 ZHONGSHAN ROAD SHANGHAI, CHINA
TEL: 021-56082266 FAX: 021-56082265

卖 方:
The Seller: TOKYO IMPORT & EXPORT CORPORATION
82-324 OTOLI MACHI TOKYO, JAPAN
TEL: 028-548-742 FAX: 028-548-743

The Seller and the Buyer have confirmed this Contract with the terms and conditions stipulated below.

DESCRIPTIONS OF GOODS	QUANTITY	UNIT PRICE	AMOUNT
WARENCH		FOB TOKYO	
HEX DEYS WRENCH	1 000 SET	USD 10.00	USD 10 000.00
DOUBLE RING OFFSET WRENCH	1 500 SET	USD 10.00	USD 15 000.00
CONBINATION WRENCH	2 000 SET	USD 20.00	USD 40 000.00
ADJESTABLE WRENCH	1 500 SET	USD 20.00	USD 30 000.00

1. COUNTRY OF ORIGIN AND MANUFACTURER: TOKYO IMPORT & EXPORT CORPORATION
2. PACKING: PACKED IN 1 CARTON OF 100 PCS EACH
3. LATEST DATE OF SHIPMENT 200920
4. PORT OF LOADING: TOKYO, JAPAN
5. PORT OF DESTINATION: SHANGHAI CHINA
6. PAYMENT: IRREVOCABLE DOCUMENTARY CREIDT AT 30 DAYS AFTER SIGHT
7. PARTIAL SHIPMENTS: ALLOWED
8. TRANSHIPMENT: NOT ALLOWED
9. INSURANCE: FOR 110 PERCENT OF THE INVOICE VALUE COVERING ALL RISKS AND WAR RISK BY THE BUYER
10. DOCUMENTS: THE SELLER SHALL PRESENT THE FOLLOWING DOCUMENTS TO THE PAYING BANK FOR NEGOTIATION:
    1) THREE COPIES OF SIGNED COMMERCIAL INVOICE INDICATING CONTRACT NUMBER.
    2) THREE COPIES OF PACKING LIST.
    3) TWO COPIES OF CERTIFICATE OF QUALITY/QUANTITY ISSUED BY MANUFACTURE.
    4) WITHIN 12 HOURS AFTER THE GOODS ARE COMPLETELY LOADED, THE SELLER SHALL FAX TO NOTIFY THE BUYER OF THE CONTRACT NUMBER, NAME OF COMMODITY, QUANTITY, GROSS WEIGHT, B/L NO. AND THE DATE OF DELIVERY.
11. INSPECTION AND CLAIMS: IF THE QUALITY/WEIGHT AND/OR THE SPECIFICATIONS OF THE GOODS SHOULD BE FOUND NOT IN LINE WITH THE CONTRACTED STIPULATIONS, OR SHOULD THE GOODS PROVE DEFECTIVE FOR ANY REASONS, INCLUDING LATENT DEFECT OR THE USE OF UNSUITABLE MATERIALS, THE BUYER WOULD ARRANGE AN INSPECTION TO BE CARRIED OUT BY THE INSPECTION BUREAU AND HAVE THE RIGHT TO CLAIM AGAINST THE SELLERS ON THE STRENGTH OF THE INSPECTION CERTIFICATE ISSUED BY THE BUREAU. ALL CLAIMS SHALL BE REGARDED AS ACCEPTED IF THE SELLERS FAIL TO REPLY WITHIN 30 DAYS AFTER RECEIPT OF THE BUYER'S CLAIM.

Buyer:
SHANGHAI IMPORT & EXPORT TRADE CORPORATION.
陈 冲

Seller:
TOKYO IMPORT & EXPORT CORPORATION
山 田

陈冲缮制开证申请书如下：

IRREVOCABLE DOCUMENTARY CREDIT APPLICATION

To: BANK OF CHINA　　　　　　　　　　　　　　Date: AUG. 27, 2009

Beneficiary (full name and address) TOKYO IMPORT & EXPORT CORPORATION 82-324 OTOLI MACHI TOKYO, JAPAN	L/C No. Ex Card No. Contract No.　TX200923
	Date and place of expiry of the credit SEP. 20, 2020　JAPAN
Partial shipments　　　　Transshipment ☒ allowed　　　　☐ allowed ☐ not allowed　　　☒ not allowed	☐ Issue by airmail ☐ With brief advice by teletransmission ☐ Issue by express delivery ☐ Issue by teletransmission (which shall be the operative instrument)
Loading on board/dispatch taking in change at/from TOKYO not later than　SEPT. 20, 2020 for transportation to SHANGHAI	Amount (both in figures and words) USD 95 000.00 SAY U.S. DOLLARS NINETY FIVE THOUSAND ONLY
Description of goods HEX DEYS WRENCH DOUBLE RING OFFSET WRENCH CONBINATION WRENCH ADJESTABLE WRENCH	Credit available with ☐ by sight payment　☒ by acceptance　☒ by negotiation ☐ by deferred payment at 　　against the documents detailed herein ☒ and beneficiary's draft for 100 % of the invoice value at 　　USD 95 000.00 　　on 30DAYS AFTER SIGHT
Packing: PACKED IN ONE CARTON OF 100 SET	☒ FOB　　☐ C&F　　☐ CIF or other terms

Documents required: (marks with ×)
1. (×) Signed Commercial Invoice in 2 copies indicating L/C No. and Contract No.
2. ( ) Full set of clean on board ocean Bills of Lading made out to 　　 and blank endorsed, marked "freight [ ] to collect/ [ ] prepaid [ ] showing freight amount" notifying [ ].
3. ( ) Air Waybills showing "freight [ ] to collect/[ ] prepaid [ ] including freight amount" and consigned to
4. ( ) Memorandum issued by 　　 consigned to
5. ( ) Insurance Policy/Certificate in copes for 　　% of the invoice value showing claims payable in China in currency of the draft, blank endorsed, covering ([ ] Ocean Marine Transportation/[ ] Air Transportation/[ ] Over Land Transportation) All Risks, War Risks.
6. (×) Packing List/Weight Memo in 5 copies issued by the quantity/gross and the weights of each packing and packing condition as called by the L/C.
7. ( ) Certificate of Quantity/Weight in copies issued by an independent surveyor at loading port, indicating the actual surveyed quantity/weight of shipped goods as well as the packing condition.
8. (×) Certificate of Quantity in 2 copies issued by [ ] manufacturer/[×] public recognized surveyor/[ ]
9. ( ) Beneficiary's certified copy of cable dispatched to the accountees within 12 hours after shipment advising [×] name of vessel/[ ] flight No./[ ] wagon No., date quantity, weight and value of shipment.
10. ( ) Beneficiary's Certifying that extra copies of the documents have been dispatched according to the contract terms.
11. ( ) Shipping Co's Certificate attesting that the carrying vessel is chartered or booked by accountee or their shipping agents.
12. ( ) Other documents, if any:

Additional instructions:
1. (×) All banking charges outside the opening bank are for beneficiary's account.
2. (×) Documents must be presented with 15 days after the date of issuance of the transport documents but 　　 with the validity of this credit.
3. (×) Third party as shipper is not acceptable. Short Form/Blank Back B/L is not acceptable.
4. ( ) Both quantity and amount 　　% more or less are allowed.
5. ( ) prepaid freight drawn in excess of L/C amount is acceptable against presentation of original charges voucher issued by shipping Co. /Air Line/or it's agent.
6. ( ) All documents to be forwarded in one cover, unless otherwise started above.
7. ( ) Other terms, if any:

Account No.: 67548211	with	BANK OF CHINA　(name of bank)
Transacted by: SHANGHAI IMPORT & EXPORT TRADE CORPORATION (Applicant: name, signature of authorized person)		
Telephone No.: 56082266		陈冲　　(with seal)

三、实训缮制要求

填 制 栏 目	填制内容和要求
1. 开证日期（DATE）	在进口申请书右上角填写申请日期
2. 致：	银行印制的申请书上事先都会印就开证银行的名称、地址，银行的 SWIFT CODE、TELEX NO. 等也可同时显示
3. 信用证的传递方式	申请书已列出几种传递方式，分别是信开（by air mail）、简电通知（with brief advice by teletransmission）、快递（by express delivery）、电传（by teletransmission）等。申请人只需在选中传递方式前面方框中打"×"即可
4. 信用证的性质	申请书已列明"不可撤销跟单信用证"（Irrevocable Documentary Credit），不必重新填写。如需增加保兑或可转让等内容，可在本栏空白处另加注
5. 信用证号码（L/C NUMBER）	编号由开证银行编列
6. 信用证的有效期及到期地点（Date and Place of Expiry）	填写信用证的有效期及到期地点；有效期通常掌握在装运期后 15 天到期，到期地点一般在议付地
7. 申请人（APPLICANT）	填写开证人的全称及详细地址，并注明联系电话、电传等号码
8. 受益人（BENEFICIARY）	填写受益人的全称及详细地址，并注明联系电话、电传等号码
9. 通知行（ADVISING BANK）	由开证行填写
10. 信用证金额（AMOUNT）	填写合同规定的总值，分别用数字和文字两种形式表示，并且表明币制。如果允许有一定比率的上下浮动，要在信用证中明确表示出来
11. 分批装运是否允许（PARTIAL SHIPMENT）	此处可打√或打×，表示同意与否
12. 转运是否允许（TRANSHIPMENT）	此处可打√或打×，表示同意与否
13. 装运地（港）及目的地（港）的名称，最迟装运日期（LOADING IN CHARGES、FOR TRANSPORTATION TO、LATEST DATE OF SHIPMENT）	如允许有转运地港，也应列明
14. 贸易条件	应根据合同成交的贸易术语在相对应的贸易术语代码前的方框中打"×"，如果是其他条件，则应先在"Other terms"前的方框中打"×"，然后再在该项目的空白处打上有关的贸易术语
15. 信用证的兑付方式（CREDIT AVAILABLE WITH/BY）	申请书上已印有四种选择，如"即期付款"（by sight payment）、"承兑"（by acceptance）、"议付"（by negotiation）"延期付款"（by deferred payment）等，可根据合同的付款方式确定选项，并在其前面的方框中打"×"

(续表)

填 制 栏 目	填制内容和要求
16. 汇票要求:（BENEFICIARY'S DRAFT）	主要包括汇票的金额、付款的期限和付款人的规定
17. 单据条款（DOCUMENTS REQUIRED）	申请人必须根据合同规定填写单据条款,不能随意提出超出合同规定的要求,也不能降低或减少合同规定的要求
18. 商品描述（COVERING）	合同规定的货物描述都必须与合同内容相一致,应具体明确表示清楚
19. 附加指示（ADDITIONAL INSTRUCTIONS）	信用证申请书已印有7条,其中第1条至第6条是具体的条款要求,如需要可在条款前的括号中打"×";内容不完整的,可根据合同规定和申请的需要填写清楚。第7条是"其他条款",对上述没有包括的条款,可视需要填写在该栏目中
20. 授权人签字（法人代表）及电话、传真等内容（NAME,SIGNATURE OF AUTHORISED PERSON,TEL NO.,FAX,ACCOUNT NO.）	申请书最下面的一栏由有关授权人签字。申请人的开户银行（填银行名称）、账户号码、执行人、联系电话、传真、申请人签字盖章等内容

单证模拟实训十

一、缮制购买外汇申请书模拟操作

上海食品进出口公司与法国的 DENSE PTE LTD. 进行洽谈,最后达成一致意见,采用 CIF 价格条件、电汇支付方式、航空运输。购货合同书签订后,刘进填写购买外汇申请书,填写汇款申请书、支付手续费办理 30% 货款的电汇。刘进持有关批文和证明材料向中国银行上海分行申请购买外汇,填写购汇申请书。

上海食品进出口公司
SHANGHAI FOOD IMPORT & EXPORT CORPORATION.
328 SHANXI ROAD SHANGHAI, CHINA

购 货 合 同 书   P/C NO.: SOT0405127
PURCHASE CONTRACT   DATE: MAR 22, 2008

买　方:
The Buyer: SHANGHAI FOOD IMPORT & EXPORT CORPORATION
　　　　　328 SHANXI ROAD SHANGHAI, CHINA
　　　　　TEL: 021-62781456　FAX: 021-62781454

卖　方:
The Seller: DENSE PTE LTD.
　　　　　6 CHANGJ NORTH STREET PARIS, FRANCE
　　　　　TEL: 65-64157986　FAX: 65-64157988

本合同由买卖双方订立,根据本合同规定的条款,买方同意购买,卖方同意出售下述商品:
This Contract is made by and between the Buyer and Seller, whereby the Buyer agrees to buy and the Seller agrees to sell the under-mentioned commodity according to the terms and conditions stipulated below.

1. 商品名称、规格、数量及单价:
COMMODITY, SPECIFICATIONS, QUANTITY AND UNIT PRICE:

商品名称及规格	数　量	单　价	总　值
WHISKY		CIF PARIS	
MACALLEN HIGHLAND MALT 18 YRS 75 cl	100 PCS	USD 1 100.00	USD 5 500.00
ROYAL SALUTE 70 cl	100 PCS	USD 1 100.00	USD 5 500.00

2. 原产地国与制造商:
COUNTRY OF ORIGIN AND MANUFACTURER: France, Dense Light Semiconductors Pte Ltd..

3. 包装:必须适合海运、防湿、防潮、防震、防静电、耐粗暴搬运的卖方标准包装,5件装1箱。
PACKING: To be packed in the Seller's standard export packing suitable for long distance ocean transport and well protected against dampness, moisture, shock, static and rough handling. Packed in 1 carton of 5 pcs each.

4. 唛头：
SHIPPING MARK：
   S. F. C
   SOT0405127
   PARIS
   C/NO. 1 – 40

5. 装运日期：2008 年 5 月 20 日前
DELIVERY：BEFORE MAY. 20，2008
6. 起运地：巴黎机场
AIRPORT OF DEPARTURE：PARIS AIRPORT FRANCH
7. 目的地：中国浦东机场
AIRPORT OF DESTINATION：PUDONG AIRPORT CHINA
8. 分批装运：不允许
PARTIAL SHIPMENTS：NOT ALLOWED
9. 转运：允许
TRANSSHIPMENT：ALLOWED
10. 付款条件：30％前 T/T、70％ T/T
TERMS OF PAYMENT：BY 30％ T/T IN ADVANCE, THE OTHERS 70％ T/T AFTER SHIPMENT
11. 保险：由卖方按发票全部金额加一成投保一切险和战争险
Insurance：For 110 Percent Of The Invoice Value Covering All Risks By The Seller
12. 单据：卖方提供下列单据：
DOCUMENTS：The seller shall present the following documents to the paying bank：
1) 签字的商业发票三份，注明合同号。
Three copies of Signed Commercial Invoice indicating contract number.
2) 装箱单三份。
Three copies of Packing List.
3) 保险单正本二份。
Two Insurance Policy of Original.
4) 空运单正本二份。
Two Air Waybill of Original.
5) 卖方应在货物发运后 12 小时将合同编号、商品名称、数量、毛重、航次及日期电告买方。
Within 12 hours after the goods are completely loaded, the Seller shall FAX to notify the Buyer of the contract number, name of commodity, quantity, gross weight, B/L No. and the date of delivery.

Buyer：   Seller：
SHANGHAI FOOD IMPORT & EXPORT CORPORATION. Dense Light Semiconductors Pte Ltd
  刘 进   Tom

刘进填写购买外汇申请书:

中国银行上海市分行
购买外汇申请书

中国银行_____分(支)行:

　　我公司为执行第_____号合同项下对外支付,需向贵行购汇。现按外汇局有关规定向贵行提出下述内容及所附文件,请审核并按实际付汇日牌价办理售汇。所需人民币资金从我公司在贵行账户中支付。

1. 购汇金额:

2. 用　　途:□进口商品　　□从附费用　　□索退赔款　　□其他

3. 支付方式:□信用证　　　□托收　　　　□汇款(□货到付款　　□预付货款)

4. 商品名称:

5. 数量:

6. 合同号:　　　　　　　　　　金额:

7. 发票号:　　　　　　　　　　金额:

8. □一般进□商品,无须批文
　　□控制进□商品,批文随附如下:
　　　　　□进口证明　　□许可证　　□登记证明　　□其他批文
　　　　　批文号码:　　　　　　批文有效期:

9. 附件:□批文　　□合同/协议　　□发票　　　　□正本运单
　　　　□报关单　□运费单/收据　□保险费收据
　　　　□佣金单　□关税证明　　　□仓单　　　　□其他

10. □请于开证时立即售汇,转存保证金专用户。

申请单位(盖章):_____

银行审核意见:

　　上述内容与随附文件/凭证描述相符,拟按申请书要求办理售汇。

　　经办人:　　　　　　复核人:　　　　　　核准人:

　　售汇日期:

　　(加盖售汇专用章)

二、缮制汇款申请书模拟操作

根据模拟操作一中的背景,刘进填写汇款申请书:

中国银行上海市分行汇款申请书
BANK OF CHINA

外汇	汇款方式 Type of Remittance	电汇 T/T	付款凭证（回单）	户名 Name of Account	
		票汇 D/D	日期 Date	账号 Account No.	

请付 Pay	牌价 Rate	请付 Remit
	@7.60	

（汇款）大写金额 （Remit）Amount in Word	

收款人 Payee	
住　址 Address	
收款人所在地银行 Beneficiary's Bank	
汇款人 Remitter	
附　言 Remarks	

（付款单位银行盖章）

复　核　　　　　经　办

三、缮制开证申请书模拟操作

上海进出口公司与 TOKYO IMPORT & EXPORT CORPORATION 进行洽谈，并与其签订购货贸易合同。合同签订后，上海进出口公司的陈冲在合同规定的开证时间内及时向中国银行上海分行申请开立信用证，为此要填写开证申请书并交纳开证费和保证金。相关资料如下：

1. S/C NO: SOT0409127   DATE: APR.26,2009
2. THE BUYER: SHANGHAI IMPORT & EXPORT TRADE CORPORATION
   1321 ZHONGSHAN ROAD SHANGHAI, CHINA
   TEL: 65-64157986
3. THE SELLERS: TOKYO IMPORT & EXPORT CORPORATION
   82-324 OTOLI MACHI TOKYO, JAPAN
4. DESCRIPT OF GOODS: 100% COTTON KNITTED SKIRT
   ART NO. H32331
   ART NO. H32332
5. Amount: USD 10 750.00   CIF SHANGHAI
6. PACKING: PACKED IN 35 CARTONS OF 100 PCS EACH
7. DELIVERY: BEFORE JUN.30,2009
8. PORT OF LOADING: OSAKA
9. PORT OF DESTINATION: SHANGHAI
10. PARTIAL SHIPMENTS: NOT ALLOWED
11. TRANSSHIPMENT: ALLOWED
12. TERMS OF PAYMENT: IRREVOCABLE DOCUMENTARY CREIDT AT SIGHT.
    The Buyers Shall Issue An Irrevocable L/C At Sight Before MAY.25,2009
13. DOCUMENTS:
    1) Three copies of Signed Commercial Invoice indicating contract number.
    2) Three copies of Packing List.
    3) Two copies of Certificate of Quality issued by manufacture.
    4) within 12 hours after the goods are completely loaded, the Seller shall FAX to notify the Buyer of the contract number, name of commodity, quantity, gross weight, B/L No. and the date of delivery.
    5) Full set of clean on board ocean Bill of Lading made out to order of shipper, and marked freight prepaid and showing freight amount.
    6) Insurance Policy For 110 Percent Of The Invoice Value Covering All Risks And War Risk By The Seller.
14. 开证形式：电开
15. 银行及账号：中国银行上海分行 45781235

上海进出口公司的外汇结算银行是中国银行上海分行，于是陈冲根据贸易合同的有关规定向该行办理开证手续，填写好开证申请书。

IRREVOCABLE DOCUMENTARY CREDIT APPLICATION

To: BANK OF CHINA　　　　　　　　　　　　Date:

Beneficiary (full name and address)	L/C No. Ex Card No. Contract No.	
	Date and place of expiry of the credit	
Partial shipments ☐ allowed ☐ not allowed	Transshipment ☐ allowed ☐ not allowed	☐ Issue by airmail ☐ With brief advice by teletransmission ☐ Issue by express delivery ☐ Issue by teletransmission (which shall be the operative instrument)
Loading on board/dispatch taking in change at/from not later than for transportation	Amount (both in figures and words)	
Description of goods	Credit available with ☐ by sight payment　☐ by acceptance　☐ by negotiation ☐ by deferred payment at 　against the documents detailed herein ☐ and beneficiary's draft for 　% of the invoice value 　at/on	
Packing:	☐ FOB　　☐ C&F　　☐ CIF ☐ or other terms	

Documents required: (marks with ×)
1. ( ) Signed Commercial Invoice in　copies indicating L/C No. and Contract No.
2. ( ) Full set of clean on board ocean Bills of Landing made out　　　and blank endorsed, marked "freight [ ] to collect/[ ] prepaid [ ] showing freight amount" notifying
3. ( ) Air Waybills showing "freight [ ] to collect/[ ] prepaid [ ] including freight amount" and consigned to
4. ( ) Memorandum issued by　　　consigned to
5. ( ) Insurance Policy/Certificate in copes for　% of the invoice value showing claims payable in China in currency of the draft, blank endorsed, covering ([ ] Ocean Marine Transportation/[ ] Air Transportation/ [ ] Over Land Transportation) All Risks, War Risks.
6. ( ) Parking List/Weight Memo in　copies issued by the quantity/gross and the weights of each packing and packing condition as called by the L/C.
7. ( ) Certificate of Quantity/Weight in　copies issued by an independent surveyor at loading port, indicating the actual surveyed quantity/weight of shipped goods as well as the packing condition.
8. ( ) Certificate of Quanlity in　copies issued by [ ] manufacturer/[ ] public recognized surveyor/[ ]
9. ( ) Beneficiary's certified copy of cable dispatched to the accountees within　hours after shipment advising [ ] name of vessel/[ ] flight No. /[ ] wagon No., date quantity, weight and value of shipment.
10. ( ) Beneficiary's Certifying that extra copies of the documents have been dispatched according to the contract terms.
11. ( ) Shipping Co's Certificate attesting that carrying vessel is chartered or booked by accountee or their shipping agents;

Additional instructions:
1. ( ) All banking charges outside the opening bank are for beneficiary's account.
2. ( ) Documents must be presented with　days after the date of issuance of the transport documents but with the validity of this credit.
3. ( ) Third party as shipper is not acceptable. Short Form/Blank Back B/L is not acceptable.
4. ( ) Both quantity and amount　% more or less are allowed.
5. ( ) prepaid freight drawn in excess of L/C amount is acceptable against presentation of original charges voucher issued by shipping Co. /Air Line/or it's agent.

Account No.:	with　　　　　(name of bank)
Transacted by:	(Applicant: name, signature of authorized person)
Telephone No.:	(with seal)

项目十一

进口官方单证

实训目标

◆ 掌握进口许可证的内容以及缮制要求,并学会独立缮制进口许可证。
◆ 掌握进口货物报检单的内容以及缮制要求,并学会独立缮制进口货物报检单。
◆ 掌握进口货物报关单的内容以及缮制要求,并学会独立缮制进口货物报关单。

工作任务一 缮制进口许可证申请表

实训背景

上海进出口贸易公司从日本 TOKYO IMPORT & EXPORT CORPORATION 进口 WARENCH。上海进出口贸易公司陈冲开始进行申请进口许可证的工作。

一、实训指南

进口许可证制(Import License System)是指实行许可证管理的进口商品,除进料加工、来料加工、来料装配、外商投资企业的进口及其他特殊规定外,都必须按国家规定的审批权限进行审批并凭批准文件向发证机关申领进口货物许可证,没有许可证一律不准进口。这种制度可以直接控制进口数量和进口国别。

二、实训样本

上海进出口贸易公司从日本 TOKYO IMPORT & EXPORT CORPORATION 进口 WARENCH。上海进出口贸易公司陈冲需要申请进口许可证。合同资料如下:

上海进出口贸易公司
SHANGHAI IMPORT & EXPORT TRADE CORPORATION
1321 ZHONGSHAN ROAD SHANGHAI, CHINA

PURCHASE CONTRACT

TEL: 021-56082266
FAX: 021-56082265

P/C NO.: TX201023
DATE: AUG. 20, 2010

买　方:
The Buyer: SHANGHAI IMPORT & EXPORT TRADE CORPORATION
　　　　　 1321 ZHONGSHAN ROAD SHANGHAI, CHINA
　　　　　 TEL: 021-56082266　FAX: 021-56082265

卖　方:
The Seller: TOKYO IMPORT & EXPORT CORPORATION
　　　　　 82-324 OTOLI MACHI TOKYO, JAPAN
　　　　　 TEL: 028-548-742　FAX: 028-548-743

The Seller and the Buyer have confirmed this Contract with the terms and conditions stipulated below:

DESCRIPTIONS OF GOODS	QUANTITY	UNIT PRICE	AMOUNT
WARENCH		FOB TOKYO	
HEX DEYS WRENCH	1 000 SET	USD 10.00	USD 10 000.00
DOUBLE RING OFFSET WRENCH	1 500 SET	USD 10.00	USD 15 000.00
CONBINATION WRENCH	2 000 SET	USD 20.00	USD 40 000.00
ADJESTABLE WRENCH	1 500 SET	USD 20.00	USD 30 000.00

1. COUNTRY OF ORIGIN AND MANUFACTURER: TOKYO IMPORT & EXPORT CORPORATION
2. PACKING: PACKED IN 1 CARTON OF 100 PCS EACH.
3. LATEST DATE OF SHIPMENT 100920
4. PORT OF LOADING: TOKYO, JAPAN
5. PORT OF DESTINATION: SHANGHAI, CHINA
6. PAYMENT: IRREVOCABLE DOCUMENTARY CREIDT AT 30 DAYS AFTER SIGHT.
7. PARTIAL SHIPMENTS: ALLOWED
8. TRANSHIPMENT: NOT ALLOWED
9. INSURANCE: FOR 110 PERCENT OF THE INVOICE VALUE COVERING ALL RISKS AND WAR RISK BY THE BUYER
10. DOCUMENTS: THE SELLER SHALL PRESENT THE FOLLOWING DOCUMENTS TO THE PAYING BANK FOR NEGOTIATION:
    1) THREE COPIES OF SIGNED COMMERCIAL INVOICE INDICATING CONTRACT NUMBER.
    2) THREE COPIES OF PACKING LIST.
    3) TWO COPIES OF CERTIFICATE OF QUALITY QUANTITY ISSUED BY MANUFACTURE.
    4) WITHIN 12 HOURS AFTER THE GOODS ARE COMPLERELY LOADED, THE SELLER SHALL FAX TO NOTIFY THE BUYER OF THE CONTRACT NUMBER, NAME OF COMMODITY, QUANTITY, GROSS WEIGHT, B/L NO. AND THE DATE OF DELIVERY.
11. INSPECTION AND CLAIMS: IF THE QUALITY/WEIGHT AND/OR THE SPECIFICATIONS OF THE GOODS SHOULD BE FOUND NOT IN LINE WITH THE CONTRACTED STIPULATIONS, OR SHOULD THE GOODS PROVE DEFECTIVE FOR ANY REASONS, INCLUDING LATENT DEFECT OR THE USE OF UNSUITABLE MATERIALS, THE BUYER WOULD ARRANGE AN INSPECTION TO BE CARRIED OUT BY THE INSPECTION BUREAU AND HAVE THE RIGHT TO CLAIM AGAINST THE SELLERS ON THE STRENGTH OF THE INSPECTION CERTIFICATE ISSUED BY THE BUREAU. ALL CLAIMS SHALL BE REGARDED AS ACCEPTED IF THE SELLERS FAIL TO REPLY WITHIN 30 DAYS AFTER RECEIPT OF THE BUYER'S CLAIM.

Buyer:
SHANGHAI IMPORT & EXPORT TRADE CORPORATION

Seller:
TOKYO IMPORT & EXPORT CORPORATION

上海进出口贸易公司填写进口许可证申请表：

中华人民共和国进口许可证申请表

1. 进口商： 代码 1368029168 上海进出口公司	3. 进口许可证号：
2. 收货人： 上海进出口公司　1368029168	4. 进口许可证有效截止日期： 　　　　年　　月　　日
5. 贸易方式： 　一般贸易	8. 出口国（地区）： 　日本
6. 外汇来源： 　购汇	9. 原产地国（地区）： 　日本
7. 报关口岸： 　吴淞海关	10. 商品用途： 　自营内销
11. 商品名称： 　扳手	商品编码： 　8204.1100

12. 规格、型号	13. 单位	14. 数量	15. 单价（USD）	16. 总值（USD）	17. 总值折美元
HEX DEYS WRENCH	套	1 000	10.00	10 000.00	10 000.00
DOUBLE RING OFFSET WRENCH	套	1 500	10.00	15 000.00	15 000.00
CONBINATION WRENCH	套	2 000	20.00	40 000.00	40 000.00
ADJUSTABLE WRENCH	套	1 500	20.00	30 000.00	30 000.00
18. 总计		6 000		95 000.00	95 000.00

19. 领证人姓名： 　　陈　冲 （上海进出口公司印章） 联系电话：021-56082266 申请日期：2010年8月12日 下次联系日期：	20. 签证机构审批（初审）： 终审：

中华人民共和国商务部监制　　　　　　第一联（正本）签证机构存档

三、实训缮制要求

填 制 栏 目	填制内容和要求
1. 我国对外成交单位(Importer)	我国具备该商品进口经营权、对外签订进口合同的单位名称及其编码
2. 收货人(Consignee)	实际收货人名称
3. 进口许可证编号(Import Licence No.)	签证机关的指定编号
4. 许可证有效期(Expiry Date)	进口许可证的有效截止日期
5. 贸易方式(Terms of Trade)	根据国际贸易惯例在合同中使用的贸易方式
6. 外汇来源(Terms of Foreign)	进口商品所需外汇的获得渠道
7. 到货口岸(Place of Clearance)	商品进口时进口商报关的口岸名称
8. 进口国(地区)(Country/Region of Export)	最初向我国发货,在中转国内不发生任何商业交易的国家或地区
9. 商品原产地(Country/Region of Origin)	根据原产地规则生产或制造商品的国家(地区)
10. 商品用途(Use of Goods)	商品进口后的用途
11. 商品名称(Description of Goods)	进口商品的名称,根据对外贸易经济合作部公布的商品名称填写
12. 商品规格、编码(Specification)	进口商品的具体规格和编号
13. 单位(Unit)	进口商品计量单位
14. 数量(Quantity)	第12项下各规格进口商品的数量值
15. 单价(Unit Price)	第12项下各规格进口商品的单位数量价格,括号内填写币别,币别按照国家标准表示
16. 总值(Amount)	第12项下各规格商品的货币金额,括号内填写币别,币别按照国家标准填写

(续表)

填制栏目	填制内容和要求
17. 总值折美元(Amount in USD)	由签证机关根据国家定期公布的汇率和统计方法,将商品金额折算成美元金额
18. 总计(Total)	进口商品的总数量,金额以及总金额折美元值
19. 备注(Supplementary Details)	由签证机关使用,作出必要的说明或其他事项
20. 发证机关签章(Issuing Authority's Stamp & Signature)	用于签证机关签字盖章
21. 发证日期(Licence Date)	填写签发进口许可证的日期

工作任务二　缮制进口货物报检单

实训背景

上海进出口贸易公司从日本 Tokyo Import & Export Corporation 进口扳手。上海进出口贸易公司陈冲根据合同规定的开证时间向中国银行上海分行办理开证后。须向出入境检验检疫局申请报检,填制报检单。

一、实训指南

入境货物检验检疫的一般工作程序是:报检后先放行通关,再进行检验检疫。入境报检时,应填写《入境货物报检单》,并提供外贸合同、发票、提(运)单、装箱单等有关单据,以及按照检验检疫的要求,提供相关其他特殊证单(如进口汽车应提供进口安全质量许可证复印件等特殊单证)。进口货物如为法定检验商品,须向出入境检验检疫局签发《入境货物通关单》。如货物的外包装是原木的,需提供熏蒸证明;如不是原木包装的,须提供出口商的非木质包装证明,否则不能入境。

二、实训样本

上海进出口贸易公司陈冲根据《中华人民共和国进出口商品检验法》及其实施条例等有关规定及时办理报检手续,填写入境货物报检单,并随附有关单据。

中华人民共和国出入境检验检疫
入境货物报检单

报检单位(加盖公章)： 上海进出口贸易公司 *编　号　8664771215

报检单位登记号：1880298666　　联系人：陈冲　　电话：56082266　　报检日期：2010年9月27日

发货人	(中文)	上海进出口贸易公司		企业性质(划"√")	☑合资	□合作	□外资
	(外文)	SHANGHAI IMPORT & EXPORT TRADE CORPORATION					
收货人	(中文)						
	(外文)	TOKYO IMPORT & EXPORT CORPORATION					

货物名称(中/外文)	H.S.编码	产地	数/重量	货物总值	包装种类及数量
扳手 WRENCH	8204.1100	日本	6 000 SETS	95 000.00 美元	60 箱

运输工具名称号码	COSCO V.861		合同号	TX201023
贸易方式	一般贸易	贸易国别(地区)	日本	提单/运单号	XY05111
到岸日期	2010.09.24	起运国家(地区)	日本	许可证/审批号	06-JZ5661168
卸毕日期	2010.09.24	起运口岸	东京	入境口岸	吴淞海关
索赔有效期至	2010.09.24	经停口岸		目的地	上海

集装箱规格、数量及号码				
合同订立的特殊条款以及其他要求		货物存放地点		上海逸仙路5号
		用　途		企业自营内销
随附单据(划"√"或补填)		标记及号码	*外商投资财产(划"√")	□是　否

随附单据		*检验检疫费	
☑ 合同 ☑ 发票 □ 提/运单 □ 兽医卫生证书 □ 植物检疫证书 □ 动物检验证书 □ 卫生证书 □ 原产地证 ☑ 许可/审批文件	☑ 到货通知 ☑ 装箱单 □ 质保书 □ 理货清单 □ 磅码单 □ 验收报告 标记及号码：N/M	总金额（人民币元）	
		计费人	
		收费人	

报检人郑重声明： 1. 本人被授权报检。 2. 上列填写内容正确属实。 签名：陈冲	领取证单	
	日期	
	签名	

注：有"*"号栏由出入境检验检疫机关填写　　　　◆ 国家出入境检验检疫局制

三、实训缮制要求

填 制 栏 目	填制内容和要求
1. 编号	由检验检疫机构报检受理人员填写,前6位为检验检疫局机关代码,第7位为报检类代码,第8位和第9位为年代码,第10位至第15位为流水号
2. 报检单位登记号	报检单位在检验检疫机构登记的号码
3. 联系人	报检人员姓名、联系电话
4. 报检日期	检验检疫机构实际受理报检的日期
5. 收货人	外贸合同中的收货人,应中英文对照填写
6. 发货人	外贸合同中的发货人
7. 货物名称中/外文	进口货物的品名,应与进口合同、发票名称一致,如为废旧货物应注明
8. H.S.编码	进口货物的商品编码。以当年海关公布的商品税则编码分类为准
9. 产国地区	该进口货物的原产国家或地区
10. 数/重量	以商品编码分类中标准数量为准,并应注明数重量单位
11. 货物总值	入境货物的总值及币种,应与合同、发票或报关单上所列的货物总值一致
12. 包装种类及数量	货物实际运输包装的种类及数量,如是木质包装还应注明材质及尺寸
13. 运输工具名称号码	运输工具的名称和号码
14. 合同号	对外贸易合同、订单或形式发票的号码
15. 贸易方式	该批货物进口的贸易方式
16. 贸易国别地区	进口货物的贸易国别
17. 提单/运单号	货物海运提单号或空运单号,由二程提单的应同时填写
18. 到货日期	进口货物到达口岸的日期
19. 起运国家地区	货物的起运国家或地区
20. 许可证/审批号	需办理进境许可证或审批的货物应填写有关许可证号或审批号
21. 卸毕日期	货物在口岸的卸毕日期
22. 起运口岸	货物的起运口岸
23. 入境口岸	货物的入境口岸
24. 索赔有效期至	对外贸易合同中约定的索赔期限
25. 经停口岸	货物在运输中曾经停靠的外国口岸
26. 目的地	货物的境内目的地
27. 集装箱规格、数量及号码	货物若以集装箱运输应填写集装箱的规格、数量及号码
28. 合同订立的特殊条款以及其他要求	在合同中订立的有关检验检疫的特殊条款及其他要求应填入此栏

（续表）

填 制 栏 目	填制内容和要求
29. 货物存放地点	货物存放的地点
30. 用途	货物的用途可以是：Ⅰ．种用或繁殖，Ⅱ．食用，Ⅲ．奶用，Ⅳ．观赏或演艺，Ⅴ．伴侣动物，Ⅵ．试验，Ⅶ．药用，Ⅷ．饲用，Ⅸ．其他
31. 随附单据	在随附单据的种类前划"√"或补填
32. 标记及号码	货物的标记号码，应与合同、发票等有关外贸单据保持一致。若没有标记号码则填"N/M"
33. 外商投资财产	由检验检疫机构报检受理人员填写
34. 签名	由持有报检员证的报检人员手签
35. 检验检疫费	由检验检疫机构计费人员核定费用后填写
36. 领取证单	报检人在领取检验检疫机构出具的有关检验检疫证单时填写领证日期及领证人姓名

工作任务三 缮制进口货物报关单

实训背景

上海进出口贸易公司从日本 Tokyo Import & Export Corporation 进口扳手。陈冲办理好报检手续后，根据进口商海运提单等有关内容填写进口货物报关单，在海关规定的时间内，及时办理进口货物报关手续。

一、实训指南

进出口货物报关单(the Import Declaration)是由海关总署规定统一格式和填制规范，由进出口货物收货人、发货人或其代理人填制并向海关提交的申报货物状况的法律文书，是海关依法监管货物进出口、征收关税及其他税费、编制海关统计以及处理其他海关业务的重要凭证。

进口报关单分为三种，但各项内容基本相同：

(1) 一般进口货物报关单(白色)。

(2) 进料加工专用进口货物报关单(粉红色)。

(3) 来料加工、补偿贸易专用进口货物报关单(绿色)。

二、实训样本

陈冲办理好报检手续后，根据进口商海运提单等有关内容填写进口货物报关单，在海关规定的时间内，及时办理进口货物报关手续。

中华人民共和国海关进口货物报关单

预录入编号：　　　　　　　　　　　　　　　海关编号：444117252

进口口岸 吴淞海关 2202	备案号	进口日期 2010.09.24	申报日期 2010.09.26
经营单位（0387124666） 上海进出口贸易公司	运输方式 江海运输	运输工具名称 COSCO V.861	提运单号 XY10111
收货单位 0387124666	贸易方式 一般贸易	征免性质 一般征税	征税比例
许可证号 06-JZ5661168	起运国（地区） 日本	装货港 东京	境内目的地 上海
批准文号	成交方式 FOB	运费 502/890/3	保费 502/990/3	杂费
合同协议号 TX200523	件数 60	包装种类 箱	毛重（千克） 175	净重（千克） 145
集装箱号	随附单据 B：T0608114		用途 外贸自营内销

标记唛码及备注
　　　　N/M

项号	商品编号	商品名称、规格型号	数量及单位	原产国（地区）	单价	总价	币制	征免
	8204.1100	WRENCH		日本			502	照章
01		HEX DEYS WRENCH	30 千克 1 000 套		10.00	10 000.00		
02		DOUBLE RING OFFSET WRENCH	30 千克 1 500 套		10.00	15 000.00		
03		CONBINATION WRENCH	40 千克 2 000 套		20.00	40 000.00		
04		ADJUSTABLE WRENCH	45 千克 1 500 套		20.00	30 000.00		

税费征收情况

录入员	录入单位	兹声明以上申报无讹并承担法律责任	海关审单批注及放行日期（签章） 张玲　2010.9.30
报关员 3101045588 陈冲		申报单位（签章） 上海进出口贸易公司 报关专用章	审单　　审价
单位地址　北京路 1000 号			征税　　统计
邮编	电话 56082266	填制日期 2010 年 9 月 26 日	查验　　放行 九汀　2010.9.30

三、实训缮制要求

填 制 栏 目	填制内容和要求
1. 收货单位	指已知的进口货物在境内的最终消费、使用单位,包括自行从境外进口货物的单位、委托有外贸进出口经营权的企业进口货物的单位
2. 征免性质	指海关对进出口货物实施征、减、免税管理的性质类别。本栏目应按海关核发的《征免税证明》中批注的征免性质直报,或根据实际情况,按海关规定的《征免性质代码表》选择填报相应的征免性质简称或代码。加工贸易报关单中,本栏目应按海关核发的《登记手册》中批注的征免性质填报相应征免性质或代码
3. 征税比例	此栏不填
4. 起运国地区	指进口货物起始发运的国家(地区)。对发生运输中转的货物,如中转地未发生任何商业性交易,则起运地不变;如中转地发生商业性交易,则以中转地为起运地填报。本栏目应按海关规定的《国别(地区)代码表》选择填报相应的起运国(地区)的中文名称或代码。无实际进境的,本栏目填报"中国"(代码"142")
5. 装运港	指进口货物在运抵我国关境前的最后一个境外装运港。本栏目应根据实际情况按海关规定的《港口航线代码表》选择填报相应的港口中文名称或代码。无实际进境的,本栏目填报"中国境内"(代码"0142")
6. 境内目的地	指已知的进口货物在国内的消费地、使用地或最终运抵地。本栏目应根据进口货物的收货单位所属国内地区,并按海关规定的《国内地区代码表》选择填报相应的国内地区名称或代码
7. 批准文号	填报《进口付汇核销单》编号
8. 成交方式	根据实际成交价格条款按海关规定的《成交方式代码表》选择填报相应的成交方式代码。无实际进境的填 CIF 价
9. 运费	本栏目填报成交价格中不包含运费的进口货物的全部国际运输费用。填报规则与出口报关单同栏目的填报规则相同。运保费合并计算的,运保费填在本栏目
10. 保费	本栏目用于填报成交价格中不包含保险费的进口货物所含的国际运输的保险费用。填报规则与出口货物报关单同栏目的填报规则相同
11. 用途	应根据进口货物的实际用途按海关规定的《用途代码表》选择填报相应的用途代码
12. 原产国地区	指进口货物的生产、开采或加工制造的国家(地区)。本栏目应按海关《国别(地区)代码表》规定,选择填报相应的国家(地区)名称或代码

除上述所列项目外,报关单上的其他项目的缮制要求,与出口货物报关单上相同项目的填报要求相同,请参照出口货物报关单的填制。

单证模拟实训十一

一、缮制进口许可证模拟操作

上海进出口贸易公司与日本 TAKAMRA TRADING CORPORATION 达成进口合同,进口 EDUCATIONAL BOOKS。为此,上海进出口贸易公司的刘进需要申请进口许可证。

合同资料如下:

SHANGHAI IMPORT & EXPORT TRADE CORPORATION.
1321 ZHONGSHAN ROAD SHANGHAI, CHINA
PURCHASE CONTRACT

TEL: 021-65788877   P/C NO.: TX201023
FAX: 021-65788876   DATE: Aug. 10, 2010

The Buyer: SHANGHAI IMPORT & EXPORT TRADE CORPORATION
1321 ZHONGSHAN ROAD SHANGHAI, CHINA

The Sellers: TAKAMRA TRADING CORPORATION
82-324 OTOLI MACHI TOKYO, JAPAN
TEL: 028-548-742   FAX: 028-548-743

Dear Sir or Madam:
We have faxed to you order for 89 books before. As follows are the terms details of the books.

Order No	Description	Quantity	Amount
SK0626215	EDUCATIONAL BOOKS	89 SET	CIP SHANGHAI USD 5 030.51

PACKING: Packed In 26 Cartons
AIRPORT OF DEPARTURE: Osaka Airport
AIRPORT OF DESTINATION: Pudong Airport Shanghai, China
PARTIAL SHIPMENT: Not Allowed
TRANSHIPMENT: Not Allowed
TIME OF SHIPMENT: Latest Date Of Shipment 100930
TERMS OF PAYMENT: 100% T/T In Advance
INSURANCE: For 110 Percent Of The Invoice Value Covering W.P.A By The Seller
DOCUMENTS: The Seller Shall Present The Following Documents:
1) Two Air Waybill.
2) Three Copies Of Signed Commercial Invoice Indicating Contract Number.
3) Three Copies Of Packing List.
4) Two Copies Of Certificate Of Quality Issued By Manufacture.
5) Insurance Policy In 2 Copies.

INSPECTION AND CLAIMS: Within the guarantee period stipulated should the quality/weight and/or the specifications of the goods be found not in with the contracted stipulations, or should the goods prove defective for any reasons, including latent defect or the use of unsuitable materials, the Buyer shall arranges for an Inspection to be carried out by the Bureau and have the right to claim against the Sellers on the strength of the inspection certificate issued by the Bureau. Any and all claims shall be regarded as accepted if the Sellers fail to reply within 30 days after receipt of the Buyer's claim.

THE BUYER:    THE SELLER: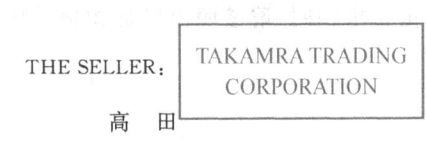
刘 进   高 田

缮制进口许可证如下：

中华人民共和国进口许可证申请表

1. 进口商：　　　代码	3. 进口许可证号：
2. 收货人：	4. 进口许可证有效截止日期： 　　年　　月　　日
5. 贸易方式：	8. 出口国（地区）：
6. 外汇来源：	9. 原产地国（地区）：
7. 报关口岸：	10. 商品用途：

11. 商品名称：　　　　　　　　商品编码：					
12. 规格、型号	13. 单位	14. 数量	15. 单价 （USD）	16. 总值 （USD）	17. 总值折美元
18. 总计					

19. 领证人姓名： 联系电话： 申请日期： 下次联系日期：	20. 签证机构审批(初审)： 终审：
中华人民共和国商务部监制	第一联(正本)签证机构存档

二、缮制进口报检单模拟操作

上海进出口贸易公司刘进申请进口许可证后,根据合同规定的开证时间向中国银行上海分行办理开证后。然后向出入境检验检疫局申请报检,填制报检单。

中华人民共和国出入境检验检疫
入境货物报检单

报检单位(加盖公章):						*编　号:	1230508111
报检单位登记号:		联系人:		电话:		报检日期:	年　月　日

收货人	(中文)		企业性质(划"√")	□合资 □合作 □外资
	(外文)			
发货人	(中文)			
	(外文)			

货物名称(中/外文)	H.S.编码	原产国	数/重量	货物总值	包装种类及数量

运输工具名称号码		合同号	
贸易方式		贸易国别(地区)		提单/运单号	
到货日期		起运国家(地区)		许可证/审批号	
卸货日期		起运口岸		入境口岸	
索赔有效期至		经停口岸		目的地	
集装箱规格、数量及号码					
合同订立的特殊条款以及其他要求		货物存放地点			
		用　途			

随附单据(划"√"或补填)		标记及号码	*外商投资财产(划"√")	□是 □否
☑ 合同 ☑ 发票 ☑ 提/运单 □ 兽医卫生证书 □ 植物检疫证书 □ 动物检验证书 □ 卫生证书 □ 原产地证 □ 许可/审批文件	☑ 到货通知 ☑ 装箱单 □ 质保书 □ 理货清单 □ 磅码单 □ 验收报告 □		*检验检疫费	
			总金额 (人民币元)	
			计费人	
			收费人	

报检人郑重声明: 1. 报检人被授权报检。 2. 上列填写内容正确属实。 签名:_____	领　取　证　单	
	日期	
	签名	

注:有"*"号栏由出入境检验检疫机关填写　　◆ 国家出入境检验检疫局制

三、缮制进口报关单模拟操作

上海进出口贸易公司办理好报检手续后,根据进口商海运提单等有关内容填写进口货物报关单,在海关规定的时间内,及时办理进口货物报关手续。

中华人民共和国海关出口货物报关单

预录入编号: 海关编号:

出口口岸		备案号		出口日期		申报日期	
经营单位(3122668874)		运输方式		运输工具名称		提运单号	
发货单位		贸易方式		征免性质		结汇方式	
许可证号		运抵国(地区)		指运港		境内货源地	
批准文号		成交方式		运费		保费	杂费
合同协议号		件数		包装种类	毛重(千克)		净重(千克)
集装箱号		随附单据				生产厂家	
标记唛码及备注							
项号	商品编号	商品名称、规格型号	数量及单位	最终目的国(地区)	单价	总价	币制	征免
税费征收情况							
录入员		录入单位	兹声明以上申报无讹并承担法律责任		海关审单批注及放行日期(签章)		
报关员		申报单位(签章)			审单		审价
单位地址					征税		统计
邮编	电话	填制日期			查验		放行

项目十二

进出口单证综合模拟操作

> **技能目标**
>
> ◆ 了解审证的依据、步骤、工作方法,掌握信用证审核与交单的注意点。
> ◆ 了解审单的依据、步骤、工作方法、审单的常见问题,掌握审单的技巧,能够正确地审核单据。
> ◆ 掌握制单的依据、基本方法、要求和重点项目,能够正确地缮制单据。

工作任务一 信用证审核综合模拟操作

一、实训指南

(一)信用证审核的依据

(1)外贸合同。信用证是依据外贸合同开立的,所以其条款应与外贸合同的条款相符。审查信用证条款是否与外贸合同的条款相符,是外贸单证员收到信用证后首先要做的工作。

(2)《UCP600》。外贸单证员审核信用证时,应遵循《UCP600》的规定来确定是否可以接受信用证的某些条款。

(3)业务实际情况。对于外贸合同中未作规定或无法根据《UCP600》来作出判断的信用证条款,外贸单证员应根据业务实际情况来审核。如信用证条款对安全收汇的影响程度、进口国的法令和法规以及开证申请人的商业习惯等。

(二)信用证审核的步骤和信用证的修改

1. 信用证审核的步骤

第一步:熟悉外贸合同各条款内容。

第二步:对照外贸合同条款,按照可操作性原则,逐条审核信用证各条款。

第三步:核对外贸合同,有无信用证漏开的外贸合同条款。

第四步:列出信用证的不符条款。

2. 信用证的修改

通过对信用证的全面审核,如发现问题,应分别情况及时处理。对于影响安全收汇,难以接受或做到的信用证条款,必须要求国外买方进行修改。

二、实训实例

上海怡愿进出口有限公司与 NU BONNETERIE DE GROOTE 公司签订了一份全棉工装裤出口的销售合同,具体内容如下:

SALES CONTRACT

THE SELLER: NO. WILL09068
SHANGHAI WILL TRADING. CO., LTD. DATE: JUNE 1, 2020
NO. 25 JIANGNING ROAD SHANGHAI, CHINA SIGNED AT: SHANGHAI, CHINA
THE BUYER:
NU BONNETERIE DE GROOTE
AUTOSTRADEWEG 6 9090 MEUE BELGIUM

This Sales Contract is made by and between the Sellers and the Buyers, whereby the sellers agree to sell and the buyers agree to buy the under-mentioned goods according to the terms and conditions stipulated below:

Commodity & Specification	Quantity	Price Terms	
		Unit price	Amount
WORK SHORT TROUSERS - 100 PCT COTTON TWILL AS PER ORDER D0900326,	3 000 PCS	CIF ANTWERP USD 10.50/PCS	USD 31 500.00
WORK SHORT TROUSERS - 100 PCT COTTON TWILL AS PER ORDER D0900327,	5 000 PCS	USD 12.00/PCS	USD 60 000.00
TOTAL	8 000 PCS		USD 91 500.00
Total amount: U.S. DOLLARS NINETEEN THOUSAND TWO HUNDRED AND FIFTY ONLY			

Packing: IN CARTONS OF 50 PCS EACH **Shipping Mark**: AT SELLER'S OPTION
Time of Shipment: DURING AUG. 2020 BY SEA
Loading Port and Destination: FROM SHANGHAI, CHINA TO ANTWERP, BELGIUM
Partial Shipment and Transshipment: ARE ALLOWED
Insurance: TO BE EFFECTED BY THE SELLER FOR 110 PCT OF INVOICE VALUE AGAINST ALL RISKS AND WAR RISK AS PER CIC OF THE PICC DATED 01/01/2009.
Terms of Payment: THE BUYER SHALL OPEN THROUGH A BANK ACCEPTABLE TO THE SELLER AN IRREVOCABLE SIGHT LETTER OF CREDIT TO REACH THE SELLER 30 DAYS BEFORE THE MONTH OF SHIPMENT AND TO REMAIN VALID FOR NEGOTIATION IN CHINA UNTIL THE 15th DAY AFTER THE FORESAID TIME OF SHIPMENT.

SELLER BUYER
SHANGHAI WILL TRADING CO., LTD. NU BONNETERIE DE GROOTE
张 平 LJSKOUT

ISSUE OF DOCUMENTARY CREDIT

27: SEQUENCE OF TOTAL: 1/1
40A: FORM OF DOC. CREDIT: IRREVOCABLE
20: DOC. CREDIT NUMBER: 132CD6372730
31C: DATE OF ISSUE: 200715
40E: APPLICABLE RULES: UCP LATEST VERSION
31D: DATE AND PLACE OF EXPIRY: DATE 200910 PLACE IN BELGIUM
51D: APPLICANT BANK: ING BELGIUM NV/SV(FORMERLY BANK
                BRUSSELS LAMBERT SA), GENT
50: APPLICANT: NU BONNETERIE DE GROOTE
              AUTOSTRADEWEG 6
            9090 MELLE BELGIUM
59: BENEFICIARY: SHANGHAI WILL IMPORT AND EXPORT CO., LTD.
              NO. 25 JIANGNING ROAD, SHANGHAI, CHINA
32B: AMOUNT: CURRENCY USD AMOUNT 19 500.00
41A: AVAILABLE WITH…BY ANY BANK IN CHINA BY NEGOTIATION
42C: DRAFTS AT… 30 DAYS AFTER SIGHT
42A: DRAWEE: NU BONNETERIE DE GROOTE
43P: PARTIAL SHIPMTS: NOT ALLOWED
43T: TRANSSHIPMENT: ALLOWED
44E: PORT OF LOADING: ANY CHINESE PORT
44F: PORT OF DISCHARGE: ANTWERP, BELGIUM
44C: LATEST DATE OF SHIPMENT: 200815
45A: DESCRIPTION OF GOODS
    + 3 000 PCS SHORT TROUSERS - 100PCT COTTON TWILL AT EUR10.50/PC AS PER ORDER D0900326 AND SALES CONTRACT NUMBER WILL09068.
    + 5 000 PCS SHORT TROUSERS - 100PCT COTTON TWILL AT EUR12.00/PC AS PER ORDER D0900327 AND SALES CONTRACT NUMBER WILL09069.

SALES CONDITIONS: CFR ANTWERP
PACKING: 50 PCS/CTN
46A: DOCUMENTS REQUIRED
    1. SIGNED COMMERCIAL INVOICES IN 2 ORGINAL AND 2 COPIES.
    2. FULL SET OF CLEAN ON BOARD OCEAN BILLS OF LADING, MADE OUT TO ORDER, BLANK ENDORSED, MARKED FREIGHT COLLECT NOTIFY THE APPLICANT.
    3. CERTIFICATE OF ORIGIN.
    4. PACKING LIST IN QUADRUPLICATE STATING CONTENTS OF EACH PACKAGE SEPARARTELY.
    5. INSURANCE POLICY/CERTIFICATE ISSUED IN DUPLICATE IN NEGOTIABLE FORM, COVERING ALL RISKS, FROM WAREHOUSE TO WAREHOUSE FOR 120 PCT OF INVOICE VALUE. INSURANCE POLICY/CERTIFICATE MUST CLEARLY STATE IN THE BODY CLAIMS, IF ANY, ARE PAYABLE IN BELGIUM IRRESPECTIVE OF PERCENTAGE.
47A: ADDITIONAL CODITIONS
    1/ALL DOCUMENTS PRESENTED UNDER THIS LC MUST BE ISSUED IN ENGLISH.
    7/IN CASE THE DOCUMENTS CONTAIN DISCREPANCIES, WE RESERVE THE RIGHT TO CHARGE DISCREPANCY FEES AMOUNTING TO EUR 75 OR EQUIVALENT.
71B: CHARGES: ALL CHARGES ARE TO BE BORN BY BENEFICIARY

48：PERIOD FOR PRESENTATION：WITHIN 5 DAYS AFTER THE DATE OF SHIPMENT，BUT WITHIN THE VALIDITY OF THIS CREDIT
49：CONFIRMATION INSTRUCTION：WITHOUT

根据信用证审核的四个步骤，提出修改意见如下：

(1) 31C　开证日期不符，根据合同，开证日期应为 200702 之前。

(2) 31D　有效期不符，根据合同，有效期应为 200915。

(3) 31D　到期地点不符，根据合同，到期地点应在中国。

(4) 59　　受益人名称不符，受益人名称应为"SHANGHAI WILL TRADING CO.，LTD."。

(5) 32B　信用证金额不符，根据合同，信用证金额应为 USD91 500.00。

(6) 42C　汇票付款期限不符，汇票付款期限应为"AT SIGHT"。

(7) 42A　汇票受票人有误，汇票受票人应为开证行(ING BELGIUM NV/SV(FORMERLY BANK BRUSSELS LAMBERT SA，GENT)或付款行，不应是开证申请人。

(8) 43P　应为允许分批装运。

(9) 44E　装运港不符，装运港应为"SHANGHAI"。

(10) 44C　最迟装运期不符，最迟装运期应为 200831。

(11) 45A　品名不符，品名应为"WORK SHORT TROUSERS"。

(12) 45A　单价币别不符，单价币别应为"USD"，不应为"EUR"。

(13) 45A　贸易术语不符，贸易术语应为"CIF"，不应为"CFR"。

(14) 45A　合同号有误，应为 WILL09068。

(15) 46A　提单运费项目应注明"FREIGHT PREPAID"，不应为"FREIGHT COLLECT"。

(16) 46A　保险单的保险金额应为发票金额的"110PCT"，不应为"120PCT"。

(17) 46A　保险险别应为"ALL RISKS AND WAR RISK"。

(18) 71B　所有费用由受益人负担不合理。

(19) 48　　交单期应为装运日期后"15 天"，不应是装运日期后"5 天"。

(20) 50　　申请人有误，应为 NU BONNETERIE DE GROOTE，AUTOSTRADEWEG 6 9090 MEUE BELGIUM。

三、实训操作要点

审 核 项 目	审 核 要 点
1. 信用证的付款保证是否有效	(1) 信用证明确表明是可以撤销的。若信用证中如没有表明该信用证是否可以撤销，按照《UCP600》的规定，应理解是不可以撤销的 (2) 审核应该保兑的信用证未按要求由有关银行进行保兑 (3) 审核关于有条件的生效的信用证情况，如："待获得进口许可证后才能生效" (4) 审核信用证密押不符情况 (5) 审核信用证简电或预先通知情况 (6) 审核由开证人直接寄送的信用证事宜

(续表)

审 核 项 目	审 核 要 点
2. 信用证的付款时间是否与有关合同规定相一致	(1) 关于信用证中规定有关款项须在向银行交单后若干天内或见票后若干天内付款等情况。对此,应检查此类付款时间是否符合合同规定或公司的要求 (2) 若规定信用证国外到期,有关单据必须寄送国外。由于我们无法掌握单据到达国外银行所需的时间且容易延误或丢失,有一定的风险,通常我们要求在国内交单付款
3. 审核信用证受益人和开证人的名称和地址是否完整和准确	受益人应特别注意信用证上的受益人名称和地址应与其印就好的文件上的名称和地址内容相一致
4. 检查装运期的有关规定是否符合要求	超过信用证规定装运期的运输单据将构成不符点,银行有权拒绝付款
5. 检查能否在信用证规定的交单期交单	如来证中规定向银行交单的日期不得迟于提单日期后若干天,如果过了限期或单据不齐有错漏,银行有权不付款
6. 检查信用证内容是否完整	应核实内容是否完整
7. 检查信用证的通知方式是否安全、可靠	信用证一般是通过受益人所在国家或地区的通知/保兑行通知给受益人的。如果不是这样寄交的,应该首先通过银行调查核实信用证的真实性
8. 检查信用证的金额、币制是否符合合同规定	信用证的金额应该与事先协商的相一致,信用证中的单价与总值要准确,大小写并用,内容要一致
9. 检查信用证的数量是否与合同规定相一致	除非信用证规定数量不得有增减,否则,在付款金额不超过信用证金额的情况下,货物数量可以容许有5%的增减。特别注意的是,以上提到的货物数量可以有5%增减的规定一般适用于大宗货物,对于以包装单位或以个数为计算单位的货物不适用
10. 检查价格条款是否符合合同规定	不同的价格条款涉及具体的费用如运费、保险费由谁分担
11. 检查货物是否允许分批出运和转运	除非信用证另有规定,货物是允许分批装运的,也是允许转运的
12. 检查有关的费用条款	信用证中规定的有关费用如运费或检验费等应事先协商一致,否则,对于额外的费用原则上不应承担;银行费用如事先未商定,应以双方共同承担为宜

(续表)

审核项目	审核要点
13. 检查信用证中有无陷阱条款	应特别注意下列信用证条款是有很大陷阱的条款,具有很大的风险:1/3正本提单直接寄送客人的条款(如果接受此条款,将随时面临货、款两空的危险);将客检作为议付文件的条款(接受此条款,受益人正常处理信用证业务的主动权很大程度上掌握在对方手里,影响安全收汇)
14. 保险条款	若来证要求的投保险别或投保金额超出了外贸合同的规定,除非信用证上表明由此而产生的超保费用由开证申请人承担并允许在信用证项下支取,否则应予修改。若保险加成过高,还需征得保险公司同意,否则应予修改
15. 单据条款	要仔细审核信用证中的单据条款,特别要注意一些软条款,如商业发票经买方复签生效、1/3正本提单直接寄给买方等
16. 银行费用条款	一般情况下,出口方银行费用由受益人承担,进口方银行的费用由开证申请人承担。关于银行费用承担,进出口双方应在谈判时加以明确
17. 检查信用证中有无矛盾之处。	如:空运却要求提供海运提单;价格条款是FOB,保险应由买方办理,而信用证中却要求提供保险单
18. 检查有关信用证是否受UCP600的约束	明确信用证受《UCP600》的约束可以使我们在具体处理信用证业务中,对于信用证的有关规定有一个公认的解释和理解
19. 检查信用证规定的文件能否提供或及时提供	一些需要认证的单据特别是使馆认证等能否及时办理和提供。由其他机构或部门出具的有关文件如出口许可证、运费收据、检验证明等能否提供或及时提供

工作任务二 单据审核综合模拟操作

一、实训指南

在信用证结算方式下,外贸单证员审单的原则是单货一致、单证一致、单单一致;银行审单的原则是单证一致、单单一致。在托收结算方式下,外贸单证员审单的原则是单货一致、单约一致、单单一致;银行审单的原则是审核单据的名称、份数是否与托收申请书一致,并无审核单据内容的义务;在汇款结算方式下,外贸单证员审单的原则是单货一致、单约一致、单单一致。

二、实训实例

ABC皮具进出口公司外贸单证员制作好信用证项下的单据后,请根据信用证以及《UCP600》审核单据。

资料:

BENEFICIARY: ABC LEATHER GOODS CO., LTD.
　　　　　　　123 HUANGHE ROAD TIANJIN, CHINA
APPLICANT: XYZ TRADING COMPANY
　　　　　　456 SPAGNOLI ROAD, NEW YORK 11747 USA
...

DRAFTS TO BE DRAWN AT 30 DAYS AFTER SIGHT ON ISSUING BANK FOR 90% OF INVOICE VALUE.
...

YOU ARE AUTHORIZED TO DRAWN ON ROYAL BANK OF NEW YORK FOR DOCUMENTARY IRREVOCABLE CREDIT NO. 98765 DATED APR. 15, 2020. EXPRITY DATE MAY31, 2020 FOR NEGOTIATION BENEFICIARY.

AVAILABLE WITH ANY BANK IN CHINA BY NEGOTIATION
...

FULL SET OF CLEAN ON BOARD OCEAN BILLS OF LADING, MADE OUT TO ORDER, BLANK ENDORSED AND MARKED FREIGHT PREPAID NOTIFY APPLICANT.
...

INSURANCE POLICY/CERTIFICATE IN DUPLICATE FOR 110 PCT OF INVOICE VALUE COVERING ALL RISKS AND WAR RISK OF THE PICC DATED01/01/1981
...

GOODS: 5 000 PCS OF LEATHER BAGS PACKED IN 10 PCS/CARTON
...

合同号:ABC234

信用证号:DT905012

发票号:1234567

发票日期:2020年5月5日

发票金额:USD108000 CIF NEW YORK

装运港:TIANJIN, CHINA

目的港:NEW YORK,USA

装船日期:2020 年 5 月 15 日

开船日期:2020 年 5 月 15 日

发票签发人:ABC LEATHER GOODS CO.,LTD.

    ALICE

G.W.:2 408 KGS

N.W.:2 326 KGS

MEASUREMENT:21.70 CBM

NO OF PACKAGES:500 CARTONS

船名、航次号:SUN V.126

提单号码:CNS010108895

集装箱号/封号:YMU259654/56789

运输标记:XYZ

1234567

NEW YORK

NOS.1-500

保险单号码:HMOP09319089

 1. 汇票

BILL OF EXCHANGE

凭   信用证号

Drawn under:XYZ TRADING COMPANY   L/C NO. 89765

日期

Dated:May 15,2020

号码   汇票金额   中国天津

No. 123456 Exchange for USD 108 000.00   Shanghai,China Date:June 1,2009

见票   日后(本汇票之副本未付)付交

At ****** sight of this FIRST of Exchange (Second of Exchange being unpaid)

pay to the order of BANK OF CHINA, TIANJIN BRANCH

金额

the sum of US DOLLARS ONE HUNDRED AND EIGHT THOUSAND ONLY

此致

To:XYZ TRADING COMPANY   ABC LEATHER GOODS CO.

                      ALICE

2. 提单

Shipper Insert Name, Address and Phone ABC LEATHER GOODS CO., LTD. 123 HUANGHE ROAD TIANJIN, CHINA		B/L No. CNS010108895	
Consignee Insert Name, Address and Phone XYZ TRADING COMPANY 456 SPAGNOLI ROAD, NEW YORK 11747 USA		中远集装箱运输有限公司 COSCO CONTAINER LINES TLX: 33057 COSCO CN FAX: +86(021) 6545 8984 ORIGINAL	
Notify Party Insert Name, Address and Phone XYZ TRADING COMPANY 456 SPAGNOLI ROAD, NEW YORK 11747 USA			
Ocean Vessel Voy. No. SUN V. 126	Port of Loading SHANGHAI CHINA	Port-to-Port **BILL OF LADING**	
Port of Discharge LONG BEACH	Port of Destination	Shipped on board and condition except as other…	
Marks & Nos. Container/Seal No.	No. of Containers or Packages	Description of Goods	Gross Weight Kgs	Measurement
XYZ 1234567 LONG BEACH NOS. 1 – 500 YMU259654/56789	5 000 PCS	LEATHER GOODS FREIGHT PREPAID	2 400 KGS	20.70 CBM
		Description of Contents for Shipper's Use Only (Not part of This B/L Contract)		
Total Number of containers and/or packages (in words) SAYFIVE THOUSAND PCS ONLY				
Ex. Rate:	Prepaid at	Payable at LONG BEACH	Place and date of issue TIANJIN MAY 30, 2020	
	Total Prepaid	No. of Original B(s)/L THREE (3)	Signed for the Carrier COSCO CONTAINER LINES +++	
LADEN ON BOARD THE VESSEL DATE: MAY. 30, 2020 BY: COSCO CONTAINER LINES +++				

3. 保险单

货物运输保险单
CARGO TRANSPORTATION INSURANCE POLICY

总公司设于北京　　　一九四九年创立
Head Office Beijing　　Established in 1949

发票号（INVOICE NO.）123456　　　　　保单号次
合同号（CONTRACT NO.）ABC234　　　　POLICY NO. HMOP09319089
信用证号（L/C NO.）DT905012
被保险人（INSURED）XYZ TRADING COMPANY

中国人民财产保险有限公司（以下简称本公司）根据被保险人的要求，由被保险人向本公司缴付约定的保险费，按照本保险单承保险别和背面所载条款与下列特款承保下述货物运输保险，特立本保险单。

THIS POLICY OF INSURANCE WITNESSES THAT PICC PROPERTY AND CASUALTY COMPANY LIMITED (HEREINAFTER CALLED "THE COMPANY") AT REQUEST OF THE INSURED AND IN CONSIDERATION OF THE AGREED PREMIUM PAID TO THE COMPANY BY THE INSURED, UNDERTAKES TO INSURANCE. THE UNDERMENTIONED GOODS IN TRANSPORTATION SUBJECT TO THE CONDITIONS OF THIS POLICY AS PER THE CLAUSES PRINTED OVERL AND OTHER SPECIAL CLAUSES ATTACHED HEREON.

标记及号码 Marks & Nos.	包装数量 Quantity	保险货物项目 Description of Goods	保险金额 Amount Insured
XYZ 1234567 NEW YORK NOS. 1-500	5 000 PCS	LEATHER BAGS	USD 108 000.00

总保险金额 TOTAL AMOUNT INSURED: US DOLLARS ONE HUNDRED AND EIGHT THOUSAND ONLY

保费：　　　　　　　　起运日期：　　　　　　　　　装载运输工具：
PREMIUM: AS ARRANGED　DATE OF COMMENCEMENT MAY. 30, 2020　PER CONVEYANCE: "SUN" V. 126
自　　　　　　经　　　　至
FROM TIANJIN VIA *** TO LONG BEACH

承保险别：
CONDITIONS
　　　COVERING ALL RISKS AS PER CIC OF THE PICCC DATED 01/01/2009.

所保货物，如发生保险单项下可能引起索赔的损失或损坏，应立即通知本公司代理人查勘。如有索赔，应向本公司提交保单正本（本保险单共有3份正本）及有关文件。如一份正本已用于索赔，其余正本自动失效。

IN THE EVENT OF LOSS OR DAMAGE WHICH MAY RESULT IN A CLAIM UNDER THIS POLICY, INNEDIATE NOTICE MUST BE GIVER TO THE COMPANY'S AGENT AS MENTIONED

HEREUNDER CLAIMS, IF ANY ONE OF THE ORIGINAL POLICY WHICH HAS BEEN ISSUED IN ORIGINAL TOGETHER WITH THE RELEVENT DOCUMENTS SHALL BE SURRENDERED TO THE COMPANY. IF ONE OF THE ORIGINAL POLICY HAS BEEN ACCOMPLISHED. THE OTHERS TO BE VOID.

中国人民财产保险股份有限公司上海市分公司

赔款偿付地点　　　　　　　　　　PICC Property and Casualty Company Limited, Shanghai
CLAIM PAYABLE AT/IN TIANJIN IN USD

出单日期　　　　　　　　　　　　　　　　　　×××
ISSUING DATE MAY 16, 2020　　　　　　　　GENERAL MANAGER

　　根据审单的几个方法,依据信用证审核各种单据,得出以上单据存在以下不符点:

汇票改错:

(1) Drawn Under：后应为 ROYAL BANK OF NEW YORK。

(2) 信用证号应为 DT905012/98765（两者选其一）。

(3) 开证日期应为 APR. 15, 2020。

(4) 汇票编号应为 1234567。

(5) 金额小写应为 USD 97 200.00。

(6) 出票日期：不早于 2020 年 5 月 15 日,不晚于 2020 年 5 月 31 日。

(7) 汇票期限应为 At 30 days after sight。

(8) 金额大写应为 US DOLLARS NINETY-SEVEN THOUSAND TWO HUNDRED ONLY。

(9) 受票人应为 ROYAL BANK OF NEW YORK。

(10) 出票人应为 ABC LEATHER GOODS CO., LTD.。

(11) 出票地点应为 TIANJIN。

提单改错:

(1) Consignee 应为 To Order。

(2) Port of Loading 应为 TIANJIN。

(3) Port of Discharge 应为 NEW YORK。

(4) 唛头中的目的港应为 NEW YORK。

(5) 包装件数应为"500 CARTONS",不应是"5 000 PCS"。

(6) 品名应为 Leather Bags。

(7) 毛重应为 2 408 KGS。

(8) 尺码应为 21.70 CBM。

(9) 大写件数应为 SAY FIVE HUNDRED CARTONS ONLY。

(10) 运费支付地点应为 TIANJIN。

(11) 提单签发日期应为 MAY 15, 2020。

(12) 装船日期应为 MAY 15, 2020。

保险单改错：

(1) 发票编号应为 1234567。

(2) 被保险人应为"ABC LEATHER GOODS CO.,LTD."。

(3) 包装件数应为 500 CARTONS。

(4) 保险金额应为 USD 118 800.00。

(5) 保险金额大写有误，应与小写金额一致。

(6) 起运日期应为"MAY 15，2020"。

(7) 目的港应为 NEW YORK。

(8) 险别应为一切险加战争险。

(9) 保险赔付地点应为 NEW YORK。

(10) 保险单出单日期应不晚于 2020 年 5 月 15 日。

(11) 保险人应为天津分公司。

(12) 保险单份数为两份。

三、实训操作要点

审核单据	审核要点
1. 商业发票	(1) 除非信用证另有规定，商业发票的出具人与汇票的出票人应相同，在绝大多数情况下为信用证的受益人 (2) 除非信用证另有规定，抬头为开证申请人 (3) 不得为"形式发票"或"临时发票" (4) 货物描述和信用证的商品描述相符 (5) 没有表现出来任何附加的、不利的货物描述涉及物状态或价值的 (6) 发票上包括信用证所提及的货物细节、价格条款 (7) 发票上提供的其他资料如唛头、号码、运输通知等与其他单据是否一致 (8) 发票上的货币与信用证一致 (9) 发票金额与汇票金额一致 (10) 发票金额不超过信用证可使用的余额；如不允许分批装运，发票应包括信用证要求的整批装运金额，如允许分批装运，金额在总、分之间互不矛盾，并与信用证规定、汇票相符 (11) 按照信用证要求发票已被签字、(或公证人证实、合法化、签证等) (12) 有些资料关于装运、包装、重量、运费或其他有关的运输费用符合其他单据上所载明的 (13) 提交正确张数的正本及副本 (14) 显示的合同号与信用证规定一致 (15) 注意上下浮动幅度
2. 装箱单、重量单	(1) 单据的名称和份数必须和信用证要求相符 (2) 货物的名称、规格、数量及唛头等，必须与其他单据相符，可以相互补充，不可互相矛盾 (3) 数量、重量及尺码的小计必须吻合，并与信用证、提单、发票等单据相符 (4) 提供的单据份数不能少于信用证规定的数量

(续表)

审核单据	审 核 要 点
3. 运输单据	(1) 运输单据的种类必须与信用证规定相符 (2) 运输单据应具备法定条件并由运输公司(如船公司、航空公司等)或其代理人签名 (3) 除非信用证另有规定,必须提交全套提单 (4) 收货人和被通知人名称、地址、起运港、目的港、装运日期等,应符合信用证规定 (5) 除非信用证另有规定,发货人(Shipper)通常为受益人或转让信用证中的受让人,但若是受益人以外的一方作为发货人,也可接受 (6) 提单货物描述一般符合信用证所说明的货物描述,货名可以用统称(General Term)、唛头、数量、重量、船名、线路等应与信用证相符,并与其他单据一致 (7) 提单上价格条款或有关运费的记载必须与信用证及其他单据一致。如CIF、CFR,相应的费用记载应为"Freight Prepaid"(运费已预付)或"Freight Paid"(运费已付);FOB,相应的费用记载应为"Freight Collect"(运费到付)或"Freight Payable at Destination"(目的地支付运费) (8) 提单抬头若为"To Order Of Shipper"、"To Shipper's Order"、"To Order",均应作背书 (9) 收妥备运提单(Received B/L),必须于货物实际装船后,加注"On Board"(已装船)字样及已装船日期
4. 保险单据	(1) 应明确保险单的全套正本份数,并且除非信用证另有规定,必须提交全套正本保险单 (2) 保险单据必须由保险公司(Insurance Company)或承保人(Underwriters)或他们的代理人(Agents)开立及签署,除非信用证另有规定,银行不接受由保险经纪人(Broker)签发的暂保单(Cover Note) (3) 保险单日期必须早于或等于提单日期 (4) 除非信用证另有规定,保险单显示的金额、币别必须与信用证要求一致 (5) 投保的险种必须符合信用证的要求,若信用证使用了含义不明确的条款,如"通常险别"(Usual Risks)或"惯常险别"(Customary Risks),银行当按照所提示的保险单予以接受 (6) 除非信用证另有规定,银行将接受证明受免赔率(Franchise)或免赔额约束的保险单据 (7) 当信用证规定"投保一切险"时,银行应接受含有任何"一切险"批注或条文的保险单据,不论其有无"一切险"标题,甚至表明不包括某种险别 (8) 保险单的船名、航程、装运港、目的港、唛头等应与提单、发票等其他单据一致 (9) 应表明赔付地、在目的地的支付赔款代理人、支付的货币种类,信用证如无此项规定,赔付地点可以选择在进出口人的任何一方 (10) 信用证要求保险单(Insurance Policy)时,不得以保险凭证(Insurance Certificate)代替;反之,则可以 (11) 份数完全符合信用证规定的数量
5. 产地证	(1) 它是独立的单据,不要与其他单据联合起来,必须由信用证指定的机构出具,若信用证无此规定,可以由包括受益人在内的任何人出具 (2) 按照信用证要求,它已被签字、公证人证实、合法化、签证等 (3) 内容必须符合信用证的要求,并与其他单据不矛盾;如信用证规定货物为某地生产,则产地证必须表明为某地生产 (4) 载明原产地国家,应该符合信用证的要求 (5) 含有检验意义的产地证的日期不能迟于提单;特殊产地证的格式必须符合进口国惯例的要求 (6) 份数不能少于信用证规定的数量

（续表）

审核单据	审核要点
6. 汇票	(1) 汇票载有正确的信用证参考号码 (2) 它有当前的日期 (3) 签字及/或出票人的名称与受益人的名称一致 (4) 开至正确的付款人，不能是开证申请人 (5) 金额大小写一致，并与信用证规定、发票相符 (6) 汇票的期限就是信用证所要求的 (7) 收款人应是受益人或交单银行 (8) 如果需要背书，是否已被正确地背书 (9) 是否有限制性背书 (10) 是否包含信用证要求的条款 (11) 所开立的金额不超过信用证可以使用的余额
7. 其他单据	如进口许可证、商检证书等，均须先与信用证的条款进行核对，再与其他有关单据核对，做到单同一致、单证一致、单单一致

工作任务三 单据缮制综合模拟操作

一、实训指南

制作和审核出口单证的主要依据是买卖合同、信用证、有关商品的原始资料和国际惯例，报关报检单据还需要按照国内有关职能机构的规定，另外，贸易对方来往的函电的有关内容必要时也可参照使用。

二、单证缮制的实际操作流程

缮制单据是按货、证、船、款的程序进行制单。

(1) 货：受益人依契约和信用证的规定，将货物的规格、性能、数量、核查清楚，并确认货物与契约的规定完全相符。

(2) 证：依信用证规定缮制和配齐所需单据，应认真不疏忽，全面不遗漏，完整不缺欠，准备无差错，防止有货无证无单，延误收款。

(3) 船：租船定舱，必须提供全部所需的单据，依其单据、船主或其代理人方可提供船期、航程、装船等事宜，防止有货无船或有货无单据而造成延误。

(4) 款：契约的当事人依银行业务规定，保证受益人提交规定的单据（其中包括代表物权的提单在内）向银行办理业务，开证申请人依信用证规定，付款赎单，凭单提货。

三、单证缮制操作要点

单证缮制步骤	操 作 要 点
1. 掌握各项制单资料并加以归纳整理	了解合同、工厂交货单、信用证等信息,及时掌握各项制单的基础资料,加以归纳整理,仔细核对
2. 审核制单资料	如果已经有出运货物明细单的,必须对此单进行仔细审核,即从报关托运单证和结汇单证两个方面来检查出口货物明细表。将信用证相关内容进行归类,找出涉及单据的信用证条款。将所需单据列一份清单,并在副本信用证上作适当的标注,形成一份信用证单据条款备忘录,以提高工作效率
3. 单证信息录入	单证信息录入应体现单证操作的逻辑顺序。出口单证一般以商业发票、装箱单为基础单据,发票是中心单据,应先录入商业发票内容。然后按照发票内容分别录入装箱单、产地证、报关单、出口货物订舱委托书、海关发票、投保单等单证。如果有需要时,再作出口商证明、装船通知、船公司证明、汇票等,分别将单据交有关方面。制单人员对各种单据的用途、单证中每一栏应该填制的事项以及哪些是必要事项,哪些是一般事项必须熟悉。制单完毕后,制单人员最好先审一遍,发现差错,立即更正
4. 单据标识	对单据作业过程进行标识,是使单证作业过程处于受控状态并不断改进,为此,单证标识应体现过程的记录及可追溯的特点

单证模拟实训十二

一、信用证审核模拟操作

根据合同内容审核信用证,指出不符之处并提出修改意见。

山东亿海进出口有限公司与 LINSA PUBLICIDAD, S. A. 公司签订了一份牛皮出口的销售合同,具体内容如下:

SALES CONTRACT

THE SELLER:
SHANDONG YIHAI IMP. & EXP. CO. , LTD.
NO. 51 JINSHUI ROAD, QINGDAO, CHINA
THE BUYER:
LINSA PUBLICIDAD, S. A.
VALENCIA, 195 BAJOS. 08011. BARCELONA, SPAIN

NO. YH08039
DATE: DEC. 1, 2008
SIGNED AT: QINGDAO, CHINA

This Sales Contract is made by and between the Sellers and the Buyers, whereby the sellers agree to sell and the buyers agree to buy the under-mentioned goods according to the terms and conditions stipulated below:

Commodity & Specification	Quantity	Price Terms	
		Unit price	Amount
CARDHOLDER DYED COW LEATHER BLACK BROWN	5 000 PCS 8 000 PCS	FOB QINGDAO USD 1. 45 PCS USD 1. 50 PCS	USD 7 250. 00 USD 12 000. 00 USD 19 250. 00
Total amount: U. S. DOLLARS NINETEEN THOUSAND TWO HUNDRED AND FIFTY ONLY			

Packing: 1PC/POLYBAG, 500PCS/CTN
Time of Shipment: DURING JAN. 2009 BY SEA

Shipping Mark: L. P.
BARCELONA
NOS. 1 - 26

Loading Port and Destination: FROM QINGDAO TO BARCELONA
Partial Shipment and Transshipment: ALLOWED
Insurance: TO BE EFFECTED BY THE BUYER.
Terms of Payment: THE BUYER SHALL OPEN THROUGH A BANK ACCEPTABLE TO THE SELLER AN IRREVOCABLE SIGHT LETTER OF CREDIT TO REACH THE SELLER 30 DAYS BEFORE THE MONTH OF SHIPMENT AND TO REMAIN VALID FOR NEGOTIATION IN CHINA UNTIL THE 15th DAY AFTER THE FORESAID TIME OF SHIPMENT.

ISSUE OF DOCUMENTARY CREDIT

27: SEQUENCE OF TOTAL: 1/1

40A: FORM OF DOC. CREDIT: IRREVOCABLE

20: DOC. CREDIT NUMBER: 103CD137273

31C: DATE OF ISSUE: 081215

40E: APPLICABLE RULES: UCP LATEST VERSION

31D: DATE AND PLACE OF EXPIRY: DATE 090202 PLACE IN SPAIN

51D: APPLICANT BANK: BANCO SANTANDER, S. A.
      28660 BOADILLA DEL BARCELONA, SPAIN

50: APPLICANT: LINSA PUBLICIDAD, S. A.
    VALENCIA, 195 BAJOS. 08011. BARCELONA, SPAIN

59: BENEFICIARY: SHANDONG YIHAN IMP. & EXP. CO. , LTD.
    NO. 51 JINSHUI ROAD, QINGDAO, CHINA

32B: AMOUNT: CURRENCY EUR AMOUNT 19250.00

41A: AVAILABLE WITH…BY ANY BANK IN CHINA BY NEGOTIATION

42C: DRAFTS AT… 30 DAYS AFTER SIGHT

42A: DRAWEE: LINSA PUBLICIDAD, S. A.

43P: PARTIAL SHIPMTS: NOT ALLOWED

43T: TRANSSHIPMENT: NOT ALLOWED

44E: PORT OF LOADING: ANY CHINESE PORT

44F: PORT OF DISCHARGE: VALENCIA, SPAIN

44C: LATEST DATE OF SHIPMENT: 090115

45A: DESCRIPTION OF GOODS
  GOODS AS PER S/C NO. YH08036 DATED ON DEC. 1, 2008
  CARDHOLDER DYED COW LEATHER
  BLACK COLOUR/8 000 PCS AT USD1.45/PC FOB QINGDAO
  BROWN COLOUR/5 000 PCS AT USD1.50/PC FOB QINGDAO
  PACKING: 200 PCS/CTN

46A: DOCUMENTS REQUIRED
  1. SIGNED COMMERCIAL INVOICE IN 3 COPIES
  2. CERTIFICATE OF ORIGIN GSP FORM A ISSUED BY OFFICIAL AUTHORITIES
  3. PACKING LIST IN 3 COPIES
  4. FULL SET CLEAN ON BOARD BILLS OF LADING MADE OUT TO ORDER MARKED FREIGHT PREPAID AND NOTIFY APPLICANT
  5. INSURANCE POLICY/CERTIFICATE IN DUPLICATE ENDORSED IN BLANK FOR 110% INVOICE VALUE COVERING ALL RISKS AND WAR RISK AS PER CIC

47A: ADDITIONAL CONDITIONS
  BILL OF LADING ONLY ACCEPTABLE IF ISSUED BY ONE OF THE FOLLOWING SHIPPING

COMPANIES: KUEHNE-NAGEL (BLUE ANCHOR LINE) VILTRANS (CHINA) INT'L FORWARDING LTD. OR VILTRANS SHIPPING (HK) CO., LTD.
71B: CHARGES: ALL CHARGES ARE TO BE BORN BY BENEFICIARY
48: PERIOD FOR PRESENTATION: WITHIN 5 DAYS AFTER THE DATE OF SHIPMENT, BUT WITHIN THE VALIDITY OF THIS CREDIT
49: CONFIRMATION INSTRUCTION: WITHOUT

经审核信用证需要修改的内容如下：

二、单据审核模拟操作

根据已知资料指出下列单据中错误的地方。

南京金陵纺织品进出口公司外贸单证员制作好信用证项下的单据后，请根据信用证以及《UCP600》审核单据。

SALES CONTRACT

Contract No.：NJT090218
Date：Feb. 18, 2009
Signed at：Nanjing, China

The Seller：NANJING JINLING TEXTILE CO., LTD.
Address：UNIT A 18/F, JINLING TOWER, NO. 118 JINLING ROAD, NANJING, CHINA.
The Buyer：DEXICA SUPERMART S. A.

Address: BOULEVARD PACHECO 44, B-1000 BRUSSELS, BELGIUM

This Sales Contract is made by and between the Sellers and the Buyers, whereby the sellers agree to sell and buyers agree to buy the under-mentioned goods according to the terms and conditions stipulated below:

Commodity and specifications	Quantity	Unit Price	Amount
GIRLS GARMENTS	10 800 PCS	CIF BRUSSELS EUR 5.00/PC	EUR 54 000.00

10% more or less in quantity and amount are acceptable.

Packing: IN CARTON   Shipping Mark: N/M

Time of Shipment: Within 30 days after receipt of L/C.

From NINGBO PORT CHINA to BRUSSELS, BELGIUM.

Transshipment and Partial Shipment: Allowed.

Insurance: to be effected by the Seller for 110% of full invoice value covering all risks up to port of destination and war risks included with claim payable at destination.

Terms of Payment: By 100% Irrevocable Letter of Credit in favor of the Sellers to be available by sight draft to be opened and to reach China before APRIL 1, 2009 and to remain valid for negotiation in China until the 21 days after the foresaid Time of Shipment. L/C must mention this contract number L/C advised by BANK OF CHINA JIANGSU BRANCH. ALL banking Charges outside China are for account of the Buyer.

The Seller   The Buyer

NANJING JINLING TEXTILE CO., LTD.   DEXICA SUPERMART S. A.

钟　山   ALICE

其他资料：

(1) 装运信息：指定 APL 承运，装期 2009 年 4 月 19 日；船名 PRINCESS；航次 V.018。

(2) 装箱资料：合计 108 箱，装入 1×20' 集装箱。

(3) 商业发票号：NJT090218-09，签发日期 2009 年 4 月 10 日。

(4) 信用证号：CMKK9180205。

1. 一般原产地证

ORIGINAL

1. Exporter DEXICA SUPERMART S. A. BOULEVARD PACHECO 44 B – 1000 BRUSSELS, BELGIUM	Certificate No. CCPIT 091810528 **CERTIFICATE OF ORIGIN** **OF** **THE PEOPLE'S REPUBLIC OF CHINA**
2. Consignee NANJING JINLING TEXTILE CO., LTD. UNIT A 18/F, JINLING TOWER, NO. 118 JINLING ROAD, NANJING, CHINA	
3. Means of transport and route FROM NANJING PORT, CHINA TO BRUSSELS, BELGIUM BY AIR	5. For certifying authority use only
4. Country/region of destination CHINA	

6. Marks and numbers DEXICA S/C NJT090218	7. Number and kind of packages; description of goods LADIES GARMENTS PACKED IN (108) TWO HUNDRED AND EIGHT CARTONS ONLY. **********************	8. H. S. Code 6204430090	9. Quantity 10 080 DOZEN	10. Number and date of invoices NJT090218 APR. 9, 2009

11. Declaration by the exporter 　　The undersigned hereby declares that the above details and statements are correct, that all the goods were produced in China and that they comply with the Rules of Origin of the People's Republic of China. NANJING JINLING TEXTILE CO., LTD. ZHONG SHAN 　　　　　　出口商 　　　　　　申请章 NANJING APR. 15, 2009	12. Certification 　　It is hereby certified that the declaration by the exporter is correct. CHINA COUNCIL FOR THE PROMOTION OF INTERNATIONAL TRADE JIN LIAN CHENG 　　　　　　CCPIT 　　　　　　签证章 NANJING CHINA APR. 16, 2009
Place and date, signature and stamp of authorized signatory	Place and date, signature and stamp of certifying authority

2. 保险单

中国人民保险公司江苏省分公司
THE PEOPLE'S INSURANCE COMPANY OF CHINA JIANGSU BRANCH

货物运输保险单
CARGO TRANSPORTATION INSURANCE POLICY

发票号(INVOICE NO.) NJT090218-09   保单号次 PYIE2006080
合同号(CONTRACT NO.) NJT090218   POLICY NO.
信用证号(L/C NO.): CCPIT 091810528
被保险人: Insured: NANJING JINLING TEXTILE LTD.

中国人民保险公司(以下简称本公司)根据被保险人的要求,由被保险人向本公司缴付约定的保险费,按照本保险单承保险别和背面所载条款与下列特款承保下述货物运输保险,特立本保险单。

THIS POLICY OF INSURANCE WITNESSES THAT THE PEOPLE'S INSURANCE COMPANY OF CHINA (HEREINAFTER CALLED "THE COMPANY") AT THE REQUEST OF THE INSURED AND IN CONSIDERATION OF THE AGREED PREMIUM PAID TO THE COMPANY BY THE INSURED, UNDERTAKES TO INSURE THE UNDERMENTIONED GOODS IN TRANSPORTATION SUBJECT TO THE CONDITIONS OF THIS OF THIS POLICY ASPER THE CLAUSES PRINTED OVERLEAF AND OTHER SPECIL CLAUSES ATTACHED HEREON.

标记 MARKS & NOS	包装及数量 QUANTITY	保险货物项目 DESCRIPTION OF GOODS	保险金额 AMOUNT INSURED
DEXICA S/C NJT090218	10 800 DOZEN	LADIES GARMENTS	USD 54 000.00

总保险金额 TOTAL AMOUNT INSURED: US DOLLARS FIFTY FOUR THOUSANDS ONLY

保费   起运日期   装载运输工具
AS ARRANGED   DATE OF COMMENCEMENT: APR. 9, 2009   PER CONVEYANCE: PRINCESS V.018
自   经   至
FROM: NANJING PORT CHINA VIA --- TO BRUSSELS, BELGIUM
承保险别: CONDITIONS: Covering F. P. A up to PORT OF DESTINATION.

所保货物,如发生保险单项下可能引起索赔的损失或损坏,应立即通知本公司下述代理人查勘。如有索赔,应向本公司提交保单正本(本保险单共有 __3__ 份正本)及有关文件。如一份正本已用于索赔,其余正本自动失效。

IN THE EVENT OF LOSS OR DAMAGE WITCH MAY RESULT IN A CLAIM UNDER THIS POLICY, IMMEDIATE NOTICE MUST BE GIVEN TO THE COMPANY'S AGENT AS MENTIONED HEREUNDER. CLAIMS, IF ANY, ONE OF THE ORIGINAL POLICY WHICH HAS BEEN ISSUED IN __3__ ORIGINAL (S) TOGETHER WITH THE RELEVENT DOCUMENTS SHALL BE SURRENDERED TO THE COMPANY. IF ONE OF THE ORIGINAL POLICY HAS BEEN ACCOMPLISHED. THE OTHERS TO BE VOID.

中国人民保险公司广州市分公司
THE PEOPLE'S INSURANCE COMPANY OF CHINA JIANGSU BRANCH

赔款偿付地点
CLAIM PAYABLE AT Nanjing, CHINA   王天华
出单日期
ISSUING DATE: APR. 20,2009   Authorized Signature

一般原产地证缮制错误的地方有：

保险单缮制错误的地方有：

三、单据缮制模拟操作

请根据银行来证及货物明细，缮制出口单据。

A. 货物明细

商品名称：Trolley Cases

货号			
	TS503214	TS503215	TS503216
产地		Dalian China	

（续表）

商标		TAISHAN	
包装	1 pc in 1 PE bag；3 pcs/CTN		
箱子尺寸	53.5×37×79.5 cm 0.157 3 cbm	53.5×34.5×82 cm 0.151 cbm	48×32.5×78.5 cm 0.122 5 cbm
箱子尺寸（总）	57.886 4 cbm	57.833 cbm	58.8 cbm
净重/毛重（个）	4 KG/4.6 KG	3.5 KG/4 KG	3 KG/3.5 KG
净重/毛重（总）	4 416 KG/5 078.4 KG	4 021.5 KG/4 596 KG	4 320 KG/5 040 KG
数量	1 104 PCS	1 149 PCS	1 440 PCS
单价	USD 6.50	USD 6.00	USD 5.80
金额	USD 7 176	USD 6 894	USD 8 352
集装箱容量	Qty/40' FCL：368 ctns	Qty/40' FCL：383 ctns	Qty/40' FCL：480 ctns

发票号码：TSI0801005　　发票日期：2008-8-5　　授权签字人：张平
装运船名：DONGFENG　　航　次：V.369　　装船日期：2008-8-23
运输标志：ORTAI
TSI0601005
NEW YORK
C/NO.1-1231
原产地标准："P"

B. 信用证相关内容

27：Sequence of Total：1/1

40A：Form of Documentary Credit：IRREVOCABLE

20：Documentary Credit Number：N5632405TH11808

31C：Date of Issue：080715

31D：Date and Place of Expiry：080909 CHINA

51D：Applicant Bank：CITY NATIONAL BANK
133 MORNINGSIDE AVE NEW YORK, NY 10027 Tel：001-212-865-4763

50：Applicant：ORTAI CO., LTD.
　　　　　　30 EAST 40TH STREET, NEW YORK, NY 10016
　　　　　　TEL：001-212-992-9788 FAX：001-212-992-9789

59：Beneficiary：DALIAN TAISHAN SUITCASE & BAG CO., LTD.
　　　　　　66 ZHONGSHAN ROAD DALIAN 116001, CHINA TEL：0086-0411-84524789

32B: Currency Code Amount: USD 22 422.00

41D: Available With/By: ANY BANK IN CHINA BY NEGOTIATION

42C: Drafts at: SIGHT

42D: Drawee: ISSUING BANK

43P: Partial Shipments: NOT ALLOWED

43T: Transhipment: NOT ALLOWED

44E: Port Of Loading: DALIAN, FCHINA

44F: Port Of Discharge: NEW YORK, U.S.A.

44C: Latest Date of Shipment: 080825

45A: Description of Goods and/or Services:
CIF NEWYORK TROLLEY CASES AS PER S/C NO. TSSC0801005

46A: Documents Required
+MANUALLY SIGNED COMMERCIAL INVOICE IN 2 COPYES INDICATING L/C NO. AND CONTRACT NO. CERTIFYING THE CONTENTS IN THIS INVOICE ARE TRUE AND CORRECT.
+FULL SET OF ORIGINAL CLEAN ON BOARD MARINE BILLS OF LADING MADE OUT TO ORDER, ENDORSED IN BANK MARKED FREIGHT PREPAID AND NOYIFY APPLICANT.
+PACKING LIST IN 2 COPYES ISSUED BY THE BENEFICIARY.
+ORIGINAL GSP FORM A CERTIFICATE OF ORIGIN ON OFFICIAL FORM ISSUED BY A TRADE AUTHORITY OR GOVERNMENT BODY.
+INSURANCE POLICIES OR CERTIFICATES IN DUPLICATE, ENDORSED IN BANK FOR 110 PERCENT OF INVOICE VALUE COVERING ICC CLAUSES(A).
+MANUFACTURER'S QUALITY CERTIFICATE CERTIFYING THE COMMODITY IS IN GOOD ORDER.
+BENEFICIARY'S CERTIFICATE CERTIFYING THAT ONE SET OF COPIES OF SHIPPING DOCUMENTS HAS BEEN SENT TO APPLICANT WHTHIN 5 DAYS AFTER SHIPMENT.

47A: Additional Conditions
+UNLESS OTHERWISE EXPRESSLY STATED, ALL DOCUMENTS MUST BE IN ENGLISH.
+ANY PROCEEDS OF PRESENTATIONS UNDER THIS DC WILL BE SETTLED BY TELETRANSMISSION AND A CHARGE OF USD50.00 (OR CURRENCY EQUIVALENT) WILL BE DEDUCTED.

49: Confirmation Instructions: WITHOUT

57D: Advise Through Bank: BANK OF CHINA DALIAN BRANCH

72: Sender to Receiver Information:

DOCUMENTS TO BE DESPATCHED BY COURIER
SERVICE IN ONE LOT TO CITY NATIONAL BANK

C. 制单

1. 质量证明

DALIAN TAISHAN SUITCASE & BAG CO. , LTD.
66 ZHONGSHAN ROAD DALIAN 116001, CHINA
TEL: 0086 - 0411 - 84524789

2. 商业发票

Issuer	商业发票 COMMERCIAL INVOICE		
To	Invoice No.		Date
Transport Details	S/C No.		L/C No.
Marks and Numbers	Description of Goods	Quantity	Unit Price	Amount

TOTAL VALUE IN WORDS:

3. 装箱单

Issuer	装箱单 PACKING LIST	
To	Invoice No.	Date
	S/C No.	L/C No.

Marks and Numbers	C/NOS	Number and Kind of Packages; Description of Goods	Quantity	G. W. (KGS)	N. W. (KGS)	MEAS. (CBM)
Total						

TOTAL PACKAGES IN WORDS：

4. 普惠制产地证

1. Goods consigned from (Exporter's full name and address, country)	Reference No. T200510819 GENERALIZED SYSTEM OF PREFERENCES CERTIFICATE OF ORIGIN (Combined declaration and certificate) **FORM A** Issued in _____ (Country) See Notes. Overleaf
2. Goods consigned to (Consignee's Full name, address, country)	
3. Means of transport and route(as for as known)	4. For certifying authority use only

5. Item number	6. Marks and Numbers of packages	7. Number and kind of packages; Description of goods	8. Origin Criterion (see Notes Overleaf)	9. Gross Weight or other Quantity	10. Number And date of invoices

11. Certification It is hereby certified that the declaration by the exporter is correct. **CIQ**	12. Declaration by the exporter The undersigned hereby declares that the above Details and statements are correct, that all the Goods were produced in _____ and that they Comply with the origin requirements specified for those goods in the Generalized System of preferences for goods exported to _____ (importing country)
Place and date, signature and stamp of Certifying authority	Place and date, Signature and stamp of Authorized signatory

5. 受益人证明

DALIAN TAISHAN SUITCASE & BAG CO., LTD.
66 ZHONGSHAN ROAD DALIAN 116001, CHINA
TEL: 0086 - 0411 - 84524789

参 考 文 献

[1] 邵红万.国际商务单证实训教程[M].南京:东南大学出版社,2009.
[2] 林萌芳,等.国际商务单证实训[M].北京:清华大学出版社,2009.
[3] 王胜华.国际商务单证操作实训教程[M].重庆:重庆大学出版社,2009.
[4] 杜素音.国际商务单证实训教程[M].北京:北京交通大学出版社,2010.
[5] 陆梦青.单证员岗位实训[M].北京:高等教育出版社,2008.
[6] 何剑.国际商务单证模拟实训教程[M].北京:北京出版社,2007.
[7] 郑淑媛.实用进出口单证[M].北京:电子工业出版社,2005.
[8] 童宏祥.进出口贸易业务——模拟实训与操作指南[M].上海:上海财经大学出版社,2008.
[9] 童宏祥.新编外贸单证实务[M].上海:华东理工出版社,2007.
[10] 姚大伟.国际商务单证理论与实务[M].上海:上海交通大学出版社,2010.
[11] 姚大伟.国际商务单证实务习题集[M].北京:清华大学出版社,2009.
[12] 屈韬,何秉毅.外贸单证实务[M].上海:上海财经大学出版社,2011.
[13] 全国国际商务单证专业培训考试办公室.国际商务单证专业培训考试大纲及复习指南[M].北京:中国商务出版社,2011.